Y0-CCT-604

THE
LONGEST
WAY
HOME

THE
LONGEST
WAY
HOME

Chief Alfred C. Sam's
Back-to-Africa Movement

by

William E. Bittle
UNIVERSITY OF OKLAHOMA

and

Gilbert Geis
LOS ANGELES STATE COLLEGE

with the research assistance of
Donald F. Parker

Detroit, 1964
Wayne State University Press

Published simultaneously in Canada by Ambassador Books, Limited,
Toronto, Ontario, Canada

Library of Congress Catalog Card Number 64-10596

Acknowledgment is made to J. J. Augustin, Inc., Publishers, Locust Valley, New York, for permission to quote from Down-East Spirituals and Others, *edited by George Pullen Jackson (1943). Some of the material in this book was published earlier as essays in* Phylon *Quarterly, and is included here with the permission of* **Phylon.**

Grateful acknowledgment is made to the FORD FOUNDATION *for financial assistance in the publication of this book.*

CONTENTS

FOREWORD

THE PRESENT WORK is the almost accidental outgrowth of a larger study in which the two of us became involved several years ago. At that time, both on the University of Oklahoma campus but teaching in different academic fields, we found our research interests converging on certain aspects of American Negro behavior. Of particular interest to us was the rise and growth of all-Negro communities, not only in Oklahoma, but in other states as well. These curious racial enclaves seemed to call to us out of their own peculiarity, since they were relatively few when compared to the large number of biracial communities, and because they were distributed almost entirely in the so-called border states. It occurred to us that not only must subcultural and historical factors have been unique in these areas to allow for the development of such communities, but also that a contemporary study of Negro behavior in these "racial islands" might throw considerable light on Negro behavior in general.

Thus interested, we jointly began library research to recover the details of the founding of certain of these communities in Oklahoma. Working with old newspapers, many of them dating back to territorial days, we tediously read the events of the years leading up to the period under consideration in the present work. At length, we came across

1

scattered references to Chief Sam and the movement which he sponsored. With each issue of each newspaper, we found a fantastic tale unfolding, but we somehow felt that the movement and its elaborate preparations would both come to nothing. But the movement prospered, and great numbers of Negroes were attracted to it, and we found ourselves committed to tell the story.

Once having exhausted local resources, we worked with newspaper files in New York and Texas, trying to fill the gaps in our materials. Lacking personal information, we interviewed many people who had been connected with the movement, wrote hopefully to alleged survivors and their descendants in Africa, and plagued governmental agencies, both domestic and foreign, with inquiries about the movement. Little by little the story took shape, and we were able to see the development of the movement from beginning to end.

As far as we have been able, we have sacrificed jargonized analysis in the interests of readability. The narrative is interpreted only when interpretation seems absolutely necessary. In general, though, we feel that the events are self-explanatory, and that the motives of the people involved may be inferred as easily (and probably as accurately) by the reader as by us. The story is an amazingly poignant one which illustrates again the desperate hopes of an utterly desperate group of people.

Our indebtedness for assistance in the research and writing of this book is enormous. Without question, our most profuse and sincere thanks must go to the Faculty Research Committee of the University of Oklahoma, which financed most of the work involved during the research on materials. This committee graciously answered our constant requests for additional assistance, and literally made possible the completion of the work. The Department of Anthropology of the University of Oklahoma also has provided financial assistance, though of a more indirect sort.

Of the individuals who were of assistance, Donald F. Parker must certainly head the list. He spent many tireless and unremunerated hours in the blinding task of reading aging newspapers, and his interest in the project was often greater than our own during those periods when the number of yet unread sources seemed too great to contemplate. His comments on the work, during the many conversations we have held on the African movement, have also been helpful and enlightening.

To Mrs. Louise Cook, librarian of the newspaper division of the Oklahoma Historical Society, we also give our thanks. She tolerated us for months on end, and never complained about the piles of bound newspapers which we constantly dragged across her otherwise neat reading room.

To our colleague, Norman Jackman, our thanks are due for having read an earlier version of the manuscript, and for having made many helpful suggestions; similarly, to Martha Kobler and Estelle Chodor, our thanks are due for comments.

The newspaper divisions of the New York Public Library, the State Capitol Libraries of Oklahoma and Texas, the University of Texas Library, and the University of Oklahoma Library were also helpful to us. We are especially indebted to Mrs. Irma Tomberlin and Miss Opal Carr of the latter library for their assistance. Both of these women have the remarkable ability to find in a moment things which would have taken us months to locate.

But perhaps the greatest debt of all, and one that we feel cannot be acknowledged by name, is to the many persons throughout Oklahoma who tolerated us on many occasions, and who answered our questions about their participation in the movement without flagging, and despite our invasion of their privacy. We have taken up many hours of their time, jogging their memories for details; and they have, to a person, responded with amazing skill. These were the people who made the movement in the first place, and they were also the people who have made it possible for us to document many aspects of it.

Two technical notes are necessary. First, we have reproduced exactly the spelling found in our sources. Second, a quotation may be attributed in the text to one newspaper but cited in the Notes as having been taken from another. Except for a few copies of the Boley *Progress,* the most important original sources of information on the movement, the *Progress* and the *African Pioneer,* are no longer extant. On many occasions, then, we have had to depend on quotations from these sources which ultimately appeared as reprints in other papers in the country.

The lack of primary materials has plagued us, too, in our search for information on specific details of the crossing, and the brief residence of some of the colonists in Africa. One survivor of the trip, now living in Tulsa, kept a written diary of her experiences which would have been invaluable. But the diary was consumed in a fire which destroyed her home.

The files which the Post Office Department accumulated during the time its inspectors were investigating Sam have also been destroyed.

Perhaps the most difficult obstacle has been the immutable British rule against permitting information on Africa subsequent to 1902 to be released to the public. Though Mr. E. G. Taylor of the Foreign Office provided us with a photostatic copy of the description of the landing as it appeared in the Gold Coast *Leader,* he was not able to permit us access to the many additional records with which we could have filled the remaining gaps in this story.

WILLIAM E. BITTLE
GILBERT GEIS

Norman, Oklahoma
May 1963

1

"*I Could Have Walked*"

$\mathbf{S}$HORTLY AFTER FOUR O'CLOCK in the morning, on August 21, 1914, the *S.S. Liberia,* flying a British flag and carrying sixty passengers, cleared the Port of Galveston and steamed off into the Gulf of Mexico, bound for the Gold Coast Colony, British West Africa. The passengers were all Negroes, intent upon resettling in a location where life might be easier and where political and social equality would be their right. They were, they believed, returning home to their own people and to the promise of a better existence.

The leader of the group was Alfred Charles Sam, a short, unprepossessing brown man who had spent the past year recruiting emigrants from back-country cotton farms in eastern Oklahoma. Speaking slowly, ungrammatically, and with a marked accent, Sam claimed to be an African tribal chief, born in the interior of the Gold Coast, and ruling over a town in West Akim. Everyone seemed to believe him; they all called him "Chief Sam."

Left behind as the *Liberia* pulled slowly away from her buoy in Bolivar Roads were some five hundred persons, part of Sam's followers who could not make the African trip this first time. These people, now standing on the pier and waving their farewells, would soon return to the houses they were sharing with permanent Negro residents of Galveston, and talk and wonder about the progress of the vessel which they had just seen sail away. They would wait and they would plan for the day when the *Liberia* would return to carry them off to join the others in Africa.

Another body of Sam's faithful was abandoning the camp at "South Gold Coast," a pathetic and sordid settlement at Weleetka, Oklahoma, where for eight months they had collected, hoping to be included among those departing for Africa. Though Sam had repeatedly warned his followers not to sell their lands and their possessions until the affairs of the movement were in order, many had disregarded his warnings, and had converged on the Weleetka camps. Now landless and impoverished, with no place to call home save the tent camps, they devoutly followed the movements of the ship in Galveston.

The movement from South Gold Coast camp followed one of the coldest winters in Oklahoma history. Disease, which had earlier threatened the camp, now threatened again, and the incessant shouting, singing, and lusty praying of the campers had begun to wear on the heretofore patient white citizens of Weleetka. The campers had been ordered to disperse; and they were complying with the order, moving slowly off to smaller towns, searching out relatives who would take them in, or, when possible, drifting back to the farms they had earlier abandoned.

Persons other than Sam's followers also noted the departure of the *Liberia* with no little interest. From his diplomatic post in Washington, Sir Cecil Arthur Spring-Rice, Britain's ambassador to the United States, had continuously tried to abort Sam's colonization project. To Spring-Rice, his own government threatened with involvement in a European war, the Sam affair could not have been more trivial. Yet, the possibility of a Negro exodus from the United States to a British colony posed an embarrassing prospect to the ambassador; and acting on frantic orders from London, he had moved to stem the migration.

The attention of the U. S. State Department was also focused on this patently improbable project, as was that of the Governor of Oklahoma and various minor functionaries throughout his state.

From the Gold Coast, too, came an expression of concern. The Governor of the colony urged that "every effort should be made to prevent the continuance of Sam's operations in the United States . . . for were he to succeed in inducing a number of American negroes to attempt colonisation in the Gold Coast his victims would be fore-doomed to disappointment." [1]

The warning was futile. British and American authorities, despite their often petulant but thorough methods, were able neither to block Chief Sam nor to discourage his devoted followers. The Chief had violated no statutory injunction; and his scheme, impractical and far-fetched though it seemed to the secure white dignitaries, was legally unassailable.

The exodus, then, began early on a warm August morning, with the *Liberia* carrying its Negro passengers to anticipated freedom in their ancestral home. It was an exodus born of desperation and colored by fantastic hopes. It was an exodus that represented for the passengers the ultimate rejection of a country which they could no longer regard as their own. Conceived by a Negro, and conceived for Negroes, it was a program in many ways unique in American history and in the tortured history of the Negro people in the United States.

Only stray memories of Chief Sam's turbulent upheaval of local life persist today in the areas where he recruited most heavily for his back-to-Africa movement. The intervening forty-nine years have si-phoned off a large number of people who shared in the project. Usu-ally marginal Negro farmers, and often sharecroppers, their comings and goings are largely unknown; their movements are not noted in any permanent records save as anonymous statistical units in the great urban migrations which took place after the First World War. Their brief share in an exciting, but passing, protest movement is only a part of the people themselves; and most of these people are now dead.

Yet, there are still some who remember Chief Sam though, as one of them said blandly, many of these ancients "rightly oughtn't be alive." Most recall him only vaguely, with hazy recollections of great mass meetings, of unnatural talk and activity in the area, of unique vitality among their people before things settled down once again to the enervating routine.

Others know of Sam second-hand, through small talk carried through nearly half a century. One man, a post-office worker in Clearview, re-calls that his father boasted of a property bargain he had gotten "from old man Garrett" when Garrett sold out to take his family to Africa with Sam.

A few people, though, remember Sam with a preternatural clearness and vividness. An eighty-eight-year-old Negro woman, living in a dilapidated brown-sided house in the colored section north of Weleetka, recalls with precision the dates when Chief Sam held his meetings in her town, the amounts of money taken in through stock sales in his trading company, the date on which the *Liberia* sailed, and an endless array of picayune details associated with the movement. She talks of Sam as a man sent by God to deliver the Negro from his fettered existence in the New World and to lead him off into deliverance in an African Canaan.

She remembers a meeting in Clearview, a "big meeting when Chief Sam told all about Africa, how pretty it was." She remembers that a man came in laughing from the railroad station that night, with a Fort Smith newspaper proclaiming Chief Sam to be a fraud who had absconded with all of the Negroes' money. She tells how Sam held the newspaper up to his devout followers, and how they all laughed together at the white man who wanted so much to believe his own lies that he printed them in the newspaper to make them more real.

She remembers Chief Sam talking about the "sugar cane as big as stove pipe" that grew in the Gold Coast, and his telling the people that they were needed in Africa to teach the natives about work—the kind of work they had learned to do in America.

Chief Sam, she recalls, was a religious man. He didn't "talk loud at meetings," like some religious people, "just soft-like, and the people went for him." The eyes of the old woman softened as she told the story of a white man who asked Chief Sam if he intended to ruin the country by carrying off all the Negroes.

"No," said Sam calmly. "I might leave a few around for you to lynch and burn."

The old woman worked on a farm near Weleetka while the campers swarmed about the area, barely subsisting on the food handouts that they received from sympathetic farm Negroes. Her family helped many of them. These people came to Weleetka with money, she recalls, but they poured most of it into the expedition. Then the British and American authorities hamstrung and frustrated the Negroes in their efforts to make the voyage to Africa.

"They held the ship up five months in the east," she complains, in an outburst of irritation that is still sharp despite the long lapse of time. "They wouldn't inspect the ship in Galveston, and finally Chief Sam had to move it out into the ocean because the campers came on board and ate free. They just couldn't afford to pay for their food. Sam couldn't afford to pay the port fees neither."

"We worked hard here, worked day and night, to send money to take care of that ship standing still." To emphasize her last point, she repeated it another way. "It's hard to take care of a ship standing still."

Despite her complaint there was a note of obvious pride in her voice as she recalled her own contribution to the movement. Sam wanted to carry only twelve delegates, she says, but the other people were so anxious to go to the Gold Coast that they insisted he take them, too. The delegates were supposed to explore the African country and report back to the people waiting here on its suitability for settlement. But the rest of the people were too impatient, and did not understand why any preliminary inspection had to be made.

Most vividly, though, she remembers and tries to re-create the feeling that hung in the air during the days when Sam was in their midst, a feeling that never before had been nor had ever since returned. It was electric, she says, and it was warm and all-embracing. She showed no embarrassment in her support of Sam's plans when she talked of them, and she often rose to her feet to lend greater authority to the point she was making.

"I will and do say to you that the Negro people here for the first time in my long life came together and acted like they loved one another."

She was poignant in her own feelings about the exodus to Africa. "I wanted to go so bad," she said simply, "I could have walked."

Not everyone remembers Sam with the same kindness. A neighbor, tending her grandchildren in a neat, well-kept house in the same Negro section, told of Sam with a resurgence of old bitterness. Her father-in-law had become deeply involved in the movement, and she believes he contributed more than $2,000 to assist it. He joined the group in Galveston, and later she and her husband had to send money to him so that he could return to Weleetka.

"Chief Sam was a deadbeat," she pronounces unhesitatingly. "He promised people they could live in Africa without working, and they went ahead and believed him."

Sam was a superstitious man, too, she thinks. One time she got on a train between Clearview and Weleetka, and Sam was sitting there by a window. "I sat down next to him," she relates, "and he jumped to his feet and ran to the rear of the car, a wild look in his eyes, just like he was scared to death. I guess he knew I didn't believe in him, and he was afraid to be near me."

"At the meetings," she continued, obviously enjoying herself, "he would tell us about Africa, and sell people them bonds. He talked like a foreigner, with a big accent. But he was a deadbeat."

Then why had the Negroes flocked to Chief Sam if his scheme was so patently fraudulent? The answer was indirect.

"I'm from Mississippi," she said. Then she told a story:

"Mississippi wasn't so bad. We always liked it there. Though I see a lot about it in the newspapers now, it wasn't so bad then. We lived out of town and folks let us alone. Maybe they don't let my people alone down there now, but they let us alone then.

"One day all of us were sitting on the front porch when a bunch of white men began going by the house, two at a time, and all with guns. My mother was scared, and she said to my daddy: 'Bob, they aim to lynch somebody.'

" 'No, they don't,' my daddy said. 'They're just huntin.' "

But one of the whites soon cleared up the dispute.

" 'Bob,' he called out. 'Come here. We want to tell you something.'

"My daddy went out to the men.

" 'Bob, we're going to lynch Jerry,' they told him. 'You're all right, though.'

"My daddy came back to the porch. He didn't sit down, he just fell down. He just fell down!

"Jerry lived behind us a bit. My father could of cut back through the woods to Jerry's house and warned him so that he could get away in time, but they would of killed him and all of us.

"My mother asked him: 'What are they doing?'

" 'They're just huntin',' my daddy said.

"Later, we heard the shots. Jerry was still alive when the white men came back by our house.

" 'You can go to him now,' they told Daddy. 'He won't live.' "

That was the end of the story proper, but the woman added a terse postscript:

"We left Mississippi four days after that."

The story had not quite answered the question; so we asked it again. If things were not so bad for the Negro at the time, why had he fallen in with Chief Sam's repatriation plan?

The half-smile returned, saying that we would be given a no more direct answer. "We've always liked Weleetka," the woman said with no apparent trace of sarcasm. "They've been very nice to us here. They've let us alone."

Then she went back to her previous theme. Sam was a fraud, she repeated. Just to look at him, to listen to him talk made this obvious. He was a deadbeat. "I just couldn't get it in my mind the way he told about it," she recalled.

At Clearview, a community populated entirely by Negroes, a retired doctor remembered the Weleetka camps which he had visited during one of the frequent outbreaks of disease among the colonists. The doctor, too, said that Sam was a fraud. He had been offered four shares of Sam's stock at one time in order that the trading company might use his name as a sponsor for the movement, but he had refused to accept the shares. He did not want to be involved in what he was certain was a shady scheme.

He told of the meetings in Clearview. Sam, talking without the flamboyance of the stereotyped "people's leader," but with intensity and conviction, described the wonders of Africa. The crowd was always carried away with visionary enthusiasm as the story unfolded. In this hot, dusty, and dilapidated town, Africa seemed even more lush and desirable than Sam described it. But for the physician, middle-class, practical, and secure, the account was uninteresting and obviously exaggerated. In his retelling of the events there is notably lacking the passion of the others who assert that Sam was a charlatan, for the doctor had been relatively unaffected by Sam and his movement.

But the physician may have underplayed his own involvement, like the school-bus driver in the corner of a general store in Macomb, Oklahoma, a man who said altogether too casually that his association with Sam had been slight and of little importance. He granted, finally, that he and his brother, who is now the owner of a block of Negro enterprises in a metropolitan Midwest city, had been in Galveston when the *Liberia* departed, and that his parents had later migrated on their own to Africa, intending to settle there.

The brothers had traveled to Galveston because their father wanted them to be there to see the movement get under way, the bus driver insisted. Since he had recently married and had no job, he could see no objection to going to the Gulf port city and trying to find employment. He was there when the *Liberia* sailed, but he did not get up early enough that morning to see her off.

His father had sold their farm east of Earlsboro, Oklahoma, and claimed that he netted some $11,000 from the sale, though the son now avers that he had "never seen any of that money."

"I told my daddy that a man with all that money *in his pocket* didn't have much money." But the father wanted to go to Africa, even though he might not make the trip with Sam.

The busman claims to remember Chief Sam's meetings only vaguely. Sam wore "American citizen clothing." He talked mostly of Africa, and of "the diamonds that you could find in the ravines after the rain, and the ivory on the elephants' tusks."

"The fact of the matter is," the man concludes, "some of them wanted to go to Africa bad. I didn't want to go, so I didn't pay too much attention to all of the things that went on."

There were many others who remembered Sam, including persons who grinned happily over blurry, photostatic copies of his picture from the newspapers, and who looked as if the pictures brought home to them a flood of pleasant memories, memories that often shadowed anything that had happened to them before or since. These pleased, open grins represented the distillation of the memories of Sam's ephemeral flash across the individuals' otherwise drab lives.

A seventy-two-year-old woman, hunched and slow-moving, wondered if there might be a "premium" for the last remaining survivor among the *Liberia*'s passengers. If so, she was certain that she would win it. She sat in a high-backed chair in an odd triangular room beneath a walk-up hotel in the Negro section of Tulsa. Her children, who shared the rooms adjoining hers, passed in and out during the interview.

She had gone with Chief Sam because her husband wanted to make the trip. Both of them had been working "like two men" on their farm in Beggs, and they had some money, but no home of their own. Sam had made "good talk," and that was why she and her husband followed him.

An old woman and her son in Shawnee, finally, illustrate the ways in which a part of themselves and a part of the confusion which presently surrounds the movement have inextricably combined in many persons who retain memories of Sam's sojourn among them.

Loud and overwhelming, the son told about the project: "My father put $30,000 into that sucker scheme," he said. "If you want to get it back for me then I'll help you all you want. That's why I'm a poor man today, because of that Chief Sam."

"My father practically gave away everything he had to join with Chief Sam," he continued. "He sold 200 head of chickens and 300 head of turkeys at twenty-five cents apiece. We had 100 hogs weighing about 150 pounds each, and he sold them for a dollar apiece."

Six blocks away, in the same city, we interviewed the mother of this ebullient little man and asked her about Sam.

"I didn't want to go to Africa," she recalled. "There are too many wild animals there."

She remembers Sam, and she bitterly remembers that her husband had bought one share of stock, valued at $25, in the company. For some reason she had kept the certificate, and she finally dug it out of a clutter of papers hidden away in a valise under her bed.

"Yes," she stated emphatically in answer to a question, "this is the only money my husband gave Sam."

And so it went with the people who were involved, directly or indirectly, wittingly or unwittingly, in the scheme. To watch the flickering, erratic mind attempting to revive a lost emotion, to stand by while still another mind protects its owner with gross factual distortion, is the kind of drama that any attempt at the re-creation of a long-past, subjectively important event, evokes. But this, in short time, too easily deteriorates into dilettantism. An array of recalled emotions is not a social history; an awesomely old, chronically disillusioned woman lamenting a failure is not an adequate answer to the movement's appeal.

The point is really this: the Sam movement, quite apart from its local, human interest, contains much significant material on the social conditions of the time and place at which it occurred. It tells much about the people who were involved in it, and in turn, as much about the people who rejected any involvement. It tells both of the blacks and the whites, the latter structuring the lives of the former and creating, in large measure, their discontents.

This movement provides the germ of an explanation for the social unrest of an historically inarticulate group of people, a group which could not easily verbalize this discontent in florid protests, which could not pour its feelings into a concrete mold to be viewed by future historians. The story of Sam's movement is the story of a group of people who probably knew that they could make no perceptible dent in the world about them, and who, therefore, remained passive and silent with reference to that world. This passivity and silence leads too easily, however, to an interpretation of acquiescence; and acquiescent the Negroes were not. The Sam movement illustrates an ultimate stage of passivity: not utter resignation, but the final and extreme, the most vigorous and only feasible protest—the emigration to a distant, fictionalized homeland, the rejection of an American residency.

This rejection, carried out in the face of opposition, bitterness, facetiousness, all of the weapons which the white majority could muster and exhibit, was, for the Negroes, a matchless resolution of their problems. Not only did they remove themselves from the source of their difficulty, but they sternly indicted a situation which the whites had created and with which the Negroes could never hope to cope in any other terms.

African returns by Negro groups infrequently dot the history of the American nation. In colonial times, the deportation of Negroes to African colonies, either real or to be established for such purposes, was often suggested to remove these social anomalies from the American scene. Most often such programs involved only Negro freedmen, whose presence among their bound brothers posed certain delicate problems for both the North and the South. It was feared, among other things, that these freedmen might become either public charges or public menaces. Though removal to the North was a possibility, and often was laid down as condition for manumission, many northern states soon adopted countervailing regulations to keep out such freedmen. "The North," Frederic Bancroft has tartly observed, "wished the South to free her slaves and keep her freedmen, while the South was determined to make emigration a requisite for freedom."[2]

This impasse to internal relocation of Negroes left Africa as a single, feasible possibility. Perhaps the first coherent proposal for the wholesale removal of American Negroes to Africa was made in 1714.

The plan conceived of the Negro's new role in Africa as that of missionary among his more benighted fellows. The plan was elegant in its economy and simplicity. Each master was to subscribe a sum of money when he manumitted his slaves, so that each Negro could be sent to "his own country." Though the plan received wide support in the North, there is no indication that Southern masters took kindly to the scheme, nor that any manumitted slaves ever reached Africa under its terms.

Early in 1773, Rev. Samuel Hopkins, pastor of the First Congregational Church of Newport, Rhode Island, proposed to his friend Ezra Stiles the education of Negro students who might go to Africa to christianize the natives. Accompanying these several missionaries would be a vanguard of some forty persons who would found a colony in Africa which might eventually expand with manumitted slaves. Though two Negroes were ultimately sent under this program, the Revolutionary War interrupted further migration plans.[3]

In one of the most famous and fantastic colonization ventures ever undertaken by a European nation, Sierra Leone was established as a putative haven for British Negroes, some of whom had served the redcoats during the American Revolution, and had preferred to return to London rather than to remain as traitors in a country which could not make up its mind about them. These Negroes, once freed on British soil, had become something of a problem in the London slums, and had been as unable to find acceptance and integration there as they had been in the United States. In 1787, the first party, consisting of 411 settlers, among them some sixty white prostitutes shanghaied from dock bordellos, sailed from England and landed in the British protectorate. Though the Sierra Leone settlers were intermittently supplemented from Newfoundland and the United States during succeeding years, through a series of melodramatic misadventures the colony declined and its appeal to overseas Negroes was negligible.[4]

In the early 1800's, the American Colonization Society found in Liberia what it hoped would be a refuge for American freedmen. The story of this territory is well known; it attracted more than ten thousand American Negroes, despite the fervid opposition of most Negro leaders who reviled the plan. They called both the society and its scheme "anti-Christian in character and misanthropic in its pretended sympathies," and its leaders "arrant hypocrites" conducting an organization that was obviously "one of the Negro's worst enemies." [5]

One of the most ardent supporters of repatriation of the American Negro was Abraham Lincoln, who conceived of such a program as being the most humane and kind type of treatment that could possibly be afforded to a race of people who had not been assimilated effectively into American life. Lincoln went so far as to circularize various governments, asking them to indicate the degree of hospitality they would extend to resettled American Negroes. Negro colonization appeared to Lincoln to be as important as emancipation; and in late 1862, a few months before he issued the famous proclamation, he called together a group of prominent free Negroes and asked for their support of a colonization program.

"Your race suffered greatly, many of them by living among us, while ours suffer from your presence," he bluntly told them. "In a word we suffer on each side. If this be admitted, it affords a reason why we should be separated." [6] Only the lack of a general response to his suggestions appeared to dim Lincoln's enthusiasm for relocating the Negro group and solving, thereby, the "Negro problem" in the United States.

African returns conceived and implemented by Negroes are, however, excessively rare. The only known project of this type was one led by Paul Cuffe, a mixed Indian-Negro sea captain from New England. Cuffe carried thirty-eight passengers, among them twenty children, to Sierra Leone in 1815 aboard his brig, the *Traveller,* but the colonists soon blended in with the ill-fated British repatriates and failed to found an American colony of Negroes which might be attractive to their erstwhile countrymen.[7]

It appears, then, that the first large-scale back-to-Africa movement, conceived exclusively by a Negro, and made manifest as well by Negroes alone, was the one which is documented in this book. Sam's movement was, for its time, unique; and it still stands as the only plan which posed emigration to Africa as its primary goal.

The Garvey movement of a few years later included not only emigration to Africa (almost an afterthought), but also the founding of the Universal Negro Improvement Association to put the Negro into commerce and industry, and to provide a context for the development of the Negro which might be equal to that of the whites. Unlike

Garvey, Sam had no major plan save to rescue his American brothers from the situation with which they were confronted, and to return them to their homeland.

Because of their significance, back-to-Africa movements by the Negro merit more serious consideration and attention than they have generally received. It is true that charlatans and fakers have frequently organized emigration schemes which, in their course, often run like ornate comic operas, hilarious event following upon improbable motive. But once the patent absurdity of the superficial framework is brushed aside, the movement is seen as an index of a state of mind of the Negro; as such, it deserves much closer inspection.

Gunnar Myrdal pinpoints this need for documentation of such movements in a penetrating statement in *An American Dilemma*. Writing of the Garvey movement, Myrdal reminds us of the importance of the response from the Negro masses:

> Negro intellectuals, for understandable reasons, show certain inhibitions to deal with the topic as do white students of the Negro problem. But it is worthy of historical investigation and careful reflection. For one thing, it proves that it is possible to reach the Negro masses if they are appealed to in an effective way. It testifies to the basic unrest of the Negro community. It tells of dissatisfaction so deep that it amounts to hopelessness of ever gaining full life in America. It suggests that the effective method of lining up the Negroes into a mass movement is a strongly emotional race-chauvinistic protest appeal. Considering the caste conditions under which Negroes live, this is not surprising.[8]

The records of these African returns can re-create what happened; but one must, as Myrdal suggests, read carefully and reflect well before one knows why these things happened. The documents offer little more than broad clues because the words and dates in the records must be meaningfully combined with emotions, attitudes, beliefs, with states of being, those fleeting data of history which spring from an individual's mind and then refuse the invitation of time to persist.

Unfortunately, the people involved cannot tell you why a thing took place, for they really never know the total reason. To those who acted out the movement at the proper time and place, the context of the situation led inevitably to the feeling that the action was right and logical. For the undoubting colonists aboard the *Liberia,* the course of events which put them there was not a sequence of historically and temporally unique factors, each piling one upon the other and providing, finally, an impelling motive to act. For them, their fate was natural, reasonable, and unquestionably right; and their actions were the result of a vague awareness that they should act in that way.

The analyst cannot deal altogether in these "feelings," though they may ultimately be important in the understanding of a social movement. For him, the task is more difficult. He must, of necessity, assume that the sequence of events leading up to the action, each placed neatly in some order, provided the set of determinants which motivated the final action.

In the following chapters, then, we have presented what is essentially a summary of the known events of Sam's arrival in Oklahoma, his movements while in the state, his method of contact with Negroes, the events which followed when his party of colonists sailed for Africa, and the ultimate outcome of the movement. But more than that, we have attempted to portray the backdrop against which the movement itself was acted out, the backdrop of Oklahoma in 1913, and the Negro-white relations which were characteristically a part of that period. The importance of those factors which reinforced the Negro's belief that withdrawal was the only reasonable alternative has also been indicated. Moreover, we have described the role which Sam, as an individual, played in the movement, though in all truth, Sam's soil was more fertile than even he could have known when he happened upon it.

2

*"Happy is the Man"**

> He rises in the morning,
>   With the lark he tunes his lays,
> And offers up a tribute,
>   To his God and prayer and praise.
>
> And then unto his labor,
>   He cheerfully repairs,
> In confidence believing,
>   His God will hear his prayers.
>   *(From "Happy Man")*

OKFUSKEE COUNTY, where Sam did a major share of his recruiting for the back-to-Africa movement, sprawls errantly across the area of Oklahoma known locally as the "black belt." The county lies on the eastern side of the State, on the edge of the Sandstone Hills region. Though local farmers often characterize their land as "hilly," as indeed it may seem from behind a plow, the term "rolling" would be more apt.

Since shales and sandstones constitute the principle underlying rocks in the county, the low places exhibit rather extensive outcrops which form flat, gently contoured prairies. The harder shales frequently outcrop in barren ridges, interrupting the softer, densely foliated hills. In driving along the section roads in the eastern part of the county, you

---

* The epigraphs, and the titles of Chapters II-IX are quoted from *Down-East Spirituals and Others,* ed. George Pullen Jackson (Locust Valley, New York: J. J. Augustin, Inc., 1943).

have the feeling of traveling by a miniature mountain, as the road often follows along a fifteen-foot high overhang of shale.

The region as a whole is favorable for agriculture. As a result, much of the county has come under the plow, though some portions still bear the native tangle of blackjack and post oak and still look to the passerby like a wilderness.

The county, like many others in eastern Oklahoma, was carved out of the old Creek nation after the federal government, through the Dawes Commission, ended its century-long experiment in ethnic isolation. By 1898, the commission had secured an agreement from the Five Civilized Tribes to dissolve their tribal governments; and the lands had been opened for legal settlement by whites.

Oklahoma was, at this period, the last easily accessible frontier in the United States. It was the farthest east of those states which came into the Union in the twentieth century, and by a great degree, the least arid. The area embraced by the state was acquired originally in 1803 as a part of the Louisiana Purchase. Soon thereafter, it was set aside as a permanent home for many of the Indian groups which had aboriginally inhabited the now densely populated southeastern states. At the time of the removal of the Five Tribes from their original homes, each was given a title to a portion of land in the new Indian Territory in the Southwest; and each was promised protection from the encroachment of whites.

The Five Tribes erred fatally during the Civil War by siding with the Confederacy, with whom they had both cultural and economic ties. As a result they fared badly after Appomattox. Prior treaties were now invalidated and new treaties, less favorable to the Indians, drawn up.

The Indians were forced to give up their western lands, previously inviolate territory, and this area was now opened for further settlement by whites and other Indian tribes. In addition, the Indians were made to grant rights-of-way to the swiftly expanding railroads. And, in line with the post-war amendments to the Constitution, the Indians were made to free the slaves that they then held in bondage.

From the Indian point of view, these treaty concessions were fatal to their continued existence as autonomous, culturally homogenous groups. Now fallen rebels, they no longer held any bargaining power to negotiate with the government which they had, by definition, betrayed. Though in earlier times the Indians might have gainfully played the part of victims of broken treaties (an all-too traditional role with the American aborigine), they themselves were now treaty-breakers in the Union's eyes.

Only protected in a largely ineffectual and token manner by the federal government—and often themselves more than reluctant hosts to outsiders—the Indians soon found themselves being infiltrated by persons without legal right to be in their territory. By the early 1870's, cattlemen from Texas and Kansas had begun to graze their herds on Indian lands. Indian Territory was rich by contrast to much of Kansas and Texas; and from the point of view of the whites, it was ridiculously underpopulated. In addition, the whites knew that "only Indians" occupied that land. Federal protection was lax and desultory, and there was no indication that it would in the near future become more stringent. Those cattlemen who did not simply move in occasionally made casual agreements with the Indians for grazing privileges, but more often such rights were simply usurped. Soon huge cattle herds were moving back and forth across the territory bound from the Texas range to midwestern markets.

The railroads began to build during this same period, and laborers and their families came into the territory for construction work. By 1880, there were nearly five thousand people in the territory who, under no imaginative stretch of treaty agreements, had a right to be there. In addition to those whose settlement was outrightly illicit, thousands of others were operating in the territory under vague permits issued—often with abandon—by Indian tribal governments.

Day by day, white immigration into the territory increased. The Indians made feeble and largely ineffectual efforts to stem the tide by occasional local legislation which forbade the leasing of Indian lands to whites for farming purposes. But the land covenants failed to deter many tribesmen, all too eager to realize some profit on their otherwise fallow land. By 1889, there were 108,000 whites out of a total population of 175,000. Towns, even cities, sprang up, all under the domination of non-Indians.

Negroes, too, were fairly numerous in the territory. It has been estimated that between four and five thousand Negroes were brought into the land as slaves by the Indians. Of this number, a more than proportionate share was held by the Creeks, the original inhabitants of Okfuskee County. The Creeks were easy masters; often it was difficult to distinguish socially between slave and master as they worked side by side and shared the same food and dwelling. Many Negroes from slave-holding states to the east fled to Creek holdings in Indian Territory where they found masters not so white and labors not so tedious.

The place of the Negro among the Indians was a unique one. Experience in the Deep South had provided the Negro with a certain *savoir faire* that the Indian notably lacked, so that Negroes were often relied upon to deal with whites. These Negroes, sometimes called "linksters" because of their ability to speak English and their knowledge of white customs, inevitably gained a prominent position in Indian councils.[1] The isolation—often by choice, sometimes by coercion —of the Indian had ill-prepared him for dealings with the whites; the Negroes were better acculturated to the country of their forceful adoption than its original inhabitants. One Creek Negro summed up the contrast to the traditional southern slave: "I was eating out of the same pot with the Indians, going anywhere in this country I wanted to while they was still licking the master's boots in Texas."[2] Discrimination against the Negro was not absent in Indian Territory, but the Negro here obtained an importance which he did not have in the slave-holding states.

After the Civil War, many Negroes moved westward into Indian Territory in search of land and opportunity. They operated under the same restrictions as did the whites in their quest for Indian lands, but they had as little difficulty in eventually alienating these lands from the Indians through circumvention of existing statutes. When the Dawes Commission finally acted in 1898, then, the settlement of the Indian Territory was an accomplished fact, and the commission simply moved to legalize it.

The final opening of the Indian Territory is a familiar bit of Americana. The magnet of available farming land drew thousands of people, previously reticent about settling illegally in the territory, from the more densely populated southern and border states. This new frontier was comparatively near. But this was not the only advantage. Eastern Oklahoma was environmentally similar in many respects to the southern states. Cotton could be grown in both places, along with other traditional southern crops. Further, there were cultural, even spiritual, connections between the Indian Territory and the South. The Five Tribes were immersed in the slave-holding tradition, as well as in other aspects of the antebellum southern economy. The whites, too, who had "soonered" into the territory were predominantly southerners. For the relocating family, crossing out of Louisiana, Arkansas, or Texas, eastern Oklahoma was but an annex to the South which they recognized and with which they were equipped to cope. Indeed, present-day Oklahomans still employ the term "Little Dixie" for the eastern part of the state.

Kansas was represented, too, in the territory, but not to nearly as great an extent as the southern states. Kansans tended to seek their own environmental level, and peopled the Plains regions to the west.

From an early period that portion of eastern Oklahoma which ultimately became Okfuskee County had an ethnically mixed population. The Creek freedmen, the one-time slaves of the Indians, had early contributed the Negro component. This element was quickly supplemented, and eventually inundated, by the inrush of what later came to be called state Negroes, persons who, like the whites, had moved into the territory in search of new and available land. The freedmen tried to keep their distance from the state Negroes, whom they considered to have a lower status. They called them "Watchina," a corruption of Virginia—meaning "white man"—with the connotation of "white man's Negro." But the Creeks, in large part influenced by the ideology of the white men with whom they had been thrust into contact, began to turn their backs on the former slaves they had treated so leniently and with whom they had intermarried so casually. The freedmen soon became psychologically marginal and quantitatively insignificant. Only occasionally could they establish their independence of the Negro status being pressed upon them. One of them commented, for example, that "When you get as much money as Johnny (a freedman) you're an Indian not a Negro."[3] But mostly they suffered the discrimination imposed upon all Negroes and complained bitterly: "It was those state niggers from Texas that spoiled it for us, bowing and scraping and scratching the head."[4] There were at first social sanctions against marriage between the freedmen and the state Negroes, but these soon broke down in the face of the hostility of both the whites and the Indians toward the Indian freedmen.

When the Fort Smith and Western Railroad began to build through

Okfuskee County, running from the Oklahoma-Arkansas border to the territorial capital at Guthrie, Negro laborers from many parts of the South came to work on the right-of-way. The Negroes came with their families, and often with vague ideas of permanence, hoping to settle in this region, where the racial etiquette was still more ambiguous than it was in the deep southern states. The sale of land was ultimately under federal jurisdiction, and it appeared that racial distinctions would not be relevant.

In the course of time, however, old antipathies between the Negroes and whites were aroused and began to exhibit themselves. Negroes laboring on the railroads were segregated into special camps, each crew overseered by a Negro foreman. The situation was reflected by the system of building adopted by the Fort Smith and Western, as described by an early settler:

> The Ft. Smith and Western was going through where Dustin is now. Frew and Bambrick Construction Company was the main contractors for the grading. There was no town but later they started one and called it Spokoggee. One sub-contractor would have one mile to grade and his crew lived in a huddle of tents, then another sub-contractor had the next mile, and so on. There would be someone on all of the track bed. There was a mixture of people, not any one nationality. There were a few negroes, but they didn't work with the white men, their sub-contractors were negroes.[5]

The railroad encouraged settlements along its right-of-way, offering the attraction of commodity transportation. The way for extensive settlement was finally cleared by President Roosevelt's proclamation of April 20, 1904, which allowed the freedmen to put their lands on the market for sale. Speculators, both Negro and white, took advantage of the potentially profitable situation, and began to develop sites along the railroad paths in the county. As far as racial lines were concerned, two important facts were evident: settlers in the new territory had every intention of imposing upon it the pattern of residential segregation and inferiority that had been prevalent in the South; and secondly, there was, at the moment, no rigid, inflexible system of racial settlement in the youthful Indian Territory. Both provided the opportunity for an attempt to develop a new resolution of the racial problem within the limits of the superimposed segregation ethos. The result was the rapid growth in various areas of the territory, and particularly in Okfuskee County, of a number of Negro enclaves, begun with fantastically high hopes of political and social freedom of self-direction and self-fulfillment.

A political entity all their own was not an altogether new concept for the colored people of Oklahoma. They had earlier rallied around a figure who had promised them their own sovereign unit on a large scale. This figure was Edwin P. McCabe, at one time the state auditor of Kansas.

In the 1880's, McCabe had founded a newspaper, the *Herald,* which he edited from his home in the Negro community of Langston. The *Herald* was single-mindedly devoted to the establishment of the Negro state of Oklahoma.

McCabe planned to petition the President to be appointed governor of the Oklahoma Territory. It was his hope that the territory would eventually be admitted to the Union as a Negro state, ruled and governed entirely by his racial peers. The movement seemed, for a time, to gain strength.

The Indianapolis *Freeman* editorialized as late as 1905:

> The more we think about the subject the more we are convinced that it is not only possible, but it would be an easy matter for the colored people to make Oklahoma and Indian Territory a state under their own control and management; where all the opportunities of any other American would be theirs.[6]

But close observers of the prospects for such a development had long since abandoned hope. One of them wrote in 1890:

> I commenced to see the tide changing . . . The people were ordered to stop going into the Territory . . . it was not made a Negro state; McCabe was not appointed governor. . . . [The Negro] must still remain where he does not desire to stay.[7]

Though the Negro had been forced to abandon plans to control the state, he could still hope for a limited suzerainty over local towns and, perhaps, a county, where he could demonstrate his capacity for self-government and his ability to develop a society equivalent to, if not superior to, the white culture in the remainder of the country. It was out of such vision that the city of Boley, the dominant Negro community in Okfuskee County, came into existence.

The generally accepted story on the founding of Boley attributes its existence to a discussion between two white railroad officials on the potentialities and capabilities of the Negro for self-government. These two gentlemen were supposedly discussing the race question. One of them, Lake Moore, of Weleetka, maintained that Negroes could accomplish their own government with success if they were provided with a reasonable context in which to operate. The other individual, in typical anecdotal fashion, argued the contrary. "The result of the argument," as reported by Booker T. Washington, "was Boley." [8] The name was taken from that of W. H. Boley, a popular official of the Fort Smith and Western Railroad. Land was purchased from a freed-woman, who had been permitted to sell her holdings under Roosevelt's proclamation.

The Railroad made Thomas M. Haynes the townsite manager. Haynes, an uneducated but extraordinarily capable Negro, had migrated to the new area from Vernon, Texas, and was employed on the railroad right-of-way, along which he maintained a makeshift cabin. He had made the acquaintance of the whites by bedding them overnight in his cabin when they had finished a day's work on the roadbed too far out from the towns to conveniently make it back for the night.

With Boley established and thriving by 1904, just two years after the incorporation of Okemah (which was eventually to become the Okfuskee County seat) it was becoming increasingly apparent that the county was to have a large Negro component, and the townsite promoters were making the most of it. In March 1905, the first issue of Boley's local newspaper, the *Progress,* advertised the town with something less than restrained exuberance:

> Situated on the Ft. Smith and Western railroad about . . . seventy-five miles east of Guthrie, Oklahoma, and . . . twelve miles from the Oklahoma Territory line is the charming and thriving little town of Boley. It is situated in a belt of fertile land that is well adapted for agricultural purposes. Cotton, corn, wheat, oats and potatoes produces abundantly.[9]

The *Progress* continued to relate that "old settlers" had asserted droughts to be practically unknown in that part of the country. It rhapsodized:

> Great opportunities await the colored people here where their children

can educate and find an opening to execute same. We have men and women of nearly every profession and still there is room for more. There are bright prospects here for farmers. There are twenty thousand acres of land, the finest in the Creek nation, surrounding Boley to be leased and bought by Negroes.

Prospects were indeed bright, not only for farmers, but for the professional and mercantile men and women who would ultimately settle and serve those farmers.

The *Progress,* never one to leave much to its readers' imaginations, spelled out the business opportunities in its first issue: "Openings for investments in Boley: Good Lumber Yard, Press Brick Plant, Jewelry Store, Furniture Store, Hardware Store, Harness Shop, A Bank, Dry Goods and Notion Store, Good Barber Shop."

The situation was thoroughly appealing. The difficulties inherent in residence in a biracial community were absent for the Negro in Boley and the other Okfuskee County enclaves. He was no longer obliged to find himself reminded, in a thousand humiliating *vis-à-vis* encounters each day, that he was second-rate. His contacts with the whites, when such contacts were necessary, were cordial, as if he were a visitor from a distant planet. This was the "frontier"; a new land without the trammels of the old South, where contacts between the races could, it seemed, be sufficiently infrequent to make it unnecessary for either Negro or white to be obliged to implement his historically defined racial attitudes.

The Negroes, further, would have their first opportunity on the North American continent for self-determination. They were clearly interested in more than being left alone in their remote Hamitic outposts. For the Negro, this residence in a land not yet even a state was a racial experiment, offering a field for "the propagation, culture and consummation of his refined ideas," as well as "the means whereby he can transmit to his children the gift of man and womanhood, in the sense of equal fitness for the multitudinous avocations of life." [10] It offered a chance he had not before been allowed during his tormented residence in the New World. Each may well have felt something of pride in the knowledge, however bookish, of his African ancestors who had, before European colonization, maintained an orderly society without white assistance.

The whites in the county apparently shared this view, or were, at least, disinclined at first to hinder its implementation. White towns were relatively unmarred by Negro residents and white lives therefore less complicated by the colored man's presence. "Having the colored people all to themselves beats the Guthrie system," the Weleetka *American* commented. In Weleetka, a citizen did not have to send his children to the same school with the Negroes, nor was he "forced to refresh himself at a bar where the colored man's money was good." [11] There was also something appealing to many of the whites in the knowledge of exclusively Negro towns, operated by colored people. A manager of a cotton gin in Oklahoma City, visiting Boley in its early days, articulates this appeal:

> One day I was at Okemah buying cotton and the man I had made a deal with told me that I might make a good deal at Boley. I called the gin man at Boley and made an appointement to meet him the following day. When I arrived the man was at the train to meet me, and to my surprise he was a negro. After our business was finished he suggested that I meet the mayor. I went with him to the city hall where I received another surprise when I was introduced to the mayor and found he was a negro. [12]

An often reprinted story, first published in the St. Louis *Globe-Democrat* in 1912, some years after the founding of Boley, disclosed the predominant feeling of the whites toward the all-Negro community, at least during the early days of its existence.

> This is a very interesting town . . . Boley is what is known in Oklahoma as a "nigger town." It has not a single white resident in it. . . . Here at last I was to find the negro question solved. In a few minutes, I found myself delving into the workings of one of the most important colonization problems ever undertaken in this country, and I am glad to say that I was pleased with my investigation. [13]

The editor of the *Independent* in nearby Okemah was equally well impressed with the initial development of Boley. He described Boley after a visit in 1904 in glowing terms:

> The town occupies a unique position and is an object of considerable interest to students of political economics and those who have given any thought to the race problem. The citizens of Boley appear to be solving the race problem in a most satisfactory manner. . . . The experiment of founding a colored colony has in the case of Boley proven an unqualified success. . . . Any white man called to Boley on legiti-

mate business is assured the most courteous treatment. The vicious negro is not found in Boley.[14]

Apparently going concerns, assured of eventual success and prosperity, the pre-statehood all-Negro towns, with Boley in the lead, began their own systems of recruitment and attempted thereby to swell and strengthen their numbers. Boley was by far the most articulate, appealing regularly to out-of-state Negroes to "come to Boley." The *Progress,* widely distributed throughout the South, argued each week:

Now is the time for you to come before speculators flood the country. Come and help prove to the caucasian race and not only the caucasian race but the world that the Negro is a law-making and law-abiding citizen, and help us solve the great racial problem that is now before us.[15]

Editorial comment, too, was vigorous and appealing. But revealing also of the Negro's attitude was the bitterness which often crept into his comment, betraying the wariness and uncertainty he felt with his apparent emancipation on this new frontier. After a glowing tribute to the state of affairs in Boley, for example, the *Progress* suddenly, from mild complaint about white attitudes, erupted into a seemingly uncalled-for bitter lament: "Is there no spot where the Negro can escape the slime, froth, and derision of our superiors, who feast and grow fat on prejudice?"[16]

The Negroes democratized themselves and their towns almost to the point of caricature. In its first issue, the *Progress* carried this item, typical of the process which epitomized the early social life in Boley: "The Union Literary Society had quite an enthusiastic meeting last Thursday evening. The subject for debate was: Resolved, that the Negro should celebrate George Washington's birthday." After an evening of lively discussion, the resolution failed. The Negroes continued to bask luxuriously in this atmosphere, and to live life in a fashion which had previously occurred to them only in fantasies.

Now firmly established, the Okfuskee Negro sought out his brothers errant, desperately wanting to show them the results of his efforts, to reveal his gains and to share these with them. Brochures were sent to Negro preachers, who in many cases apprised their congregations of the wonders of Boley. In 1905, the *Progress* told readers outside of the area that "you should take advantage of these opportunities":

What are you waiting for? If we do not look out for our own welfare, who is going to do so for us? Are you always going to depend upon the white race to control your affairs for you? Some of our people have had their affairs looked after by the white man for the past 30 years, and where are they today? They are on the farms and plantations of the white men . . . with everything mortgaged so that they cannot get away and forever will be so long as they are working upon their farms and trading in their stores.[17]

Many Negroes from the surrounding states did, in fact, ask themselves what they had been waiting for. Apparently, their reasons were often not convincing, for by April 1905, there were over two thousand Negroes in the Okfuskee area, each with hopes high, and believing that he would, at last, be able to enjoy all the rights and privileges accorded to every American citizen.[18]

In these days before statehood, the situation in the county was relatively good for the Negroes, even in the areas where they were in closer proximity to the whites. As one survivor remembers, "before the Jim Crow law was perfected, the children of that vicinity, the whites, Indians and Negroes, played and romped together with their occasional fights and scratches." Before the rigid caste ethic was really well formulated and solidified and "before the laws were made prohibiting Negroes from mixing with the other races, this mixing together was never thought of as anything wrong." [19]

The *Progress,* almost invariably viewing the situation with grandiose optimism, summarized a feeling that was undoubtedly general with its masthead motto: "All Men Up . . . Not Some Down."

By mid-April of 1905, a vague hope had begun to crystallize. The editor of the *Progress* noted that at the following session of Congress, both Oklahoma and Indian Territories would be admitted to the Union as a state. He argued that the time was now ripe for an attempt to colonize sufficient Negroes in Boley and vicinity to be able to control a county when local governments were set up.

"If we fail in this effort," he accurately warned, "we will never have the opportunity again, there is not another spot so desirable in this country, where the Negro has a chance to settle down in a little community of his own and sleep under his own vine and fig tree." [20]
In terms of the swelling Negro population, such a plan for county

control hardly seemed over-optimistic, particularly in the face of the apparent acceptance of things as they were by the whites in the area.

Further support was given to the hopes of numerical Negro strength in the county in March, when H. B. Lewis, chairman of the committee on location of the American Colony Company, visited Boley from Atlanta, seeking a suitable place to relocate the headquarters of the company. Apparently pleased with what he found in this thriving community, Lewis announced that he would recommend Boley as the new site. Two weeks later, a contract was drawn up and signed to formalize the arrangement.

The *Progress* took this move as the basis for a stepped-up campaign to gain population:

> The effort of the American Colony Company to settle enough Negroes in a community to have a Negro county is meeting with such success . . . the office of the company has already been removed to Boley, the wonderful Negro town. . . . In all probability the Indian Territory will be admitted as a state when congress meets again, and it is hoped before this is done the Negroes will have swelled the population of the district so that a county may at once be organized.[21]

The paper cited the present population of Boley at between six and eight hundred persons, with two thousand Negroes in the immediate area. The American Colony Company had hoped to import an additional two thousand people.

While the Negroes in the Boley area spun their plans for colored control of their destiny, less-involved Negroes elsewhere were mindful of what they believed to be the inevitable end of the frontier joy ride of the Boley people. Meeting in Muskogee, the Western Negro Press Association adopted a resolution to be sent to President Roosevelt, "the greatest chief executive since the great emancipator, Lincoln":

> It . . . being considered the settled policy of the white people of the southern states to abridge the political rights of colored people, and thereby nullify the 15th amendment, a memorial shall be presented to the president and to congress opposing statehood for the two territories unless an absolute guarantee can be given that no "Jim Crow" coach laws and other laws discriminating between the races in public places . . .[will be enacted].[22]

The Negroes attending this convention, principally from biracial communities, were obviously more in contact with white reality than the relatively isolated Okfuskee settlers. Certainly, their aspirations were less flamboyant than those of the territory's settlers in the all-Negro communities.

But the Boley residents were unconcerned. They saw no reason to imagine the hostility that would spring up once their own plans came into direct conflict with those of their white neighbors, and once their own aspirations touched upon white sensitivity and white prejudice. Alone and isolated, they could be tolerated; otherwise, they would have to be suppressed, particularly as their possible power in the area became manifest.

Suppression, however, was not in the immediate offing, and Uncle Jesse found reason for eloquence when he sang:

> Say have you heard the story,
>   Of a little colored town,
> Way over in the Nation
>   On such lovely sloping ground?
> With as pretty little houses
>   As you ever chanced to meet,
> With not a thing but colored folks
>   A standing in the streets?
> O 'tis a pretty country
>   And the Negroes own it, too
> With not a single white man here
>   To tell us what to do—
>   In Boley.

> And I will tell that fellow
>   Whoever he may be
> If you don't think we are colored
>   Just come here and see.
> Get on the Fort Smith and Western
>   The train will bring you here.
> Take any of the coaches
>   You have no cause for fear.
> Here a Negro makes your dresses
>   And a Negro makes your pants
> And hands your mail out
>   If you'll give him half a chance—
>   In Boley.[23]

Political activity got underway in 1906, and the joy ride was on its way to a detour from democracy. On the surface, things were both quiet and promising for the Negroes of the area. They participated fully in the election of representatives to the constitutional convention, some three hundred of them exercising their right to vote in the Boley district. The freedom with which they were allowed to cast their ballots reinforced their hopes for full participation in citizenship after statehood.

But the results of the election carried an ominous warning for the white people in the region surrounding Boley. Boley had been included in the 79th district for the purpose of electing delegates to the convention called to piece together Oklahoma's subsequent constitution. The gerrymandered district included the comparatively large towns of Weleetka, Henryetta, and Okemah, which together could muster 875 votes. But these votes were almost evenly divided between the Republican and the Democratic candidates for convention delegates, 397 going to the former and 350 to the latter, while the Socialist candidate drew 128 votes from the three towns.

Boley, on the other hand, with a voting force of three hundred citizens, cast 265 votes for the Republican candidate and only 26 for the Democrat. Six votes were given to the Socialist. Thus, when the Republican won by a mere margin of 172 votes, it was clear that the Boley majority of 239 votes had more than carried the day for the Republicans. The Negro settlement, united and determined to stay united in its franchise, held the key to the area's strength. It had to be dealt with and dealt with forcefully and decisively.

But this would not become manifest at once. The ominous sound of William Murray's remarks to the membership of the constitutional convention on the inferior place of the Negro in Oklahoma seemed to pass Boley by. The Negroes consolidated their gains, held their second local city election, and stabilized the expanding community. Business was good; and farming, largely of cotton, was equally prosperous.

It was soon apparent that the convention would remove Henryetta from consideration in the new county arrangement, which would include Boley. It also became very obvious that the county seat would go to either Okemah or Weleetka, both white towns of about the same size as Boley. Okemah was finally designated as the temporary seat, her permanence in this regard pending a future election. Certainly, there was no sympathy whatever in the Democratic-controlled convention for Boley's once-resplendent dreams of county control. The honeymoon days of condescending indulgence for the Negroes were over, now that the stark question of power and gain was involved. At best, the Negroes could hope to court favor by a judicious leasing of their ballot strength to their most obvious white friends.

The whites were not unaware of this. In late December, the Okemah *Independent,* with warm concern for the Negroes, and with an equally deep interest in securing the county seat for Okemah, reminded its readers that the local Commercial Club had earlier promised the colored people of Boley that it would provide a rooming house for them in Okemah so that they might be comfortable when doing business in that town.

The *Independent* moralized:

> It looks like this would be the proper time to commence this move again, after making this promise we would lose the confidence of those Negroes if we failed to fulfill, and Okemah is not the town to lay down on a promise.[24]

But early in 1907, the house of John Hogan, the only Negro then living in Okemah, was dynamited. This act of violence could hardly go unnoticed. The *Progress* mustered its fullest indignation, and argued that Okemah was a dubious choice for a county seat since Negroes were obviously far from safe there. It interpreted this move as an outright rejection of the Negro by the townspeople of Okemah:

> Okemah certainly shows from her actions at least that they do not want the support of the Negroes in Okfuskee county. The dynamiting of the colored man's house there a week ago, is enough to set any colored man thinking.[25]

March was uneventful. No further incidents of violence occurred, and the situation provoked by the dynamiting trailed into April, unresolved. For the whites, most of whom had certainly not been involved, the incident was trivial. For the Negroes, with the passage of time, it came to represent but a random attack on their race, and one which they doubtless felt need not reflect the attitude of most whites toward them.

On April 4, 1907, the Republican call for the county organizational meeting went out. Throughout the spring and summer, arrangements were made by local committees; and each was briefed for the fall convention.

For the Okfuskee Negroes, this was the first real election. That they had not prevailed in securing the county seat for themselves did not seem, in retrospect, unreasonable. Their hopes had simply been too ambitious. After all, they were outnumbered by the whites in the new county; and assuredly they could not hope that a group such as the delegates to the convention, drawn from all segments of the new state, would be sympathetic to their aims. But now their function in politics, their electoral weight, would become clear. They would, in this first state election, walk to the conventions and ultimately to the polls and make their wishes felt through their numbers. This is what they had been preparing for.

The Republicans were, of course, traditionally the Negroes' friends. Indeed, as early as 1892, in the Oklahoma Territorial Republican Delegate Resolutions, they had "welcomed to free homes in Oklahoma, the honest, frugal, and intelligent colored people." [26] In the same set of resolutions, they had offered to the Negro the full enjoyment of all constitutional, civil, political, and religious rights which the whites themselves would have had in this new land.

In the middle of August, the Republican convention, heavily attended by Negroes, met in Okemah to nominate a slate for county offices. A white chairman was elected and a Negro secretary named to the permanent organization. Difficulties began shortly after ten in the morning, when the convention was called to order. Two contesting delegations from Weleetka and Paden, called the "black" and the "white" delegations, presented themselves, each demanding the right to be seated. The committee on credentials met hastily and soon reached a compromise. Both delegations would be seated, it ruled, but each member would be given half a vote.

The "white" delegations from Paden and Weleetka, on learning of this decision, bolted the convention. That left fifty-eight Negroes and twenty-four whites to determine the Republican ticket. Most of the nominees were white, but two of the three county commissioners finally named were Negroes.

The Weleetka *American,* at this period Democratic and violently anti-Negro, wrote a scathing report of the convention:

Is it any wonder that the self-respecting white voter has tabooed the republican county ticket?

A common water bucket on the platform from which both black and white drank, using the same dipper.

Will any self-respecting white man cast a vote for anyone who is willing to place himself on the level with a thick-lipped son of Ham in an endeavor to secure a county job? [27]

Another note in the same paper showed the tremendous hostility aroused by the Negroes now that they had come into the same arena, as competitors, with the whites:

Don't forget that R. J. Dixon, nominee for representative on the nigger ticket, favors allowing the thick-lipped Boley bucks to ride in the same coach or even in the same seat with your wife or daughter, or the kinky-headed pickaninnies to attend the same school with your children, and if he should, by any chance, go to the legislature he will oppose the separation of the races.

Apparently, many a "self-respecting" Republican was willing to "place himself on a level with a thick-lipped son of Ham" for the powerful Negro support upon which he knew he could count and without which his political chances were nonexistent. The Negroes, for their own part, wanted no connection with the Democratic party. For the Oklahoma Negro, as indeed for most southern Negroes, the Democratic party meant "white supremacy"; and this was completely unacceptable to the Negro in terms of his own conception of his post-emancipation status.

For the whites, the situation was becoming alarmingly clear. The Negroes were no longer passive pawns in the resolution of an academic argument on their abilities to govern themselves. They were no longer the characters in an amusing anecdote, which even in the telling had now grown somewhat tedious. They were threatening the whites of the county with their active participation in politics. What was infinitely worse for the Democrats, the Negroes had the power to transform this threat into actual control of the county. A Negro county with Negro officials to operate it, all in conjunction with white Republicans, was an appallingly likely prospect.

Despite the obvious gravity of the situation, the Democrats were for the moment in control, in a position to use—or more reasonably, to abuse—power that they had secured in a somewhat pre-emptory fashion during the constitutional convention. Each county election was to be supervised by a three-man election committee. To this committee the convention had named two Democrats and one obviously emasculated Republican. The committee was in a position to head off the Negro's political ambitions.

With the aim of disenfranchisement agreed upon, the Democrats swiftly maneuvered to manipulate the election. In September, the county election board met to pass upon the list of nominations for offices which had been filed with it. The Democratic ticket, it found, was eminently complete and acceptable. But the Republicans lacked candidates for two critical positions: the county weigher and the coroner. In addition, the Negro nominees from Boley who had been duly named by the Republican convention were not certified properly, the election board decided, and would, therefore, be left off the ticket. The Okemah *Ledger* noted that "a lily-white set of nominees from Paden who had regularly filed were certified to." [28] The same failure to provide proper certification was found in the other townships in the county. Either the Republican ticket as a whole was discarded, or the Negro nominees were replaced.

The election board took one further step to protect the white, Democratic interests of the county, gerrymandering the precincts to make Negro voting as difficult as possible. Though Boley boasted a population of 824 on September 12, with Okemah listing only 1,027, and other townships considerably less, the election board ruled that there were not sufficient voters in Boley to justify the establishment of a voting precinct there. Boley voters were informed that they would have to cast their ballots at Van Zandt, a town some twelve miles distant from their homes.

The next day, the *American* provided the rationalization for this recent move of the election board, noting that if the whites did not stand together in the election, regardless of their political beliefs, the Negroes would "run things with a high hand." It reminded readers that the present situation was extremely dangerous, and it scolded white Republicans who were compounding the danger and "either do not realize the full force of negro domination, or who are so rabidly partisan that they are willing to recognize negro equality to gain political supremacy." Moved by its own Cassandra cries, the *American* continued:

> Crush the insolence of the negro now. Rebuke the white men who have encouraged and abetted them in their efforts to make themselves the peer of the white race, and you will have checked the influx of negro populations, guarded the purity of your homes, and provided safety and honor to your wives and daughters.[29]

Three Boley citizens filed a petition to compel the county officials to establish a voting precinct at a place nearer to Boley than Van Zandt, but the Democratic commission was hardly likely to grant such relief. Instead, they placed a white election inspector in frightening vigilance over the unrelocated Van Zandt ballot box. Despite these efforts, however, the Negroes were not to be denied so easily their franchise in this, their first opportunity to exercise it.

On the morning of September 17, when Walter Klutts, the election inspector, arrived at the Van Zandt precinct, he found a handful of white men there and some 100 to 150 Negroes. Many of the Negroes had camped at the voting place on the night prior to the election, and many others poured into the area "in wagons, buggies, and on horseback," marching "from the filthy claws of the gerrymander to his ugly head at Van Zant." [30] Klutts began erecting booths and preparing for the election. The Negroes demanded that they have a representative on the local election board which supervised the voting, fearing that otherwise their ballots would not be honored. There was a heated discussion, with the Negroes claiming that an attempt was being made to defraud them.

Klutts, fearing for his life, according to the outraged Okemah papers, mounted his horse, preparing to flee from the scene. Before he left, the Negroes demanded the keys to the ballot boxes; afterwards, they quietly filed to the polling place, ultimately marking their ballots for the Republican candidates who had not been removed by the county election board, or writing in the names of those candidates who had. Klutts later returned to claim the box but was hissed from the precinct.

The result of the election was a clear-cut plurality for the Republicans in Okfuskee County. The county election board, having been frustrated in its efforts to avert the Republican victory by failing to certify its ticket, and by gerrymandering the Negroes, still had no intention of recognizing the elections returns. It simply ruled that the Van Zandt votes were illegal, and that the 395-vote Republican majority in this precinct was not to be counted.

Hysterical with delight, the *American* crowed:

> After hearing the evidence in the Van Zant case the board of commissioners threw out the vote in that precinct. According to evidence introduced, the niggers chased out the white judge, took charge of things and allowed every nigger, little, big, old and young to vote as often as they desired. They violated every single rule of election and the result was a republican majority in that precinct . . .[31]

The Republicans were irritated that their efforts had failed. The Negroes, however, were outraged. For them, this was not a matter of politics alone, but a glaring betrayal of their dream. Not only had they been obliged to vote with difficulty; but the very results of this vote were now dismissed as invalid, in obvious and flagrant violation of every law and every shred of morality which they could call to mind. They appealed the case almost at once. But through an endless series of legal manipulations, a decision was not reached for more than a year.

From the point of view of the whites, the Negroes had now engaged them in open battle for supremacy in the county. The Negroes could clearly not be gently manipulated, and were prepared to assert their rights at the ballot box, in the courts, or wherever their definition of right might lead them. This threat had to be met head-on.

For the Negroes something horrible had occurred. Although they had not done anything untoward, they now found themselves slapped hard for doing it. In making their voices heard in the election, they had simply followed their own conception of their place; in marching, "as of old," to the polls, they had simply followed the lead of the whites, who had allowed them to develop this conception. The gerrymandering of the precincts might be a partisan move; the ominous election supervisor might again be a partisan move; but the dismissal, illegal as it obviously was, of the results of their vote could not be interpreted by them as a simple Democratic maneuver for control. The whites were now prepared, it was evident, to take any steps which might occur to them to prevent the Negro from participating in politics; and the extremes to which these people might go to keep him subservient could only be guessed at in frightening prospect by the Negro.

3

"Though Darkness Should Cover"

Though age and misfortune press hard on my feelings,
I'll fly to the Bible and trust in the Lord,
Though darkness should cover his merciful dealings,
My soul is still cheered by his heavenly word.
(From "Blessed Bible")

THE VAN ZANDT election affair was probably the most important single event in sharply demarcating the line between the untoward hopes of the Okfuskee County Negroes and the realities of second-rate citizenship from which they would not be allowed to escape. Even their willingness to segregate themselves into racial ghettoes proved of little value in their relations with the whites. But though the evidence of white hostility was clear and unmistakable, the Negroes could hardly yield their dreams quickly and cleanly. They held tight to these dreams, sometimes in the face of overwhelming evidence against their achievement, and they twisted their minds through endless subjective labyrinths in their attempts to remain convinced that they still had a chance to gain greater autonomy and democracy in their new homes.

But the Negroes were slowly forced to give ground, reacting to each new indignity with either incredulity or passive withdrawal. Occasionally, they rebounded with a renewed optimism which was hardly warranted by the slight advance they had made or the brief period of relative serenity they had been granted by white inertia. There was no question, though, that Negro discontent was growing; and although its development might be slow and erratic, even temporarily assuaged by a flickering hope, it would never again be quieted completely. Despite the wavering course of the Negro's reaction to the situation, an easily discernible line began to run through the story, a line of continued defeat, growing disillusionment, and nascent groping toward a resolution.

The Van Zandt dispute remained in the courts throughout the next year, settled alternately one way and then another. But by the end of 1907, two events occurred which eclipsed the local interest in this suit, and more clearly detailed the mood of the times.

In December, George W. Washington, a wealthy Muskogee Negro, made plans to depart for Africa, where he hoped to visit various Negro countries. Washington explained that the purpose of his trip was to determine what part of the African continent was best suited for settlement by "a free and self-governing race of Ethiopians."[1] He told the press that he was convinced that ultimately the white race would occupy the whole of the United States, and that the population would be so dense that coresidence with the Negro would be impossible. Washington reported that he proposed to head a movement in Oklahoma to transport the Negroes of the United States to Africa if he were satisfied with the prospects for development on that continent. "He is a man of prominence among the colored race," one newspaper noted, "and the Negroes of this section will lend a willing ear to his scheme." [2]

In the same month that Washington left for his exploratory visit, the new state of Oklahoma had its first lynching. It took place at Henryetta, a town just outside of Okfuskee County.

James Gordon, a Negro, had become involved in an argument with the white owner of a livery stable, who had refused to rent him a rig. Gordon borrowed a revolver from another Negro and shot the white man to death. Gordon was captured and jailed, but a Henryetta mob soon gathered, took him from the jail and hanged him to a telephone pole. The body was riddled with bullets by the crowd.

The reaction to the lynching was immediate and intense, and for a time it appeared that a race riot would ensue. The Okemah *Independent* noted that there were reports from "negro settlements . . . that negroes were arming in hot haste" and preparing to march on Henryetta.[3] Bloodshed, the paper warned, might result at any time.

While their political and social fortunes ebbed, Okfuskee Negroes were still making economic gains. In Boley, the *Beacon* (the town now supported two weekly newspapers) reported a scarcity of housing in the city. Hotels were doing an overflow business and the Citizen's League was compelled to hold a mass meeting in an effort to devise plans for providing better accommodations for home-seekers during their initial period of residence in the city. The *Beacon* remarked that as towns in the county were going, "Boley is a live one." [4]

Early in 1908, the state legislature seated the Democratic candidate who had been elected by the elimination of the Van Zandt returns. The Democratic county officers had also taken their oaths of office, though the Republicans still held grimly to their hopes of eventual victory in the courts, warning "the thinking class" of people to be careful in doing business with the officials because they might eventually be turned out of office. [5]

To add to Negro problems, a recently enacted law, segregating Negroes and whites in railroad cars, was about to be tested in the courts; and the colored people of the state were frantically collecting money to support the case. The *Independent,* a sometime editorial friend of the Negro, was in a dilemma over the attitude it should take toward the act.

It could sympathize, it felt, with the Negroes who would be "made to ride in the coach the front part of which . . . will often be filled with drunken whites," and it could agree that the Negroes "are justly entitled to protection against drunken brawlers"; but at the same time the paper felt that "no scheme has ever yet been devised to effectually protect white men and white women when travelling by rail, from the annoyance and even danger of coming in contact with whiskey crazed fiends." Under these circumstances, it seemed that the "negro will have to continue to 'tote' his end of the burden so long as whiskey is distilled." [6]

The second Republican county convention was held the same month, and the change in racial attitude was evident. The Republicans were now trying to unload the Negroes from "white party councils and control" without losing them at the polls. [7] It was a delicate plan to effect. The Republicans knew that the state legislature had begun to implement its attempts to completely disenfranchise the colored voters by adopting a "grandfather clause," an amendment to the state constitution, which would define the right of franchise in terms of ancestry. The major problem with which the state representatives had been confronted was the framing of an act which would keep the Negroes from voting without "knocking out the Indians also." [8] The *Independent* bitterly commented: "The gang entrusted with the work ... probably will be equal to the emergency. It is doubtful if they will be hampered with many scruples in the wholesale disenfranchisement of citizens." [9]

Despite the almost certain passage of the grandfather clause, the Republicans had to act cautiously in their dealings with the Negroes since they could not be certain how many might ultimately be able to circumvent the provisions of the clause.

At the convention, the Boley delegation was cut into halves, and one segment was assigned to the Van Zandt whites. This realignment of delegates allowed the whites to outnumber the Negroes in this precinct, and to trim sharply the Negro potential at the convention. The plan was also deemed to have the long-range effect of preventing the Negroes from Boley, Clearview, Weleetka, and other small towns from controlling the next nominating convention and placing Negro candidates on the Republican ticket.

Despite this maneuver, a mixed delegation was named to the state convention. One Republican summed up this development with some resignation when he said, "It was a bitter pill to take, but you know the grandfather law will not shut out all the negro votes and we want 'em." [10]

Boley still hoped for a solution to her growing political problems in the continued recruitment of Negro population. The white newspapers imagined they saw a plot underway to systematically increase Negro colonization in the county, the details of which they passed on to their readers.

The plan was "simple and direct." It was alleged that a Boley banker and several realtors approached the white farmers in the vicinity of Boley. The delegation supposedly made the farmer a higher than reasonable offer for his land and suggested that he might be more comfortable in an area where he would have fewer Negro neighbors. The white farmer, it was said, would usually sell at a good profit and a new Negro family would be invited to buy the vacated land, and "thus, the black population is spread." [11]

It was further reported that during the preceding two months, under this nefarious system, more than one hundred white farmers had sold their leases to Negroes. In several localities the population had doubled within the past year, a large percentage of this increase being Negro.

The *Progress* righteously denied the allegation, calling it a patent absurdity. It argued: "No one need have any worry about Boley bothering anything, or anybody politically or otherwise. If it don't concern us we leave it alone." [12]

There was the tragically familiar ring of passivism in this comment. The Negroes, having now been openly defined as threats to white supremacy in the county, had been subjected to political reprisals; and they were retreating to the pattern of subordination which their southern backgrounds had taught them to be successful. What the *Progress* said, however, though an omen, was not really a current majority view. The Negro was still very much concerned with county politics and still conceived of himself as capable of having an important role in it. The somewhat naïve soothings of the *Progress* must either have expressed only the new approach of a cautious minority or a studiously contrived reticence on the part of the editor.

In June, the Boley paper, belying its earlier disclaimer of political interest, hit out vigorously against Okemah as the permanent county seat:

> The county seat fight is now on, and Boley desires to be counted with the element that stands for a fair deal, so far as the individual rights of the citizens . . . are concerned. Boley is strictly against Okemah.[13]

The *Progress* recalled the Van Zandt affair, in which "the gang of Okemah politicians who stood for the disenfranchisement of the Negro" summarily counted out the Negro votes. The *Progress'* editor clearly entertained no fantasies about his town as a county seat; but he could not make up his mind on other places, save in his rigid and uncompromising opposition to Okemah.

"We stand for a fair campaign, a fair vote, and that each town and each citizen may stand on an equal footing," he wrote; and he was convinced that Okemah would not provide these prerequisites to democratic equality were she to gain the permanent designation as county seat. "Faithful are the wounds of a friend; but the kisses of mine enemy are deceitful," he dolefully concluded.

Okemah was indignant. The *Ledger* felt that if Boley's editor disapproved of the acts of a handful of county officials, that was his right. But it was appalled that these acts should be held against the entire population of Okemah. The newspaper was further enraged by the fact that several county editors had seen fit to reprint the *Progress'* editorial without further comment. There is "no excuse," the Okemah press believed, "for peddling broadcast the slanders of an irresponsible negro against more than 1000 citizens of Okemah who had no knowledge of the affair." The charges, it was contended, should have been directed "plainly at the men involved and not against people in no manner connected with the matter." [14]

In July, a proclamation was issued calling for an election to determine the permanent site of the county seat. Though Okemah residents feigned surprise at any doubt of the election's outcome, and though they reassured the rational people of the county that Okemah was so conveniently located that "none could be found who would desire or seek to change it," they nonetheless made hasty overtures to woo the Boley vote back into their camp.[15] The county officials in Okemah, for example, reconsidered their earlier high-handed dismissal of the Negroes' request for a polling place more convenient than Van Zandt and turned their attention to the establishment of a precinct at Boley. When they had concluded their deliberations, not one, but two precincts had been established, Number 18 at North Boley, and Number 19 at South Boley.

The Negroes bit hard at this ill-concealed bid for their support. Over five hundred persons met at the Antioch Baptist Church in Boley, where many town leaders addressed the crowd. After much discussion, a resolution was submitted and unanimously adopted. Into this resolution were crowded many rationalizations. It stated that the removal of the county seat "would work a hardship upon the people who have made investments in Okfuskee County." It might also occasion the costly disorganization of the county government, to the detriment of a large number of citizens. It would "create a feeling that would operate to the disadvantage of business interests in the county." [16]

Telling, too, of the tragic recognition by the Negro of his declining status in the county was the comment in the resolution that Boley residents wanted the county seat at Okemah rather than at a town nearer to Boley:

> . . . since the relations of the races have been such as to warrant the Negro . . . to guard against any movement that would tend to encourage large numbers of other races of people to dwell and become too closely allied in interests to large numbers of Negroes and to the detriment of both.

But the clue to the unanimous adoption of the resolution lay in its final paragraph. This asserted that the Negroes were deeply appreciative of the action of the County Election Board in establishing voting precincts for the citizens of Boley, "thereby insuring peaceable and fair elections with satisfaction to all parties concerned."

A boon had been granted; a temporary concession had been given by the whites. Okfuskee County Negroes, seduced by their own hopes for better times, had fallen in line with Okemah and once more the atmosphere in the county had apparently improved.

The Paden *Press* remarked on this development:

> Once the darkey was not allowed to have his habitat in the town [Okemah] and he was discouraged by high explosives. . . . But now in the eyes of Okemah boosters the colored man is the "fairest among ten thousand, and one altogether lovely." All he has to do is ask and it will be given unto him.[17]

Despite Weleetka's free barbecue for "colored citizens," the Negroes remained steadfastly behind Okemah. By the end of August, Okemah had won the county seat election, and it was reported that though the "election was quite spirited . . . no trouble had been reported from any precincts."[18] This was the last election for many decades in which the Negro would vote without contest.

Several days later, George W. Washington returned from his ninemonth tour of Liberia. He had been much impressed by a nation of Negroes seeming to live under laws which they had themselves enacted. Once again in Oklahoma, he began to solicit interest from local Negroes in migrating to Liberia. Washington scheduled an October convention to review his plan for a removal to Africa.

The *Independent,* recognizing the present camaraderie between the Negroes and the whites to be but a temporary lull, took some positive interest in the scheme.

> In no other state in the Union are negroes so rich and prosperous as in Oklahoma, where the freedmen share with the Indians in the distribution of lands and vested funds. In spite of this wealth these . . . negroes . . . would welcome a return to Africa and there endeavor to solve the destiny of the colored race.[19]

The convention, drawing delegates from Negro communities around the state, presented a resolution to Oklahoma's Senator Thomas Gore, who in turn presented it to Congress. The petition asked for federal money to aid in the transport of those Negroes from the United States who wanted to colonize in Liberia. The resolution gained some support in Congress, but a general feeling was shortly expressed that the "more highly educated negroes would take advantage of the chance" while the less desirable Negroes would remain in the United States.[20] Since many of the senators felt that this latter group was precisely the element which the country would wish to be rid of, they saw little merit in the proposal.

At the end of April 1909, more than a year and a half after the general election had been held, the first high court decision on the Van Zandt case was handed down. Judge Frank M. Bailey, of Chickasha, had been appointed by the state supreme court as a special judge to hear the case. He ruled that no undue duress had been put upon the white election official and that no intimidation of voters had taken place. The election inspector's fear of the Negro assemblage was the result of his own unreasonable interpretation of the situation. The election was, therefore, entirely legal.

Effectively, then, the entire Republican ticket of 1907 was elected. But since the ticket had carried two Negroes to office as county commissioners, a situation which would have been unacceptable even to the Republicans, a compromise was reached and, on May 20, when the Republicans finally were installed in the offices to which they had been elected, all of the county commissioners were white. Though the case was soon appealed to the state supreme court, and Bailey's decision reversed, no change in county officers took place. The next election was too near, and the compromise had obviously satisfied all parties concerned.

During the period of political quiet that existed between the elections the Negro communities attempted simply to maintain themselves in the face of growing white antipathy. The sheriff's force from Okemah began to make periodic raids on Boley, ostensibly to clear out gambling joints and other undesirable places, but more functionally to intimidate the Negroes during the interim period and to indicate to them without question the place they were destined to occupy.

The raids forced the law-abiding citizens of Boley into an unpleasant dilemma. No one was more indignant about the violations of gambling and liquor ordinances than these respectable Negro people, and they complained often to the county officials about the lawlessness in Boley. At the same time, the arrests and trials of the lawbreakers in the courts at the county seat served to reinforce the white stereotype of the Negro as disreputable and criminal. The Negro middle class tried desperately to disassociate itself from the rowdy element and align itself with the peaceful segments of the white group, a maneuver which was singularly ineffective.

The *Independent* defended the sheriff's behavior and chose to interpret the raids as a requisite part of his duties:

> Sheriff Ball and his deputies had occasion to go to Boley last week, where they raided a couple of joints and arrested a much wanted negro criminal, a bank sneak who was badly wanted. The officers went armed, as is customary when on official business, a fact which caused the Boley *Progress* to give them a lecture on the carrying of arms, especially in Boley.[21]

The editor of the *Progress* was indignant over the regular appearances of the sheriff in his town.

> The Sheriff's officers from Okemah are becoming a nuisance in Boley. Nearly every morning the train brings in a bunch of deputies (sheriffs and constables) who flaunt their big smoke poles and parade the town after the fashion of Captain Lafitte . . . the disgusting feature is the exhibition of their smoke poles. A half-naked officer with nothing on but a six-shooter, a pair of pants and shoes is not a pleasing sight. Perhaps no county tolerates these six-shooter parades so strong as Okfuskee.[22]

"It would be just as convenient," he observed, "to conduct their maneuvers down by the arsenal at Okemah."

But no other county had such a large and active group of Negroes as Okfuskee. The six-shooters had a purpose. The whites, often in this somewhat naïve and haphazard fashion, were fighting the Negroes in whatever manner they could; and the tradition of intimidation was the most familiar one to them.

Early in 1910, the Negroes again renewed their efforts to nominate a county ticket. But now that the county seat controversy had been settled satisfactorily, the commissioners had no further reason to humor the Negroes; the time had come to put an unmistakable end to their recurrent dreams. The brief honeymoon was over. In March, the county commissioners redistricted the entire county, reducing the number of townships from ten to six, and throwing Boley, along with Castle and Paden, into a single township.

The *Independent* objected strongly. It pointed out that this latest move was the crassest kind of gerrymandering and that it should certainly "excite the admiration of the state machine itself." [23] The paper tried to apply fiscal logic to a situation that was blatantly racial.

> The change in the township lines . . . will entail much needless expense on the taxpayers. . . . A thousand dollars will not cover the cost of the change. Is there any benefit to be derived? Absolutely none. Rank partisanship is responsible for this unjust and expensive move.[24]

Complaints began to pour in on the commissioners. The protests pointed out that Paden township, which once again included Boley, extended over one-third of the area of the county. The *Independent* hopefully interpreted the complaints as an "ominous roar," and believed that "dissatisfaction is widespread and increased in proportion as the people learn the exact boundaries of the townships fixed by the gerrymander." [25] Some persons averred that they would ignore the proclamation announcing the new townships. An appeal made to the commissioners was taken under advisement, but the decision on it was deferred until May.

Before the redistricting provision became effective, an election to determine the location of the state capital again vividly illustrated the need to keep the Negro voters in check in Okfuskee County. The Negroes presented a solid electoral front on the capital issue, casting 295 votes in favor of retaining the capital at Guthrie. Only one vote was cast for Oklahoma City and none for Shawnee. Guthrie thus carried Okfuskee County by 195 votes, though Oklahoma City received a plurality in the state.

The complex redistricting tactic soon proved unnecessary, for the state legislature took steps to deal with the bothersome question of Negro voting in Oklahoma.

The legislature had decided to submit the grandfather clause to a vote of the people. The tortured prose of the amendment ran as follows:

> No person shall be registered as an elector of this state or be allowed to

vote in any election held herein unless he be able to read and write any section of the Constitution of the State of Oklahoma; but no person who was, on January 1st, 1866, or at any time prior thereto entitled to vote under any form of government, or who at that time resided in some foreign nation and no lineal descendant of such person shall be denied the right to register and vote because of his inability to so read such sections of the constitution.[26]

Following the amendment on the ballot, and in small type, were the words: "For the Amendment." Anyone wishing to vote against the proposition was obliged to strike out these words with a pencil. If he did not do so, his ballot would be counted as a vote in favor of the amendment. The move was obviously, as the *Independent* noted, for the purpose of taking advantage of ignorant and careless voters. "Be sure to have your lead pencil with you," the paper reminded, for no other means of deletion would do.

Despite the obstacles posed for those who wanted to vote against the amendment, it failed to carry in Okfuskee County by more than four hundred votes. Again, the Negroes trooped to their polling places in a last-ditch effort to protect their rights. The amendment, however, carried throughout the state by a majority of almost thirty thousand votes.

The *Daily Oklahoman,* published in Oklahoma City, described through its local correspondent the feelings of the Okfuskee County whites:

> Okfuskee county white people are living in one long celebration . . . a celebration of August 2, the day on which the Negro was disenfranchised. Okfuskee county is made up largely of Negroes, and the blacks have, until this time, practically dominated politics and controlled the schools.[27]

Though grossly exaggerating the extent of Negro control in the county, the *Oklahoman* doubtless reflected the feelings of a majority of the whites in Okfuskee.

This state-wide move sanctioning discrimination against the Negroes had some violent consequences. In Delaware, a small town in Nowata County, local Negroes, many of them long-time residents of the town, were driven from their homes. A committee of white citizens was appointed to call upon each of the Negro families in town and order them to leave at once. The Negroes, terrified by this bizarre and violent turn of events, "made haste to do the bidding of the committee." [28]

With the majority of the Negroes disenfranchised, the Okfuskee County Election Board continued to play havoc with precinct lines, its revised target the Republican votes of the county. Raging at this result of the "monstrous defects of the Oklahoma election law" which abdicated all power of precinct reorganization to local election boards, the *Independent* attacked the situation with the most biting sarcasm it could muster:

> The precinct lines of this county have been changed so often that it is becoming monotonous. The voter cannot keep up with these changes without neglecting his ordinary business. He can't tell "where he is at." The map maker would work himself into a premature grave to keep up with the changes. A citizen may go to sleep in one precinct and wake up in a precinct in which he is a perfect stranger. When the citizen goes to bed his precinct may be no bigger than a good-sized farm, and wake up in the morning to find that his precinct has spread over half the county . . . he may have to swear out a search warrant and finally locate his voting place. . . . So far as is at present known no voting places have been moved entirely outside the county, but it would be well for surrounding counties to guard their boundaries, as an invasion by the Okfuskee county election board is liable to occur if further changes are contemplated. [29]

Some Negroes determined to take a stand against the grandfather clause. Early in September, A. G. W. Sango of Muskogee, described locally as a "big Negro politician," [30] called a state convention at Boley to raise funds for an organized opposition to the enforcement of the clause. Sango encountered some difficulty, however, in conducting the meeting, arising presumably out of the reluctance of the Boley group to follow an outside leader whose motives were suspect and whose reputation was anything but savory.

When he arrived at the First Baptist Church in Boley where the meeting had been scheduled, Sango found the door barred to him. He transferred the meeting to another site, only to find that a group of Negroes had perched atop an adjoining building, brandishing rocks which they had gathered to "toss down on the heads of the convention if it didn't suit them." On hand also were some two hundred Boley citizens, recently deputized for the occasion and each carrying a six-shooter.

As Sango attempted to quiet the group and to call the meeting to order, an unidentified man stood up on the sidelines and announced, "Ah am chairman of dis convention and she am adjourned." Meanwhile, many of the delegates had scattered from the meeting place to follow a "ballyhoo" band which was parading down the street.

Sango, understandably abandoning his efforts to organize the meeting, met with some of his loyal followers that evening and decided to reconvene at Weleetka the following morning. At this second meeting, the Negro Civic League of Oklahoma was organized.

When reporting on the events which occurred during the meeting at Boley, Sango declared bitterly that "you can't do any business in a nigger town and that the only place for a nigger convention to be held is where there are white officers to keep order."

The moves toward disenfranchisement of the Negro began to have secondary effects. The Boley convention, at least in terms of prior Negro aims, should have been a success. But the Negroes were confused, frightened, and disorganized; and partisan politics was beginning to split the group. Convinced that they could no longer fight the Democrats with any hope of success, Negroes found it expedient to join them. In this way they might gain local patronage favors and get in at the beginning of a new political trend in the county. It was this incipient split that contributed at least in part to the suspicion of Boss Sango's motives.

In any event, the "Grandfather Convention" came to nothing. In November, the state supreme court upheld the constitutionality of the clause. In a lengthy decision, written by Robert L. Williams, later governor of the state, the court twisted its way through the provisions of the law, attempting to find it consonant with the tenets of the Federal Enabling Act under which Oklahoma joined the Union.

The court ruled that since the Indian members of the Five Civilized Tribes had an electoral form of government prior to 1866, descendants of members of these tribes were not barred from voting by the clause; nor could Negro freedmen from northern states which had permitted them to vote before 1866 be subjected to the educational requirement as a prerequisite to voting. But the descendants of aliens from countries not granting the right of ballot, as well as "blanket Indians," whose ancestors did not participate in any representative form of government, would have to submit to the educational test before being permitted to vote.

The court handed down the summary opinion that the amendment in no way violated those provisions of the Enabling Act which protected all citizens against any abridgements of their rights on the grounds of race, color or creed. The court stated: "The people of this state in section one of the bill of rights of the state constitution reserved the right to alter or reform its government whenever the public good required it." [31]

The grandfather clause was but such a reasonable reform.

The new act was vigorously implemented in the November congressional elections. The Negro vote was "remarkably light," and the white Republicans, too, failed to come to the polls in any numbers, claiming that the election had been a thoroughgoing frame-up.

Those Negroes who decided to vote in the face of the amendment, and who were able to reach their new polling places, were denied ballots on the grounds of illiteracy. The *Independent* recorded an instance where a Negro "who could read and write not only English, but Latin and Greek as well, was turned away from the polls" by an election inspector both "ignorant and democratic." [32]

The Negroes again took to the courts in an attempt to gain redress. This time they hoped for the intervention of the federal government to overcome the local prejudice against them. Overtures to the state courts were obviously pointless. A complaint was sworn out before the United States Commissioner at Holdenville, who had been present at the Paden voting precinct, charging the election officials with refusing the right of suffrage in a national election. The officials were arrested and shortly released on $1,000 bond. The *Independent* pointed out the obvious merits of the Negroes' case:

> At Paden Negroes who could unquestionably qualify under the law were refused the right to cast a ballot. The postmaster at Boley was refused a vote, also the negro agent of the railroad company . . . the Boley banker and others whose educational qualifications entitled them to vote.[33]

The literacy test case against the election officials soon came to nothing. The indictment was quashed and the judge found that no evidence of conspiracy to prevent the Negroes from voting could be demonstrated.

A few months later, the net of inequality and prejudice closed more tightly around the Okfuskee Negroes. The United States Circuit Court of Appeals, sitting in St. Louis, ruled that the "Jim Crow" railroad laws in Oklahoma were not, as five Negro complainants had charged, in conflict with the tenets of the Enabling Act. The majority decision held that the Negroes' allegations were "too vague and uncertain to constitute a case of action either in equity or at law." Judge Walter Sanborn dissented and observed, in lament, that "the statute clearly discloses that the patent intention of the Legislature of Oklahoma was to exclude . . . every colored passenger from coaches and cars occupied by white persons." [34]

While their petitions for relief from segregated facilities appeared to have reached an impasse, the Negroes still had hopes for the overthrow of the voting restrictions placed upon them by the grandfather clause. Trial cases began their long course up the hierarchical ladder of the federal court system and for a time it appeared that the clause might not stand the test of constitutionality. In May, Judge Ralph Emerson Campbell of the United States Court for the Eastern District of Oklahoma and Judge John H. Cotteral of the analogous court for the western district, handed down decisions which stated that the grandfather clause was in conflict with the Fifteenth Amendment to the United States Constitution.

The case soon went on appeal to even higher courts, but the Okfuskee whites, seeing the onset of the demise of their electoral protection from the Negroes, became uneasy. This uneasiness found an almost immediate outlet in the first lynching in the county since statehood.

Deputy Sheriff George Loney, it was reported, went to a farm near Paden to arrest a man by the name of Nelson on a larceny charge. Nelson's thirteen-year-old son stood by as the sheriff approached his father. Suddenly, the sheriff appeared to reach for his shotgun; and the young boy, believing his father's life to be in danger, shot Loney to death. The boy and his mother were both taken into custody, but the county attorney could barely gather enough evidence at the preliminary hearing to make a case against the boy on a first-degree murder charge.

Nonetheless, the mother, Laura Nelson, and her son were confined in the Okemah jail awaiting their trial on the same day the district court decision on the grandfather clause was reported to the public. A mob of masked persons approached the jail that night and took possession of the mother and son. They dragged them six miles west of town, to an iron bridge that crosses the North Canadian river at "Yarbough's crossing . . . hanging them from the middle span of the bridge." [35]

There was a strong reaction against the lynching from the "better" elements in Okemah. The *Independent* said that "the action of the mob is deeply regretted by all good citizens," noting that "there is not a shadow of an excuse for the crime." The paper expressed the hope that the local officers would make "every effort to bring the guilty parties to justice and uphold the majesty of the law."

While the *Independent* bemoaned "the terrible blot on Okfuskee County, a reproach that it will take years to remove," [36] the county judge summoned a grand jury to investigate the lynching. But the grand jury, without the help of the county attorney, could not turn up sufficient evidence to return an indictment.

The utter terror which the lynching produced in the Negroes is not difficult to imagine. Mrs. Nelson had cared for an infant while in jail with her older son, and had taken the child with her when the mob came. She had put the baby on the ground when she was forced onto the bridge by the crowd.

A woman who witnessed the scene painfully described it:

"After they had hung them up, those men just walked off and left that baby lying there. One of my neighbors was there, and she picked the baby up and brought it back to town, and we took care of it. It's all grown up now and lives here. . . ."

The Negroes had segregated themselves from the whites, but there had been no tranquil coexistence. They had been disenfranchised, then "Jim Crowed" on public facilities, and now one of their number had been lynched by a mob. The next step for the whites, and the only remaining one, was an attempted removal of the Negroes from the area. They were not long in taking this step.

By August, a covert movement became generally known to the Okfuskee County public. The farmers in the western end of the county had begun to found organizations euphemistically called Farmers'

Commercial Clubs. The purpose of these organizations was to restrict and discourage further Negro immigration into the county and to effect the withdrawal of those Negro families presently occupying land in the area.

Each member was obliged to sign a pledge:

> For the protection of ourselves and families, and for the upbuilding of a better moral and social citizenship in Oklahoma, we the undersigned citizens and land dealers in Okfuskee county, Oklahoma, do hereby agree, pledge and obligate ourselves to never rent, lease or sell any land in Okfuskee county to any person or persons of negro blood, or agents of theirs; unless the land be located more than a mile from a white or Indian resident.[37]

This last qualification was tantamount to making no qualification whatever. Except in the immediate vicinity of the all-Negro communities, the farm populations were mixed.

The pledge continued: "Furthermore, we pledge ourselves to use every honorable means within our power to avoid the hiring of negro labor and by so doing curb the emigration to this county."

Many white farmers were enlisted, believing that the movement would "doubtless prove a great benefit."[38] The *Ledger* viewed the growth of the clubs with kindness, and pointed out that, with Negro incursions into the county, land had not "advanced in value as in other communities."[39]

It was argued by the whites in the towns and rural communities that their region had "advanced ahead of the negro tenant with his log cabin and his mules to that of better homes and a good class of farmers."[40] The clubs hoped that their program might be adopted elsewhere in the state and extended over the entire eastern half of Oklahoma.

Approval of the Farmers' Commercial Clubs was not, however, entirely universal. Certain interests felt that the business of the county was bound to suffer. It was cautiously pointed out that although there were undesirable Negro elements in the county, the clubs might produce a situation in which hundreds of intelligent, honest Negro farmers would be thrown out of work and driven from their homes, and that this would "no doubt cause bitter feeling that will result, perhaps, in various kinds of losses to all."[41]

Notwithstanding these reservations, the *Independent* predicted that all "land owners and white farmers will have notices served upon them by members of the anti-Negro Farmers' Associations to not rent or lease any land to negroes." [42]

Bitter feeling did, as predicted, result. So did the exodus of Negro farmers. By the end of August the Okemah *Ledger* reported, "The movement is attracting a good deal of attention among the negroes in that part of the county and quite a number have already signified their intention of getting out as soon as they can gather their crops and dispose of their leases." [43]

The Negroes made the next move. Typically, they attempted to deal with the articulated rationalizations of the clubs, the removal of the backward and worthless Negroes, rather than with the real principle which lay behind their founding, the fiery opposition to the presence of any Negroes, whatever their characters might be. Early in November, the Negro Law and Order League was founded. Now overly conscious of themselves and their towns, the Negroes began to ferret out their own worst element, trying desperately to do the work of the clubs before the clubs had a chance to do it for themselves.

Professor John R. Hogan, of the Langston Colored Agricultural and Normal University, the president of the new league, moralistically announced to Governor Cruce:

> We want to drive the negro jointist out of existence. What we want to do and what we have to do is to eliminate the worthless negro, or the better class will be made to suffer. It is our idea to organize the negroes throughout the state into a sort of farmer's union, to work up interest among our race for agricultural pursuits. . . . There is no reason why they cannot make good farmers and fit themselves for a useful life.[44]

The situation in the county was becoming increasingly tense, with intra-group hostility growing in the Negro communities and being fed by each new white move. It was only a matter of time before the tension would break out into overt violence.

The occasion, as it must classically be, was a trivial one. Early in December, an itinerant salesman from Fayetteville, Arkansas, was in Boley peddling apples. While in a meat market, the peddler was allegedly assaulted, robbed, and struck over the head with a six-shooter.

As a final indignity, a Negro knocked him unconscious with a riding quirt. After regaining consciousness, the salesman stumbled to the railroad tracks and eventually made his way to Okemah to file a complaint.

The county sheriff's force, always eager to visit Boley, mustered a posse and left Okemah. But the reception which these men received in the Negro town was something less than cordial. The white deputy sheriff and the jailer were surrounded by some fifty armed Negroes who refused to let them take the owners of the meat market from the town. During the fracas, the mob set upon a Negro deputy who was attempting to aid the Okemah officers, and beat him severely. The sheriff's men retreated, but later the same day, the county attorney came to Boley and arrested the peddler's assailants. The men were taken before the Justice of the Peace, where they waived preliminary hearing and were thereupon placed under $2,000 bond each.

The *Independent,* in keeping with the spirit of the Law and Order League, asserted that this was the work of the "whiskey mob." [45] But the *Ledger* found cause to scoff at Boley's pretensions to be something better than the white stereotype of any Negro group: "The great negro movement with its origin at Boley to assist in maintaining law and order and cleaning the community of the criminal element seems to have been a farse as far as this case is concerned." [46]

Another Okemah paper described the incident as a near race war, which, it pointed out with relief, had fortunately been narrowly averted.

The year 1912 was an election year, and the whites turned their attention to consolidating their gains in the county. In January, the Negroes attempted, with a new and different plan, to squirm out of the political strait jacket in which they found themselves. They held a mass meeting to form an organization of independent voters. Negroes had now been excluded from the Republican party councils, since these organizations were constituted on the basis of voting strength in the 1910 elections, and the Negroes had not been allowed to vote in that year. Negroes also had a traditional antipathy to voting for Democratic candidates. Faced with an existence in a political no-man's-land, the Negro had no alternative, now, but to accept the situation and to make believe that his political "independence" was of his own choosing and represented, somehow, a higher and more noble resolution of the situation.

The local paper, its chin out and its glazed eyes forward like an oft-beaten fighter, announced that "much enthusiasm was shown" and "many telling addresses were made" at the Boley mass meeting. The new line was enunciated: ". . . the speakers declared that heretofore, they had faithfully followed the republican party, but that now we will vote for men and principles, regardless of what party they represent." [47]

This was truly democracy and freedom of choice on the grandest scale. The Negroes were no longer to be partisan voters, but only American citizens making intelligent, careful decisions in politics, and implementing these decisions with votes for men, not for meaningless political platforms and clichés.

"We are not democratics," declared one of the speakers, "but if the democratic party has a better man on its ticket than the republican party and we believe he will give us a square deal then it is our duty to vote for the man regardless of the party."

But the *Ledger,* always ready to puncture a Negro ideological bubble, accurately sized up the situation.

> The Boley negroes are prompt to talk about the vote they haven't got, and are too finding that the white republicans are using the grandfather clause against them in their own party to wrest control from them, and to keep them off of delegations and from seeking offices, all of which is very distasteful to the negro.[48]

The formal rejection from the higher echelons of the Republican party came in March when a group of Boley Negroes travelled to Oklahoma City to ask representation on the state delegation to the national Republican convention. An interview by Mr. Tolliver, editor of the *Progress,* with George H. Dodson, secretary of the Republican State Central Committee, was reported in the *Progress* on February 22.[49]

"Mr. Dodson," the editor queried, "I want to ask you whether it would be proper or improper, wise or foolish, for the negroes of Oklahoma who have always been loyal to the republican party, to ask for representation on the delegation to the national republican convention?"

"It will not do. It will not do," answered the harassed Mr. Dodson.

"Why will it not do, Mr. Dodson?"

"It will drive all the silk stocking republicans away from the party," replied Mr. Dodson.

"Mr. Dodson, whose vote is heavier: The silk stocking white republicans or the negroes?"

Mr. Dodson was apparently caught somewhat unaware.

"Well," he finally said, "that's a question."

Mr. Tolliver could not but editorialize a bit:

> Great shades of Lincoln. Here we are told point blank that it is the desire of the machine in Oklahoma to build up a "white man's party," not a party of the people. We again ask why should the negro not be independent in politics. If the socialists or the democrats or anybody else place a man on their ticket whom we believe to be a square man, who will give us a square deal, why should we not vote for our best friends?

This propositioning of the Democrats and Socialists by the Negroes was quickly rejected by the voice of the Democratic party in Okfuskee County, and the Negroes were given a "sassy-slap" in addition:

> We can say to the few Boley negroes who will be entitled to vote in the general election, that if they want to be democrats, they can demonstrate their ability to be a good one by staying home on election day and minding their own business.
>
> We don't neither need nor desire your vote. By staying at home you have much to gain and nothing to lose. Your interests would be more amply protected where you cease piling up prejudice against you.[50]

The political back of the Negro had now been hopelessly broken. Not only was he shut out of Republican politics, where he had earlier found some hope; but now the Democrats, saucy in their confidence that the Negro vote would not be cast, were prepared to reject his overtures. The grandfather clause had stripped the Negro of his suffrage right, and both the Democrats and the Republicans knew it. Neither party chose to ally with him, the Democrats because no gain was involved, the Republicans for fear that even more white votes would be lost.

The Republican abandonment of the Negro was conclusively demonstrated at the Okfuskee County Republican Convention in March, where the "darkies were conspicuous . . . by their absence." [51] They had, the *Ledger* noted with approval, "been grandfathered."

A few Negroes, probably part of that undesirable element about whom everyone was now talking, struck out in their frustration. The night passenger train on the Fort Smith and Western had been a favorite target for the people around Boley. But in mid-April, rather than simply to annoy the passengers with random stone-throwing, a determined effort was made to wreck the train. Some forty spikes were driven between the ends of the rails, and then bent up over the tracks. Though the train hit the spikes, it failed to derail, coming, instead, to a jarring stop.

No arrests were made since little could be proven. The *Ledger* philosophically observed that over the past few years the train "seems to have had its troubles coming up through the Boley territory." [52]

On June 19, Emancipation Day was celebrated at Boley, proving a welcome, if ironic, interruption to the difficulties the Negroes were encountering in gaining a full measure of emancipation. Governor Lee Cruce was promised as the principal speaker, and Judge John Carruthers was to give the welcoming address on behalf of the people of Boley. But when the great day dawned, the Boleyites were told that Cruce had been detained at the State House, while on the other side of Oklahoma, Carruthers was held up in a district court session at Holdenville. The celebration took place nonetheless, and Negroes from many parts of the state flocked to Boley to join the wilted festivities.

Late in May, the county election board gerrymandered its precincts again, and placed Boley in yet another division. Those Negroes who were able to find their polling place at the August primary were turned away on literacy grounds, the election officials scrupulously administering the conditions of the grandfather clause and creating impossible literacy burdens for those who could not be immediately turned away on the basis of ancestry.

The Negroes retaliated on as many fronts as they could, though none of their tactics proved effective, and at least one boomeranged badly. They tried to gather their forces together to appeal to the federal courts on the constitutionality of the grandfather clause, to force the election commissioners to place Boley in a reasonable voting precinct, and to secure a guarantee that the election judges would administer the literacy tests fairly. Each of these moves was blocked with ease by the white Democrats, who now controlled the election machinery and the state court system, and who had high hopes of gaining ascendancy in the federal courts after the election.

A mass meeting in Boley, aimed at organizing opposition to the grandfather clause, set off the Negro campaign. The Okemah *Ledger* reported:

> In this meeting the hearty cooperation of the negro was shown against this nefarious law known as the Grand Father Clause, throughout the State of Oklahoma. It was the sense of this meeting to urge each and every negro in the state of Oklahoma to be present himself at the polls in November for the purpose of voting, and if denied the right, to have the election officer arrested at once because this so called Grand Father law is unconstitutional.[53]

The program of harassing the election officials and obtaining redress in the federal courts had already gotten underway after the August primary. On the basis of a warrant sworn out by Negroes who claimed they had been illegally prevented from voting in the primary, the inspector, judge, and clerk of the precinct were arrested by the United States Marshal and held in custody for twenty-four hours. They were next conveyed to Holdenville, where they were arraigned before the United States Commissioner on the charge of conspiracy to prevent the Negroes from voting.

The *Ledger* saw in the move an attempt at "bluff and intimidation and in no sense an honest effort to enforce the law." It was all part of a plot to frighten election officials so that "no board where there was a heavy negro vote would dare to enforce the state election law by excluding the ignorant darkies from the poll." Again, the paranoid fear of Negro domination was called up. The *Ledger,* however, fully appraised the situation and finally found the scheme so transparent that it could be seen through by "any ten year old boy."[54]

Transparent or not, the tactic was ultimately unsuccessful and costly to the Negroes. The election officials who had been arraigned were released. As usual, the judge could find no satisfactory ground to maintain an indictment on conspiracy. The white officials had meanwhile filed a countersuit for damages, asking for $30,000. Five thousand dollars of this amount was for damage to their reputations, $50 for expenses, and $15 for loss of business time for three days. Finally, the court found the suit reasonable and awarded Henry Rich, the election judge, a $2,000 judgment against I. B. Garrett, one of the Negroes who had filed the original petition after the primary.

Shortly before the judgment had been returned, the Negroes attempted to force the election board to reconstitute the precincts so that Boley, now without a voting precinct in town, would have five election units of its own. To effect this plan, D. J. Turner, either with covert Republican sanction, as the *Ledger* claimed, or on his own initiative, applied for a preemptory writ of mandamus against the election board to compel it to establish Boley precincts.

The essence of the suit was that the six hundred qualified voters in Boley were more than a sufficient number to justify the establishment of election precincts, and that in the determination of precinct lines, the usual county practice of observing municipal boundaries should be followed.

The *Ledger* chose not to take these claims seriously. It observed, under the guise of angelic innocence, that the political campaign unfortunately would again be one of endless litigation, and that the voters of the county were weary of having their mandate so often and unreasonably challenged by a minority coalition of Republicans and Negroes. Surely no one could take seriously the claims of the Negroes. Somewhat parochially, the newspaper observed that Mr. Davison, the attorney for the complainant, "being a stranger to the county and Boley," was doubtless unaware that in the election two years prior, only fifty votes, white and colored, were cast in the two precincts between which Boley had been divided.[55]

But this reasoning, the facts of which were true, conveniently ignored the last count of population, taken in May of 1911, which had shown Boley with but sixty fewer persons than Okemah. The *Ledger* also neglected, in its amazingly poor show of historical recall, to point out that the grandfather clause had become law in 1910 and that it had been vigorously implemented during the election.

The application for the permanent writ, however, was duly filed and rejected, and Judge Carruthers handed down a decision "favorable to the election board."[56] No precincts would be established in Boley.

In the last days before the general election, reacting to the Democratic claims that the various court suits were part of Republican strategy to get the Negro vote, individual Republican candidates made a final effort openly to dissociate themselves from the Negro. The

Republican candidate for sheriff, for instance, the only Republican who would be able to win office in the county, tried to unload the death touch of Negro support onto his opponent: "Now as to the nigger vote, look at the statement of forty of the best democrats in Weleetka and see who has been catering to the nigger. . . ."[57]

The election was anticlimactic, a resounding testimony to the effectiveness of the throttle which had been placed on the Negro electoral ambitions. The *Independent* smugly estimated that probably not more than forty Negroes in the county had voted, and that these votes had been cast, in most instances, for the Socialists since this was the only political group that had bothered to make an active canvass among the Negroes.[58]

The whites could afford to relax. They were prepared, if the Negroes were now ready, to play their part in the time-honored and traditional relationship between the races which had existed in the South. They found time, for instance, to laugh a bit at the antics of their Uncle Tom neighbors, and the story of a Boley "Real Estate Deal," as the *Independent* told it:

> In 1909, H. C. Cavil bought a lot in Boley from Tucker Jones. Before Cavil bought the lot Jones took him down and showed him the lot, which had a house on it. Afterwards he placed the lot in the hands of M. A. Sorrell, who sold it to one Hill. Jones gave possession of the house to Hill, who moved in. Eighteen months afterward, one Andrew Jackson came along, and claimed the house, and then started an investigation. It was found that Tucker Jones had owned lot 14, the house was on 13, but Cavil's deed called for lot 14, as did Hill's.[59]

Who could ever have seriously believed that the Negro was ready for self-government?

To complicate their plight, the Negroes who could in the past always retreat from their political beatings into a secure economic enclave of their own, suddenly found themselves caught up in the cotton depression of 1913. Prices had dropped sharply, and there was a movement afoot to withhold the crop from the market to force the prices back up to a more favorable level. But for the small farmers, as most of the Negro farmers in the Okfuskee area were, existence was hardly possible with either a low cotton price or a crop that had to be withheld for an indefinite period of time.

In addition, Boley as a community, along with the other portions of this largely rural county, was beginning to lose population. This loss was a part of a nation-wide depletion of farm dwellers, which would get under way as a mass migration of the Negro and other marginal agriculturalists during the years of the First World War. Negro immigration into the county was by no means making up for the population losses. Oklahoma was now nearly as infamous for its Negro-white relations as the southern states, and Negroes seeking fresher air were heading North to the industrial centers where they could more readily locate employment.

Coupled with this economic burden was the total disillusionment which the Okfuskee County Negroes had suffered. They were obliged to reorient their lives completely. "All Men Up—Not Some Down" was not only meaningless but mocking. The appeal of "on to Boley" had been reduced to a hollow dream, pushed mercilessly back into the fantasy world from which it had sprung. There would be no Negro autonomy in Oklahoma, no Negro dignity, no Negro peacefulness. There would be no growing respect and admiration from white neighbors and no industrial and agricultural prosperity. Nothing had been changed during the long fight; nothing had been bettered.

Commenting upon the Negro's lot in the United States in 1910, one historian has accurately summed up the situation which now applied in Oklahoma:

> The mass of Negroes were beaten creatures, convinced by the unassailable testimony of their position of their inherent inferiority, and more than half convinced that they got from the white man no worse than they deserved. A quarter of a century later, a white Southerner, William Alexander Percy, who lived through these times, summed up the effect upon whites. "To live habitually as a superior among inferiors, be the inferiority intellectual or economic, is a temptation and a hubris, inevitably deteriorating."
>
> Voteless and voiceless, alien to and barred from the sources of liberalism, shackled by proscriptions in economic life, ridiculed with relish, lynched with impunity, more and more it seemed to Negroes that their black skins were a badge of shame, a curse of God. A paralyzing psychosis of defeatism gripped them. "It is better to die than it is to grow up and find out you're colored," the Negro Fenton Johnson lamented. "Oh, to be a Negro in a time like this!" [60]

There were but two alternatives for the Okfuskee Negroes. One was acceptance of the situation as it had developed; the other was escape. Acceptance became the solution for those who were now too tired, too timid, or too cynical to try to re-create a new dream. It also became the solution for those who still entertained hope of bettering the situation and who refused to face the reality of their position.

But there were others who churned up new visions of escape. They could go North, but there they would encounter more white Americans, as well as an industrialized atmosphere with which they were not familiar. Besides, the best the North could offer was an opportunity to be left alone; and these were not the kind of men who had envisioned condescending tolerance, but the kind who wanted an active role in the shaping of their own and their children's destiny, with no limits posed for their achievement.

One reasonable possibility remained. They could migrate once more to a place where they might hope to gain strength, power, and complete freedom. They could leave behind the unyielding pressure of the American racial code and migrate to a new continent where they would be accepted unquestioningly as equals. They could go to Africa. Their ancestors had once thrived on that continent, and now they could return, strengthened rather than weakened by their period of residence in an alien land.

At the moment, it was nothing more than a dim prospect, but its appeal and attractiveness were well rooted, the inevitable outcome of all that had gone before. Some murmurings were heard, and one group even packed and left for Africa. Others merely thought. A few wrote letters trying to find out more about their former homeland. At the moment, nothing but a fertile, fully-developed context was evolving. It might equally well develop further or expire as another unrecorded and unrealized daydream.

It was into this context that Alfred Charles Sam, emissary for the Chiefs of the Tribes of Akim, came. He could hardly have made a better choice nor come at a better time.

4

"From Egypt's Yoke Set Free"

Our bondage it shall end by and by, by and by,
Our bondage it shall end by and by,
From Egypt's yoke set free, hail the glorious jubilee,
And to Canaan we'll return, by and by, by and by,
And to Canaan we'll return by and by.
(From "Our Bondage It Shall End")

AT THE END of August 1913, an Okemah paper reported that a Negro, giving his name as Chief Sam, and alleging himself to be a bona fide chief of the Gold Coast, West Africa, was in Okfuskee County hard at work among local Negroes "on what appears to be a slick confidence game." [1] Sam was selling shares of stock in a mercantile and migration corporation, and was doing exceedingly well at it.

The newspaper report was the first public notice of Sam's activities, though Governor Lee Cruce had received a letter during the summer indicating Negro interest in Sam's migration proposals. The letter came at the end of July from Wallace, Oklahoma, and was written by Luther Fort, who described himself as a "subject to the Democrat party":

Gentlemen Hon sir Please send me a blank form petesion for the purpose of petesian for free transportation to Affrica the Negroes of Okla state wide have now united and will give up their posesion in this state to the white folks if the Government will give them free transportation to Affrica: the white race are all in favor of sending them and I wish you would Please advise me what steps to take to get all Negroes a free transpatation Thay all wont to be ready to start by June 1st 1914 furthermore send us a Blank form far the white men to sign to shown their willingness to send the Negro to Affrica Please give me all information in regarding this matter

Yours Luther Fort [2]

This information was, apparently, all new to Governor Cruce. He directed his secretary to report as much to Fort, though he did refer Fort to Senator Gore, who had earlier sponsored legislation for a back-to-Africa program.

The first newspaper report on Sam's activities also supplied some financial details on the operation. For the purchase of one share of stock, which could be obtained for the modest sum of $25, the buyer and his family would be entitled to a free passage to Africa. The paper moralized, however, that many of the local Negroes were buying shares in the company "and making no provisions for winter, so confident are they of going to Africa." [3]

Alfred Charles Sam was described variously by his followers. He was a "low brown man" to one relatively dark Negro, though "black" to a somewhat lighter man. Sam stood about five feet six inches high, and weighed some 160 pounds.

"He didn't dress fine," said one of the colonists. His speaking voice was soft and well modulated, though "he spoke broken." In public addresses, everyone agreed, Sam was far from commanding. But his uncomplicated directness and sincerity made up manyfold for his meager oratorical skill.

Though Sam was an enigma to all of the whites with whom he came into contact, and to a large proportion of the Negroes, he frequently stated that he wanted no mystery about himself. He told a reporter, in order to clarify his origins, that he had been born at Appasu, Gold Coast, and was the son of James K. Sam. His grandfather, he said, was chief of Obosse and Appasu in West Akim, a territory in the Gold Coast. Sam was the eldest son and was sent to the German Mission Seminary at Kibi. At the death of his grandfather, his uncle, Kwawin, had ascended the throne, and Sam had finally succeeded him.

As a young man, Sam engaged in the collection of Gold Coast rubber for export to the United States. During this period, he conceived the notion of establishing a trading company for the purpose of transporting African goods to America and inexpensively-produced American products to Africa. By July of 1911, the Akim Trading Company had taken shape, and had been incorporated under the laws of the state of New York with capital funds of more than $600,000. From its main headquarters in Brooklyn, the firm set out to implement a trading scheme about which it had no modesty and as little literacy. The prospectus told of the company's plans: "Our American dry goods and provisions from our Manufacturers . . . are very cheap, and our President having an over 11 years experience in West African Trade assures us to clear at least 100 percent on a dollar profit." [4] Sam was the company's president; and with six other directors, an engineering department, an attorney, and unrestrained hope, he began his trading venture.

The company held twenty square miles of territory in the Gold Coast which it hoped to develop with the assistance of its chief engineer, C. W. Chappelle, "the negro inventor of the Airship." The firm also planned to send one of its shareholders to navigation school in New York so that he might be trained as master of its vessels. The directors had "decided seriously that this is the first Negro Corporation ever conceived amongst the race" and intended to maintain it exclusively as such.

Financing would pose no problem. "This is a tangible proposition," the prospectus pointed out, "for as the civilized Negro is responsible to develop Africa," he should indicate his willingness to accept this charge by purchasing shares in the company. The price of a single share was fixed at £10.8.0; but to African Negroes, as an inducement to "get into this movement," the shares would be sold at half price.

Sam, according to the prospectus, would sail from New York on the 10th of February, 1912, in order to "open our African factories" in the Gold Coast. "All friends who will like to see him off may do so," the prospectus invited.

The Akim Trading Company apparently met with some success. According to its latter-day president, Edward E. Pettis, the company conducted commerce between New York and the Gold Coast from the middle of 1912 until the beginning of 1913 with hardly a difficulty. Sam, however, shortly made private arrangements with produce merchants in London to receive his Gold Coast goods, shortcircuiting the New York office entirely. He instructed the London firm that under no condition was it to return unsatisfactory goods to the company's New York branch. When the American office eventually learned of

Sam's maneuver, it tried to void the contracts thus independently made, but to no immediate avail. Pettis was unsuccessful in getting a hearing with the London firm, he reported, until he "turned over the matter to our lawyer for adjustment." [5]

Sam returned to New York in February of 1913 and began the formation of a new company, unembarrassedly called the Akim Trading Company, Ltd. Pettis called the shot: "Sam sought to create the impression in Africa, England, and America that the Akim Trading Company had failed and had been taken over by the Akim Trading Company, Limited." [6] Unlike the first company, the new Akim organization was dedicated to migration as well as commercial shipping. It was the culmination of one of Sam's dreams. He had, he said, always "been full of the idea" of bringing his "wandering black brothers" back to their fatherland. [7]

The new company was founded under the flexible corporation laws of South Dakota, on March 21, 1913. The incorporators, in addition to Sam, were James S. Sebree, a lawyer of Pierre, South Dakota, who apparently had been chosen to meet the requirement that at least one of the incorporators be a resident of the state, and A. E. Smith, Sam's New York agent for the new company.

The articles of incorporation could not have been broader in scope. Not only did they permit trade and other business ventures in the United States and the Gold Coast, but "in foreign countries as shall from time to time be found necessary and convenient for the purposes of the Company's business." There was also provision for the founding of a "college of agriculture and industry in all the trades of manufacturing and agriculture," and the construction, ownership and operation of "hotels, restaurants, bath houses, theaters, or other places of amusement." [8]

The principal business of the corporation was supposedly to be carried on in Pierre, but there was a provision for a business office in New York, too. The articles also mentioned the possibility of branches in Aburi, Gold Coast; Monrovia, Liberia; and Liverpool. Sam himself was never in South Dakota for the incorporation. Both he and Smith signed the papers before a notary in New York to bring into being this company with a definition of purpose that would stagger the imagination of Standard Oil.

Having provided himself with a proper legal context for his operation, Sam left New York toward the end of April for the South. He hoped to persuade former stockholders of the Akim Trading Company of the demise of that organization so that they would switch their stock to the new company. More important, he was intent on building up financial support for his current venture. The company had been incorporated for $1,000,000, this amount divided among forty thousand shares selling at $25 each.

It is not certain what drew Sam to Okfuskee County. Certainly, correspondence which Sam allegedly had with Professor J. P. Liddell, of Boley, and Dr. Dorman, of Mantee, both of whom had expressed some interest in a back-to-Africa movement, had a great deal to do with bringing Sam to the state.

Sam's plan was a simple one. He traversed Oklahoma, called meetings at which he peddled stock, and organized clubs to stimulate additional interest in his scheme. He operated primarily in the rural areas, avoiding large white settlements. On August 30, 1913, in a letter addressed "unto Governor Cruse to your excellency," Alexander Johnson of Holdenville informed the State of Oklahoma of the plan. The author of this cryptic missive told "your humble most loyal Authorities" that Negroes across the South were buying stock in the Akim Trading Company, Ltd., some paying cash, others paying in installments. Johnson alleged that over six thousand persons were standing ready to go to West Africa, and courteously invited the Governor's blessing on the movement. Johnson was an official, he reported, in two of Sam's clubs.[9]

The Governor responded:

> I do not know anything about this movement to move Negroes from Oklahoma to Africa and I don't know what I can do to assist in a proposition of this nature. It occurs to me that this is something that each negro will have to settle for himself. It occurs to me also that they ought to be very careful in paying money in installments or in any other way to persons representing themselves to be agents of a society of this nature. Many unscrupulous persons are collecting money from ignorant negroes and failing to make any proper accounting for same.[10]

Cruce's doubts were not widely shared by the Negroes. What had occurred to him had not occurred to them. They had found a Moses who would lead them out of the morass, and they were prepared to invest in him both emotionally and materially.

73

W. S. Peters, a Boley attorney, and an untiring and inveterate skeptic, was in Okemah in early September and reported that "the country Negroes around Boley are as wildly excited over Chief Sam's 'back to Africa' scheme as they are around Clearview." Peters said that some four hundred Negro families of Okfuskee County had already purchased shares in the company, and were preparing to leave at the first opportunity for new homes in Africa, where "the negroes don't have to work or even wear clothes, and where crops grow without cultivation, and life is one long, sweet, dream for the negroes." [11]

At public meetings, where the fervor of the emigration plans and the generous doses of interjected religion caught everyone in their spell, Sam reported in ornate terms the paradise he was offering. He talked of trees which bore bread, and of cotton bushes as tall as trees. The skeptics in the audience might protest, but Sam was routinely able to cope with them.

One night, during a meeting at Clearview, a local physician challenged Sam on a practical point.

"How many bushels of cotton do you get from one of those cotton trees?" the doctor asked.

"Many, many, many," said Sam, waving his hand abstractedly.

Sam told of diamonds that might be found in the gullies and ravines after a hard rain, and the Negroes took this tortured truth as evidence of unbelievable wealth on the Gold Coast.

Sam's attraction was extraordinary, and there was no denying the durability of his appeal. With each encounter, he attracted a greater number of persons to the movement. The clubs' membership grew, the number of clubs increased, and the movement spilled over from Oklahoma into Kansas, Texas, and Arkansas.

The more solid element of the Negro population, its aspirations and vested interests tied to the all-Negro communities, kept up a running fire of doubt and dire prediction about the project. Early in September, for instance, Attorney Peters was predicting that "it is likely that the authorities will look this Chief up in a few days."[12]

Peters' warning, perhaps combined with some effort to make the prediction self-fulfilling, came to realization within a few days. Earlier, Sam had been intercepted at Clearview and warned to leave the county. When this warning had no noticeable effect on the chief, it was followed by an arrest in Boley.

County Attorney Tom Hazlewood described the incident in a letter to the Governor:

> ... we filed a complaint against him in the Justice of the Peace Court at Boley, and had him arrested on a charge of having obtained money under false pretenses, but owing to the fact that the party whom we induced to swear to the complaint and all of his other victims are his friends and supporters, we could obtain no proof and therefore, the prosecution failed.[13]

Sam's followers continued to be refractory and handcuffed the authorities in their attempts at a successful prosecution on charges of fraud. They were convinced that they were not being swindled, and chose not to throw Sam to the white wolves who hounded him. Soon Sam was able to report tangible evidence of the honesty and sincerity of his scheme with news of negotiations for a ship to carry the emigrants to Africa.

The ship was the *Curityba,* an old Munson Line vessel of 2,363 gross tons, which had plied between New York and Cuba, carrying vacationers to and from the Caribbean Islands. The *Curityba* was an iron-hulled, screw steamer of the brigantine type, some 309 feet long, 40 feet broad, and 25 feet deep. It was equipped with electric lights, though at the time of purchase it lacked wireless facilities, a fact that would later prove of considerable embarrassment.

The ship had been built in 1887 in Hamburg by the Reiherstieg Schiffswerfte und Maschinen Fabrik, and operated as a German merchant vessel before its purchase by the Munson Lines.

The local papers, despite the scrambled rumors of the negotiations for the steamship, insisted that Sam was the tool of white confidence men in New York, finding it difficult to believe, interestingly enough, that a Negro could have concocted so elaborate a fraud himself. They labeled him a fake, an outright swindler, a devil who was preying on the ignorant, backward Negro of the area. But, despite the white outbursts of derision, the "ignorant" flocked to Sam's meetings and purchased his stock in great quantities.

C. G. Samuels of Boley, who signed himself as a "Ph.D. and M.T.," expressed poignantly the reasons for the Negro's interest in this Gold Coast man and his movement, in a letter to Governor Cruce:

> We are working trying to transport the colored people from the State

of Oklahoma to Gold Coast West Africa as we thinks it will be better for them since the ballot has been taken from us and we can not act as a man and am peoples are treated so crual as you no yourself our mens and womens are being lynched for most any little frivulus crime with the cord of law and we are jim Croed in the courthouse and in all publick places. So I thought that I would write you a letter to see if there is any method that you may or can or will help us in this great struggle of life in trying to make it to our native land.[14]

Africa had become the new frontier, the new hope. And this gentle, "low, brown man" who had come into the Negroes' midst was to be the vehicle that would allow them to realize the vision.

The Governor, however, regretted to inform Samuels that there were no state funds available to provide assistance to Negroes who wished to leave the United States.

The Negro press, often the most conservative force among the colored people in the United States, joined the anti-Sam forces almost immediately. At first, its reports were bemused and chiding, but as the movement gained momentum the reactions became harsher and more violent.

The Tulsa *Star* took its first notice of the movement early in October with a lengthy and somewhat inaccurate report:

Colored people in Okfuskee county are much perplexed because there resides in their midst a man who styles himself as Prince Sam, claiming to be an African king, bent on inducing as many as possible of the Colored people of this county to return to their native soil. Prince Sam says he has just completed the construction of a large steamer in the New York ship yard which he will use in transporting his American flock to the balmy climes of Africa.[15]

The *Star* reported that at least 117 families had purchased stock in the company and were prepared to migrate. It noted approvingly that "thoughtful Colored people," fearing a swindle, had corresponded with Sam's New York office, "only to find that the representations of the African chief concerning the ship and his New York company is utterly false." The paper concluded that "in all probability Chief Sam is an imposter traveling over this country fleecing people of their money."

Other Negroes, too, were much concerned about this unusual foreigner, though their motives for such concern varied greatly. The Rev. James Fair of Beggs, Oklahoma, wrote to the Governor on October 6 to express his anxiety over the disruption of communities throughout the state:

> With greatest of pleasure that I rite you these few lines with regard to the gold coast West Africa proposition which is going and are chiefly being advocated by Chief Sam from Africa and the act is growing to the extent all of the best community are shot to pieces now governor, being the chief mogul of this state, I want to know if Chief Sam have any rite to carry citizens from the united States and carry them to Africa have you given him any authority to do so now . . . if this keeps on there is likely to be a war among the negroes.[16]

The "chief mogul" was uncertain as to what attitude he should take toward the movement. He decided to tread the time-honored path of saying that he knew nothing except what he had "seen in the newspapers." Sam, he told Fair, "has no authority to represent the State of Oklahoma, in any way, and if he has any authority to represent England or any other Nation, I do not know about it." The Governor, as an afterthought, added that "he ought to be able to show proper credentials." [17]

Richard J. Hill, also of Beggs, was more direct in his approach. To Oklahoma's United States Senator Robert Owens he wrote, "Will you kindly inform me as to whether the American Negro as a whole, or those who desire to do so, can acquire title to lands in Gold Coast, West Africa, a British Colony, and if so what is the mode of procedure to do so?" [18]

Hill described to the Senator an African chief who was soliciting funds in Oklahoma, promising that on the Gold Coast "the Political and Industrial conditions will be an Hundred Folds better." Owens forwarded the letter to the State Department, whence it made its bureaucratic way to the British Ambassador and back to Governor Cruce in the State Capitol. Cruce still only knew what he had read in the newspapers.

Reinforcing information soon began to arrive at the State Department. Rev. R. C. Lee of Nuyaka, Oklahoma, the secretary of one of Sam's local clubs, had written to the Department of the Interior; and his letter had been promptly forwarded. Mr. Lee had, of late, begun to have certain misgivings about his role in the emigration scheme.

This man Sam has gotten many thousand dollars from the people tell-

ing them that they will have a home there always without price and
without taxation and that the Government is run absolutely by negroes or chief form of government. Now will you kindly inform me
that I might rightly inform the people? I would like to hear directly
from England on this subject, or you, if you are acquainted with this
special feature. I am Sec. of a club which has sent $213 to this supposed
agent in New York . . . and I feel rather shaky about the possessions
in Africa.[19]

On October 23, the first issue of a new newspaper, the *African
Pioneer,* appeared at Boley. Editorially, it explained its mission:

Our object for issuing the African Pioneer is to lessen the work of
Chief Sam by giving such information through its columns that may
benefit all clubs and friends and thus give Chief more time to devote
to new places and clubs.

Moreover, it will aid in making known to all our emigration plans
to all colored who wish to help colonize Africa. Furthermore we can
better defend our own cause through this paper.[20]

The movement had now not only a voice, but a printed organ, another concrete manifestation of its legitimacy.

Spurred by the letters which had been reaching them, the British
government now began to swing its organization to bear on the developments in Oklahoma. In a lengthy letter to Governor Cruce, the
British consul in St. Louis, C. M. Pearson, begged to bring to the
attention of the chief executive the fact that Sam was operating on a
grand scale in his state, representing himself "as an agent of the British Government.[21]

Pearson reported that after receiving notice of the movement from
his government's representatives in Washington he had attempted to
secure further information through correspondence with the mayor
of Wewoka. The mayor, however, had turned the letter over to a
"colored gentleman," E. L. Coffey, principal of the local Negro school.
Coffey, in his reply, plied the consul with questions but, according to
Pearson's interpretation, did not "seem inclined to investigate the question of the bona fides of Chief Sam."

Coffey did, however, inform the British government that Sam had
succeeded in collecting "a very considerable sum of money from ignorant negroes" and that "a great rally had been arranged for" on the

following Tuesday at Lima, where more shares would probably be
sold.

Pearson continued to Cruce:

> As the case was forwarded to me from Washington I assume that noth-
> ing is known of Chief Sam by the British representatives in this
> country. The whole story sounds very improbable and may possibly be
> a deliberate swindle in which case a large number of credulous Negroes
> have already been victimized. I have suggested to Mr. Coffey that the
> Police should interview Chief Sam and examine his credentials with a
> view to ascertaining whether the scheme is genuine or not, but I
> doubt that he will take the necessary action.

Pearson was expressing, as diplomatically as a foreign diplomat could,
his government's concern over the matter, and hinting that Cruce
might do well to stem the growth of Sam's movement in Oklahoma.

Cruce responded briefly and in typically laconic fashion. He assured
the Consul that he would look into the matter, and the same day forwarded Pearson's message to the county attorney in Wewoka asking
him to "see whether or not the man is a swindler as he appears to be,
and if you find that he is see that he is apprehended and dealt with as
he deserves to be." [22]

The Wewoka and Lima *Courier* remained for a time the sole Negro
newspaper which offered support for Sam's project. It faithfully detailed the meetings which Sam was holding, urging its readers to his
cause. The *Courier* described what must have been a typical gathering,
held at Weleetka toward the end of October. [23]

It was a passionate affair, with broad, inspiring camaraderie, racial
consciousness, and sense of religious duty and mission.

"President" Liddell, the state treasurer of the Chief Sam clubs, and
one of the men whom Sam claimed had written to him about Negro
repatriation, summoned the meeting, which was attended by more than
one thousand persons. Though the meeting was not to open until
Friday morning, many people arrived in Weleetka Thursday night,
not being able "to wait until Friday morning's dawn."

Unable to restrain the crowd, Liddell opened the meeting prematurely on Thursday evening. It began with a prayer service conducted by the pastor of the First Baptist Church. The minister's
remarks were, according to the *Courier*, "timely," and met with the
approval of all in the audience. During the course of the talk "one

could hear all over the assemblage, yes, let us get ready for the exodus."

Liddell was next on the agenda. He spoke in a "calm and deliberate way" and told the delegates that:

> Weleetka was a good town and had good people in both races. Therefore, we must not assail the white man's action or any one who does not believe as we do, but use the utmost precautions against prejudice measures and allow the spirit of God to direct every motive.

The full charisma attached to Sam was shown by an incident which had occurred earlier in the evening:

> . . . the chief was illing; this seemed to have rendered sadness to many of the delegate's hearts. As he lay on his couch greeting each delegate as he went in to see him, some would seize the cover that perchance had got over from his feet and pull it back, invoking sympathy and praying an immediate recruit.

Chief Sam, said the *Courier,* "has more local honor extended to him than any one black man we have ever beheld." At the meeting that night, the crowds pushed and shoved, trying to reach him as he made his way forward, and to touch his clothing. He had "thrown away his bad feelings" to go to the church to satisfy the delegates who "demanded his presence" at the meeting.

The crowd calmed to listen to Sam. He began to depict the conditions which awaited the Negroes on the Gold Coast and to paint an appealing picture of opportunity. He told the group that there was more than ample room in Africa for the American Negro and that they must, as an obligation to their race, go home and build a powerful kingdom. He likened himself to a Moses who had come to deliver people from their travail. He said that they were better dead than unreturned to Canaan.

The Chief talked in plain language, "without any modifiers." He told of a land flowing with milk and honey, where living streams watered the four mains of his kingdom as the Euphrates watered the Garden of Eden; where the birds and the beasts made merry, showing their Creator's appreciation for their freedom.

The *Courier* observed that he "has a power of collecting more colored people into one unit than we have ever witnessed of any flock leader. His followers are at his service no matter what the price."

A general songfest followed Sam's moving address. A "good old song" was sung, which "brought tears and great hallelujahs" from the delegates. Then there were testimonial statements from members of the group. President Liddell allowed as many as possible to testify, and asked all to listen closely to their words.

The meeting finally adjourned until Friday morning. By then, the church had been engulfed with delegates and could no longer hold the crowd which had assembled under a tree just in front of the church door. The local manager announced that the delegates could begin to buy shares in the Akim Trading Company, Ltd.

"You can take out any number of shares," he explained, "but $25 is the minimum."

The prospective colonists flocked to the manager's table. Share after share was laboriously filled out and transferred, until the manager and his colleague were exhausted. They had, in a short time, sold more than $2,000 worth of the company's embellished stock, with the globe, a ship, and an industrial site printed on its front as a reminder and symbol of the new life that was to come.

The selling was interrupted briefly for a prayer service, "which was grand." Then an evangelist led a song that made the audience "all feel uplifted." All showed great zeal for their work.

Prayer and song completed, the group returned to the table by the old tree in the churchyard, and the stock sale resumed. New people rushed to take their place in the group as soon as an opening was seen in the crowd of persons surrounding the table. The final count was astounding . . . more than $6,000 worth of stock had been sold in a few hours.

The *Courier* added its benediction to the meeting: "Now may God bless us and work all things together for good to those who love him."

On November 4, Sam held another of his mass meetings, this time at Wewoka in Seminole County. At this meeting, according to the report, $3,384.05 was subscribed by the Negroes. The story had been issued that the *Curityba* would cost $69,000 and that this sum would have to be paid by the first of the year. Sam, it was said, had already collected $15,000 toward the ship's purchase.

News of the Wewoka meeting reached Pearson, the British consul in St. Louis, by way of a news clipping sent by E. L. Coffey, "the colored gentleman" who had earlier corresponded with Pearson at the request of Wewoka's mayor. Pearson forwarded the clipping to Governor

Cruce with the wry comment, "I am not aware that the west coast of Africa is the earthly Heaven that is depicted." [24]

Sam's support from the Wewoka and Lima *Courier* soon ran into a snag. Antagonized by a real or imagined rebuke to his interests in the movement, the editor struck out at the soft points of the back-to-Africa movement in a highly critical description of a meeting at the school house in Lima. Now, the mood of the delegates was interpreted as rebellious and querulous; and the report of the program was terse and matter-of-fact, rather than flowery, except where the editor brought his own strictures to bear on the proceedings. The *Courier*'s editor was apparently peeved at the refusal of the local managers of the project to allow his newspaper to publish statistics on the financial operations of the movement.

This meeting was also well attended, with more than a thousand persons on hand. People had come "from every direction," arriving "by train, horseback and afoot." But this time, the paper alleged, their motive was "to probe into the legality of the meeting." [25]

The *Courier* had no major complaint against Sam, and noted approvingly his rebuttal to criticisms of the movement that had come from the professional Negroes in the area:

> . . . he said to pay no attention to the sceptic lawyers, doctors and school teachers, citing several instances where whites were teaching negro children in Louisiana, and that there would be nothing for this class to do after he culled the farmers from among them.

The local managers, Sorrell and Lewis, the prime targets of the *Courier*'s editor, spoke after Sam. They echoed his sentiments, adding that "the harder the public kicks the higher they would mount." The paper viewed dimly the motives of the two managers, who also published the *African Pioneer*, the voice of the movement, accusing them of attempting to impose a news blackout on rival weeklies in the area and keep all of the major information for their own columns.

"We viewed Sorrel and Lewis as the financial moor gulls of this project," said the *Courier*'s editor, adding that "we believe that Sorrel and Lewis are bias workers in that they don't want anybody except a parasite to join this financial band." The two managers were accused of not allowing "men of honest purpose to come into the project." It was, the *Courier* said, "a personal matter and not a national affair."

The editor also picked at one of the weak points of the movement, the rejection of the professionals, the people who would not, in any event, have been seduced into joining: "If we expect to build up a powerful province in Gold Coast, Africa, it will take farmers, doctors, lawyers, and men of all professions joined in one unit and asking God to lead them."

Warnings were scattered about the report, hinting at underhanded operations and shaky financing. The editor preached: "Now we say unto the thinking people who have not joined the movement look well before you jump for goats come in sheep's clothing and would deceive the very elects."

In addition to this advice on the possibilities of subterfuge, the editor had a fiscal note:

> The project runs that we pay $25.00 a share in the ship including a free trip to Africa. This is the finest and easiest way to get to Africa, were it legalized or a guarantee back of it. But not so by any means. You simply pay the money in and have their word for it. We know we have thrown away more money than this in cigars, whiskey, etc., but that is no reason why we should continue throwing money into the sea.

The *Courier* insisted, however, that it did not want its growing reservations misunderstood.

> Do not understand us to be fighting the African movement for we are not by any means. What we want is a definite understanding of the contract and a knowledge of the right of way and all of us will join for all know we must do something.

But the paper might as well have been asking for the end of Jim Crow as for the clarification of this basically unclarifiable scheme.

Possibly chagrined at its own hostility and vitriol, the *Courier* finally backtracked to a neutral corner, though it could not resist several predictions:

> The fifteenth of December though will tell the story for this is the time the first voyage is to launch. Those of you who are going prepare for the exodus in the way of money, clothing, etc., for you will need them. We now see a great host mightier than Pharoah's standing at the shores of the restless Atlantic yearning its father land, whence they have come but never seen.

In consideration of these things let us be prayerful and do nothing for spite of the other race for fear we may need some assistance before we reach the other side. Should this vessel begin sinking we would need wireless telegraph to make a report for assistance from some other vessel. Therefore let us not boast if this vessel is paid for and we come into possession of it, but thank God for our acquisition.

Who knows but what some of our status may be as those of the Titanic? If so, let us be able to sing not only "Nearer My God to Thee," but "Leaning on the Arms of Jesus."

Governor Cruce had, meanwhile, spoken with several Negroes in an attempt to supplement his meager knowledge of the movement so that he could supply more accurate information to the many persons who were corresponding with him about Chief Sam. When Cruce next wrote to Pearson, he could at least base his dire predictions upon a solid fact or two:

I have learned that there is a white man in New York behind the negro Sams in this matter, and that the money received for the shares in this ship are sent to him. Sam seems to have cast a spell over many negroes and they look upon him as a modern Moses. Under the present excitement that prevails among these negroes, it is easy for a shrewd man to take advantage of the situation and procure money from those who are able to command it.[26]

But the lieutenants of Moses were having some difficulties. In Boley, where M. A. Sorrell served in the dual capacity of justice of the peace and editor of the *African Pioneer,* many people had not taken kindly to Sam's enterprise. One November night, a mass meeting was held to discuss the impeachment of Sorrell for neglect of duty. In a broader sense, of course, the meeting was a community indictment of the entire back-to-Africa movement.

Many townspeople spoke out against Sorrell, relating the details of his participation in the movement, and spelling out his absences from Boley on missions for Sam. During the course of the meeting, the unfortunate Sorrell appeared, and "saw the handwriting on the wall." He made a short speech, and then tendered his resignation "to the delight of all present."[27]

On November 17, a dispatch from Parsons, Kansas, stated that sixty Negro families of Parsons would be among the first emigrants to leave for the Gold Coast. They anticipated sailing from New York in the middle of December. The dispatch noted that this contingent represented only a few of a large number of Negroes who would soon be leaving that section of the country.

The pace of the correspondence among the various officials interested in Sam's movement increased, with letters crossing and recrossing as the governmental agencies sought to keep each other informed of developments and to elicit action from other organizations which they themselves were incapable of initiating. Copies of letters regarding Sam systematically travelled a route that included the British Embassy in Washington, several of His Majesty's consulates, the U.S. State Department, and the Governor's office in Oklahoma City.

The Governor, in particular, was carrying on a lively correspondence with Negroes throughout the state, who bombarded his office with queries about Sam.

The general gist of these letters is indicated by one from S. W. But-ler in Sedan, Oklahoma:

> I have heard that you had order an investigation into this Progick that is now being carried on in this state concerning the ship being purchase by the Akim Trading Company and found it all right. Please take time and write me whether or not this has been done.[28]

The Governor responded in due time, indicating that he knew "very little" about Alfred C. Sam. Nor was he able "to tell whether or not his motives are pure and his intentions honorable." Finally, neither he nor the State of Oklahoma had sanctioned the movement, officially or casually.[29] But apparently the rumor was afoot, providing additional reason for the rush to purchase shares in the corporation.

A shifting theme in the African movement came to the attention of the public inadvertently a few days later, when the newspapers reported the murder of one Joe Murff, a well-to-do Negro living north of Paden. According to the *Independent,* "Murff had been elected as one of the delegates to go to Africa and look up the country in the 'back-to-Africa' movement, and was to have started in a few days." [30]

The "election" of delegates was a new twist in the migration scheme, a change forced upon Sam by the overwhelming support of his plan. It had become increasingly apparent that not ten ships, much less one, could possibly convey to Africa the growing number of pioneers who had been enlisted. Delegates were now being elected; in some cases, appointed. These persons would be taken in the first sailing and would presumably return to pass along information on the Gold Coast to the remaining stockholders.

The delegates system also served to protect Sam from the federal and local law enforcement authorities. He could now claim that he had promised essentially nothing to his stockholders save a ride to Africa to view the country.

The African delegation, meanwhile, planned a vast meeting at Weleetka for December 2. It was hoped that this meeting would be "the grandest financial snow peak of civilization, capsizing all past events of the kind." [31] The payment deadline on the *Curityba* was nearing.

No fewer than ten thousand persons were expected, and it was anticipated that $60,000 would be raised, "which will, no doubt, clear up a great deal of the indebtedness of the Company," the *Courier* reported. This would be the last meeting before the "Mighty Host" embarked, and a representative was expected from every state in the Union. As usual, the editor added a solemn note:

> Remember, some of us who shall embark for Gold Coast will never put foot on American soil any more; then how careful ought we to be in this final step which may be marked its last time by death's signal.

Despite inclement weather, thousands of people appeared at the Weleetka meeting, and "amidst the great hosts of people could be seen nothing but clock work of business, each rushing forward to pay his share when opportunity presented itself."

More than $10,000 was raised at the meeting, and its high point came when a telegram arrived from New York, stating that the *Curityba* had been paid for and that several persons had been employed as a crew for the ship. The telegram also disclosed the plan to have the Oklahoma Negroes ultimately ship from Galveston. Arrangements were to be made with the railroad companies so that special rates might be obtained for the trip to the Gulf port.

This meeting was the emotional climax of Sam's drive; the departure date for Africa stood but ten days away. During the entire previous month, Negro families had been disposing of their farms and possessions which they could not take to Africa. Once off their land, they had gathered into camps near Weleetka. Two tent cities had arisen, into which were jammed many hundred pioneers.

During the early phases of the encampment, the tents had been laid out along planned paths, with good order and adequate sanitation prevailing. As the number of proposed emigrants increased, however, conditions deteriorated quickly. The *Courier* gloomily reported that "many of the children have been horror stricken already in this preparatory exodus and we believe a great many will die of croup and other contagious diseases." [32]

On December 5, Governor Cruce, growing increasingly impatient with County Attorney Hill's delay in responding to his earlier requests for an investigation of Sam in Seminole County, and feeling the awesome press of the British government, sent an urgent note to Hill:

> I called your attention to this negro's exploits some time ago with the request that you investigate and see whether or not he is violating any of the laws of the State of Oklahoma. I wish you would advise me what your conclusions are.[33]

The Governor was beginning to be more than a little alarmed by the letters coming to his office, detailing the serious consequences of the Negro's faith in Sam if this faith should prove undeserved. He continued:

> If he [Sam] is defrauding these negroes he should be prosecuted. This matter . . . bears every ear-mark of a scheme to take advantage of the ignorance and superstition of the negroes and rob them of what little they have . . . Oklahoma in the end will be the sufferer, for we will have the negroes on our hands robbed of their property.

Cruce envisaged a situation in which the Negroes would be forced to throw themselves upon the financial mercy of the state for support after their Moses had abandoned them, taking their money with him. Worse yet was the prospect of the Negroes turning to crime to sustain themselves.

This time Hill did not delay, but wrote back to the Governor at once, excusing his prior remiss behavior by citing the demands made upon his time during the current district court term. He planned, however, to have a representative from his office at a forthcoming meeting of the African group. Hill also noted that federal authorities had been investigating Sam in that area, but they had, so far, found nothing upon which to base a prosecution. Hill further reported a salient feature of Sam's operation which, he implied, made it extremely difficult to bring a charge against the man: "It seems that Sam does not handle any of the funds personally, instead they are sent to a party in New York City, by express money order. This party's name is Smith." [34]

Hill offered a suggestion to the Governor, which the latter finally saw fit to accept:

> Sam's headquarters are at Weleetka, in Okfuskee County, and he conducts his operations from that point. I make this suggestion . . . that the authorities of that County, might be in a better position to handle the matter than this office.

Hill summarized his own attitude and the difficulties that he was encountering to the now impatient Governor:

> To date, we haven't had a negro to make a complaint to this office, on the contrary, when we talk to them they show a disposition to shield and protect the rascal. Of course after they wake up and discover that they have been fleeced, I presume that we will be flooded with complaints, in other words, they will want us to "lock the stable after the stock is gone."

Acting on Hill's advice, Cruce immediately wrote to Tom Hazlewood, county attorney for Okfuskee County. The Governor relayed essentially the same information to Hazlewood that he had earlier given to Hill and again, operating at a rapid deductive pace, he foresaw a multitude of destitute Negroes as wards of the state if Sam's clearly false scheme was not sidetracked.

Hazlewood replied to the governor in a few days. He related the story of his abortive attempt at a prosecution of Chief Sam in Boley, and told of the problems involved "owing to the fact that the party whom we induced to swear to the complaint and all of his other victims are friends and supporters." [35] Hazlewood also detailed his efforts to get somebody else to carry the burden of prosecution. He had tried to pass the case along to the federal postal authorities, and had sent them copies of letters from Smith, in New York, to prospective stock purchasers. But to date, this had had no visible effect.

Hazlewood vacillated, though, in his condemnation of Sam, and indicated in the same letter the first official doubt that Sam was an outright fake:

At first the proposition appeared to be a scheme for the sole purpose of relieving as many of the colored brothers as was possible, of the sum of $25.00, but I am informed, now, by one of Sam's chief assistants that quite a number of the more wealthy negroes have taken as much as a thousand dollars in stock in the concern. . . . They are now reporting that a ship is bought and paid for and that the first load will start from Galveston about January 1st. If this is a swindle, it is open and above board, and there is nothing secret about it.

Hazlewood concluded with the observation that if Sam was to be prosecuted, it would seem that the Post Office Department was the logical agency to undertake the court action. The Governor, relieved no doubt, agreed, and conveyed what scanty information he now had on the movement to the British consul in St. Louis.

The British Embassy in Washington soon circulated the results of its inquiries to the Colonial Office about colonization prospects in the Gold Coast. The Colonial Office pointed out that land in the Gold Coast Colony was almost exclusively under the communal ownership of the chiefs and the communities. There were but two ways in which the Oklahoma Negroes could hope to acquire land. The first possibility was to be adopted into a native community, in which instance the individual might be allotted land by the chief of the tribe. The second method was to obtain a lease from a chief or a community for a plot of land and then to have this lease validated by the Gold Coast government.

The first alternative was not feasible, the Colonial Office felt, since it "would not be likely to be acceptable to persons who are presumably Christians and civilized." The second method involved a lengthy procedure, a procedure that the Colonial Office hinted might, in fact, be indefinitely prolonged if attempted by the Oklahoma group. Under these conditions, it seemed "very undesirable for any large group of negroes to proceed to the Gold Coast before the land had been obtained." Hygienic considerations posed another barrier to the immigration. The Colonial Office felt that the American Negro would be as subject as Europeans to the deleterious effects on health of the climate of West Africa. The Office strongly urged that the United States find some means of delaying the emigration until it could be determined that "(1) the people are suitable emigrants and understand the conditions of life on the Gold Coast; and (2) that suitable land is available for them." [36]

Other Negro relocation interests shortly stirred in Oklahoma, possibly as an outgrowth of Sam's inordinate success. Toward the end of 1913, M. M. Maddin, a Johnny-come-lately Negro from New York, spoke to a crowd of 1,600 at Rentiesville, another all-Negro community. Maddin discussed his own colonization plan. He proposed to petition Congress to set aside a reservation in some thinly populated portion of the country to which American Negroes would be sent. Congress would condemn all Negro property, and pay the owners a sum representing the fair value of their land. This money would provide a nest egg for the migrants in their new home. The government would also pay the transportation costs of the Negroes to their newly created colony, where an all-Negro government would be established under the sovereignty of the United States.

Maddin's scheme was not altogether new; from colonial times various proposals had been made to resettle Negroes in remote, uninhabited sectors of the United States. But these schemes depended upon the good will and implementation of the whites, commodities which were not readily forthcoming. Sam's proposal, requiring nothing from the whites except tolerant *laissez-faire,* was much more reasonable to the Negro than Maddin's plan. Certainly, the proposal made by Maddin met with no enthusiasm in Oklahoma.

On Christmas Day, 1913, the Okemah *Independent* both wished its readers merry and reported a new development in Chief Sam's plan. According to this story, Sam was now asking Oklahoma Negroes to raise the sum of $3,000,000 "in order that he can start a bank to further his purposes." [37] The totally impossible bank, perhaps Sam's child but more likely the *Independent*'s, quite obviously never materialized.

As a last gesture for 1913, John Bassett Moore wrote from Washington to Governor Cruce, to tell him that he had found another agency upon which to foist the irritating problems connected with Sam's migration plan. The matter, Moore wrote, had been "referred to the Attorney General for such action, if any, the Department of Justice may deem advisable to take." [38]

Meanwhile, the efforts of the Negroes to obtain special rates on the railroad for their trip to Galveston to meet the *Curityba* were being rewarded. The *African Pioneer* reported that at a mid-December rally in Clearview, officials of the M. K. and T., and the Fort Smith and Western railroads, had met in person with Chief Sam and had promised to attempt to lower the fare to Galveston, which normally stood at $10.20.

More than $8,000 was raised at this meeting. The proposed day of sailing was still not settled. That elusive date had a way of retreating each time it drew near. But a delegation, to be named shortly, was to travel to New York and receive the ship. This event was planned for the 21st of January, 1914.

Business was still very good. "The secretaries are working hard trying to keep up the much business correspondence," reported the *Ledger.* "Many times the official mail exceeds 50 letters a day, all of which must be answered." [39]

Sam, too, had many problems with which to cope. Although the ship had been insured for $90,000, and the investment of the group thus protected, the difficulty of obtaining a crew for the ship was still unresolved. Sam passionately wanted an all-Negro crew for his ark. Provisions had to be purchased and coal loaded aboard. Sam was, besides, contemplating an application to the Post Office Department for permission to allow the ship to carry United States mail!

The mechanics of preparing sailing lists were also occupying the attention of Sorrell, the editor of the *African Pioneer,* who now had more time to devote to these matters since his unceremonious demise as Boley's Justice of the Peace. Presidents and secretaries of local clubs were sent blank forms, which were to be returned with haste, each man indicating the number of persons in his family who proposed to go to Africa. Feverish activity was prevalent throughout the area, and Sorrell had to spell out the moving provisions:

> Children under six years old will go free on train to ship, between six and twelve years one-half fare. State the number of live stock each family will have. Only horses and mules will go.[40]

The *African Pioneer* sounded the keynote of the moment: "Let everybody get busy."

The Tulsa *Star,* somewhat distant from the scene of these preparations and hopes, still raised its editorial voice against Sam and his activities: "In spite of the timely warnings given the colored people of Oklahoma by the colored press of the state against Chief Sam, many have become victims of his fraudulent scheme and are still hoping they will realize the truth of Chief Sam's false doctrine." [41]

Sam, the *Star* said, had announced his intention to go to Arkansas early in February to enlist the Negroes of that state. The paper quickly seized upon this item and deduced that "if the Chief expects to visit Arkansas this month and next month, when will he take the people to Africa who have paid him their $25?"

The Colored Bar Association of Muskogee also resolved against Sam, asking him to present credentials or be forced from the country. In addition to his low standing in Muskogee, one of the state's larger cities, Sam was also *persona non grata* in Tulsa, according to the *Star:* "The African Chief studiously avoids Tulsa because he knows he cannot find the usual pickings among the colored people here. He passed through this city New Year's day, but kept in hiding between trains."

Fulminating at top performance now, the *Star* reproduced a letter from W. Haluric Davis of Beggs, who said that he had known Sam in West Virginia many years before. Sam was then practicing "voodo" in the vicinity of the towns of Freeman, Good Will and Pocahuntas, according to Davis, and claiming that he had been brought to the United States from Africa by a Negro minister.

"How is it," asked Davis, "that no one hasn't discovered that he once made a tour of Oklahoma some ten years ago?"

Davis then described the activities of the Negro whom he claimed to be Chief Sam: "He then was lecturing on Africa, as an African. He carried a young crocodile in alcohol, exhibiting it as one of the gods the Africans worshipped."

The failure of the movement to get under way by the middle of January began to work hardships upon the colonists gathered in Weleetka in the camps. The weather had turned severe, and the members of the camps were in what one newspaper described as "dire straits." [42]

The tents afforded only minimal protection against the knife-like northern winds. They had not been put up with the intention of providing shelter through January, traditionally a bleak and bitter month in Oklahoma. The colonists, in addition, had little money with which to secure additional amenities. Some of the Negroes had tried to obtain employment in Weleetka to tide them through the early part of the winter, but there was very little opportunity for work in the small town. Not only was food becoming scarce, but clothing was highly inadequate. Almost all of the adults were ill-clad for a winter in the open, and many of the children were running about camp barefoot and half-naked.

A Negro physician at Clearview was called to Weleetka to minister to the unfortunate campers. The situation, as he described it, was desperate. Dysentery, typhoid fever, and other diseases beset the pioneers, and the death rate was high. The camp was overcrowded, the water of the Alabama Creek polluted, and the situation badly complicated by the cold weather.

Despite their straits at Weleetka, the pioneers held on, partly out of hope, partly out of desperation. They could not turn back now. They prayed that the *Curityba* would soon leave New York for Galveston, and that Sam would direct them south to meet the ship.

Hostility toward Sam and his followers grew throughout the state. Finally, two men, D. B. Garrett of Boley and G. W. Lane of Wewoka, sought an interview with the Governor. They wanted to convince him of the value of the colonization program, and to seek from him a letter of introduction to the British Ambassador in Washington. They accomplished at least the second half of their mission, for Cruce gave them a letter to the British, dated January 17 in which he said, in part:

> These men are interested in the enterprise being promoted in this State by . . . "Chief Sam." . . . These men will relate to you the entire plan so far as they are familiar with it. . . . I will personally appreciate it if you will grant them a conference, go into the matter thoroughly with them, advising them of the true situation so far as the representations made to them about conditions in West Africa are concerned.[43]

On the 23rd, the *Courier* reported the first definite sign that Sam's ship was ever to be ready. More than a score of persons were preparing to leave Oklahoma for New York to take charge of the *Curityba*. The delegates were to pay the remaining pending accounts against the vessel, and then sail immediately to Galveston to gather in emigrants. Between New York and Galveston, the ship was to call at Norfolk and Charleston, where "thousands will be . . . to get a glimpse of the ship that was bought by the black man; and the ship that shall traffic with the other nations of the world." In Galveston, where the membership would meet the *Curityba,* "a little girl of Oklahoma will christen the ship with palm oil from Gold Coast, Africa, in consecration of the ship to God and a mark of manliness to the co-workers." [44]

The *Courier,* moved by the optimistic signs of progress, waxed eloquent: "After this there will be thousands to step aboard, no doubt, daring the mad waves of the Atlantic, cherishing unlanguished spirit, and invigorated by the yearns of that land where a fountain never runs dry."

It was becoming more and more difficult, however, for the campers in Weleetka to hold out. In February, at the peak of the excitement, smallpox racked the tent colonies. Dr. J. C. Mahr, the state health commissioner, was called into the matter by local health officials, who reported to him that there were eight cases of smallpox in the camp already, and that the Negroes were moving freely between the camps and the town of Weleetka each day. It was urged that the Negroes be vaccinated at once. Mahr sent Peter Biewer, one of his assistants, to investigate the situation personally. Biewer vaccinated all of the Negroes in the camp, and reported that the situation would remain in control as long as the local officials kept a watch over the health conditions at the camps. While Biewer was in camp, the first major movement of the migration program began to get underway, with Sam and twenty of the Negroes packing up their belongings and leaving for New York to claim the ship.

Garrett and Lane, supported by the formal letter of introduction from the Governor, which they freely and incorrectly interpreted to all as a token of his support of the movement, reached Washington in February and were granted an interview with the British Ambassador. The results of this curious meeting between Britain's famous war-time envoy and the two Oklahoma Negroes were reported in a letter to John Bassett Moore in the State Department, to whom Spring-Rice ultimately sent Garrett and Lane.

> Messrs. Garrett and Lane, when they called here, could not be shaken in their faith in Sam's bona fides and stated that he had positive offers from native chiefs on the Gold Coast to receive them into their tribal communities; that some American negroes had already gone over and had written letters testifying to satisfactory conditions, and that as many as 6,000 American negroes intended to emigrate under Sam's auspices. [45]

To Spring-Rice this was an alarming state of affairs. He had already been informed by the Governor of the Gold Coast that local police authorities had received complaints against Sam for obtaining money under false pretenses. In addition, there was an earlier letter from the manager of the Bank of British West Africa at Accra who, confusing Sam's Akim Trading Company with his present "limited" version of that same name, indicated that Sam was wanted for fraud by certain natives to whom he had sold stock.

Spring-Rice urged that every and all efforts be made to bring Sam's operations to a speedy end. The Ambassador pointed out that should Sam accomplish his migration, and attempt to colonize American Negroes on the Gold Coast, nothing but disaster would be in store for his victims.

These measured warnings and the veiled threats of the British had little visible effect on the U.S. State Department and even less on Sam and his followers. The Negroes had a ship, and they had promises of land and freedom. They were beginning to move, to gain impetus in their quest for self-sufficiency and social equality. Most of all, they had a messiah who would lead them. Against such reality and such vision, the carping of a small-minded British bureaucracy seemed a petty matter, indeed.

5

"One Family We Dwell"

> One family we dwell in him,
> We love to sing hosanna,
> Though now divided by the stream,
> We love to sing hosanna.
> (From "One More River")

SAM AND HIS vanguard of twenty people left Weleetka on February 5, headed for New York and final possession of the *Curityba*, shortly to be rechristened *Liberia*. The group had withdrawn from local Oklahoma banks the funds which would be necessary to complete the purchase of the ship and to maintain themselves on the Gold Coast when they finally arrived. They had taken almost $70,000 with them, according to an often repeated rumor.

Meanwhile, despite their earlier opposition to the depopulation of their service territory, the railroads made plans to exploit the movement in whatever way they now could by providing for the transportation of Sam's followers to Galveston, where they were ultimately to meet the *Liberia*.

The anticipated arrival of the group in New York had provoked considerable interest. From his office on the fourth floor of the Bishop Building in Harlem, A. E. Smith, Sam's New York agent, had been issuing provocative, but obscure, statements to the press for more than a week, each one offering a new date for the imminent arrival of the Oklahoma contingent.

Smith's role in Sam's plan was a unique one. He was the sole white man involved at a high level in the movement. It was Smith who received all of the funds which **Sam** collected during his peregrinations in Oklahoma. Each meeting of the African pioneers had inevitably terminated with a trek to the nearest post office, where Sam and the local treasurer obtained a United States postal money order for the exact amount collected. These were made out to Smith and were promptly forwarded to the New York offices of the company. An erstwhile postmaster at Lima remembers the run on money orders occasioned by Sam's activities in Seminole County. In one instance, Sam came to the post office with $425 in bills which he wanted to dispatch to Smith in a single money order. The postmaster told him, however, that $100 was the largest denomination of order which he could issue, and Sam was eventually obliged to write out five different orders to send this money to New York.

Smith claimed that he transacted the business of the Akim Trading Company, Ltd., principally to give the organization a sound credit front. In an effort to clarify his somewhat ambiguous financial role in an otherwise all-Negro corporation, Smith once told reporters that "Chief Sam realized that a Negro has no standing with the white businessmen of this country." [1]

Smith was friendly and cooperative with the many reporters who visited him for information. In an interview published in the New York *Times,* February 11, Smith stated that all the company officers were Gold Coast inhabitants and that, "with the exception of Chief Sam their names are too much of a mouthful to pronounce, much less remember." He described the treasurer, vice-president, and other officers as chiefs of tribes, in a position to "influence the members of their tribes to sell to this company rather than the English trading companies."

In this last remark, Smith may well have inadvertently supplied a major reason for the British discomfort at the prospect of the emigration. Already harassed by the incessant Ashanti uprisings on the Gold Coast, which periodically closed trade routes between the coastal cities and the interior for months on end, the British could ill afford to see additional trade diverted from their hands. As it was, they had to deal with the constant nuisance encroachments of free-lance merchants in areas not directly under British suzerainty and British vigilance; and they were certainly not anxious to welcome a contingent of American Negroes, however modest it might at first seem, who had as one purpose the further diversion of Gold Coast products to non-British ports.

The *Times* reporter, still intrigued by the financial operations of the company, directed a seemingly innocent question at Smith.

"Then if the treasurer's office is in the jungles of the Gold Coast, all the money paid for stock by negroes here is sent to him?" queried the newsman.

"Oh, no," replied Mr. Smith. "All that money is received by me."

The reporter began to needle.

"Are you bonded?" he asked Smith.

"No," replied Sam's agent, reportedly with a smile. "You see, Chief Sam and his followers have faith in my trustworthiness. I paid the last installment on the steamer a week ago to-day. It amounted to $39,000, resulting from the sale of stock. The total purchase price of the *Curityba* was about $100,000."

The reporter's appetite was now really whetted. Smith had earlier asserted "emphatically . . . that neither he nor any other white man owned a single share of stock in the trading concern." Smith had also drawn a fine distinction: he was not an "officer" in the company, but merely its "agent."

The newsman, certainly doubting the implied altruism of Smith's role, finally asked, with a cultivated gift for loaded naïveté: "But if you do not own any dividend-paying stock, where will your own profits come in?"

"Well," answered Mr. Smith, "with me this is a distinctly business proposition. You see, in the first place, I have the management of the steamer. Naturally, for the small sum of $50 we cannot afford to provide food for our passengers on the trip to Africa. This they must buy on the ship. Then, when we arrive on the Gold Coast we sell them the horses and provisions with which to journey to Ashantee. There Chief Sam has 99-year leases from the chiefs of the various tribes of two tracts of lands. One tract is 120 miles square, and the other, a short distance away, is 60 miles square. This land will be leased to our immigrants."

Smith was then asked how much the rental charges would be on each acre of land. His answers were again friendly and frank, and thoroughly disarming.

"This has not yet been determined, but each immigrant can lease as much as he thinks he can work. The published reports that we will give each immigrant a certain number of acres for nothing is not true, and they all understand this perfectly."

The interview concluded with a statement on the future operating plans of the company. Smith had a facility for making these plans sound both practical and comparatively simple, quite easily capable of accomplishment. He pointed out that once the passengers had debarked in Africa, the partitions in the ship, separating the various passenger cabins from one another, would be removed, and the ship would be loaded with African products. Goat skins, mahogany, cocoa beans, rubber, coffee and ostrich feathers would be brought to the United States, where ready markets would be secured. On the return to Africa, the ship would again be outfitted for passengers, and additional emigrants would be taken to join their fellows on the Gold Coast. Since this exchange would be repeated on each voyage, it followed, thought Smith, that the company would surely prosper in due time.

Smith's calming prospectus, however, did not dim the skepticism of New York's largest Negro newspaper, the *Age*. On February 5, the very day that Sam and his group left Oklahoma, the *Age* informed its readers that Sam's arrival in New York, "anxiously awaited with interest for the past two weeks," had not yet occurred. The *Age* contacted the Munson Line to verify Smith's assertions regarding the purchase of the *Curityba*. An officer of the company "gave out the statement that negotiations have been, in large measure, completed, whereby the Akim Trading Company, Limited, has acquired one of its old steamers."[2] Only Sam's arrival, apparently, was holding up the final consummation of the sale. The *Curityba* was presently moored in the Erie Basin, Brooklyn, awaiting repairs.

The *Age* pursued its inquiries more closely into the condition of the ship, which was described as "of the old German type," and from an unnamed expert on ships acquired the estimate that it would take between $5,000 and $6,000 to make the steamer serviceable for a transatlantic run. Even though thoroughly repaired, it was observed, the ship would still be able to accommodate no more than seventy-five first class passengers and fifty second-class passengers. The *Age,* therefore, felt that it was on solid ground in doubting Sam's reported claim that he would transport some three thousand Negroes to Africa.

Sam and his delegates, all doubts of the press notwithstanding, arrived in New York sometime during the weekend of February 7. Sam had, he explained, stopped en route to give lectures and to attempt to stimulate additional interest and funds for the movement.

The Negroes were initially quartered at the Wilson House at 2148 Fifth Avenue, in the uptown Harlem section of the city. Sam, as would eventually prove characteristic, did not linger with the group, but quickly left New York for Boston, where he intended to carry on further financial proselytizing.

The delegates, finally so close to their goal, soon became impatient with the waiting. New York was bitterly cold in February; temperatures had plunged several degrees below zero, recording new lows, and transportation within the city was at a frigid standstill. Few of the delegates, accustomed to the milder climates of the southwest, ventured far from their Harlem base. But they soon could see no point in paying for their lodgings in Manhattan out of a thin financial reserve, when their own ship lay invitingly along the pier in nearby Brooklyn; so they packed what belongings they had brought and moved aboard the *Curityba* after a very few days residence at Wilson House.

The ship was hardly more comfortable, but at least it was theirs. The *Curityba* (to the pioneers, the *Liberia*), lay in a cheerless berth at the end of a long pier, surrounded by the deserted hulks of dead ships. Many of the passengers, when they ventured from their usual station around the engine room boilers, must have made mental contrasts between the wide flatlands covered with ice and snow that they could see from the cabin windows and the vivid tropical verdure of the Gold Coast for which they were destined.

Within a few days, while Sam remained absent from New York, observers had reached their verdict on the legitimacy of Sam's movement and the attitudes which they would express toward it. Most of the viewpoints were those of disbelief, mixed often with condescending amusement and occasionally intermingled with parent-like warnings about the inevitable failure of the expedition.

Duse Mohammed Ali, for example, the half-Negro, half-Egyptian editor of the *African Times and Orient Review,* taking his usual pervading interest in things African from his situation in London, added a stricture about the colonization scheme which was quickly picked up and reproduced by the New York press:

The name of Albert Sam as a chief is unknown to me. All the lands in that British Colony are tribal lands, which can neither be sold nor given away by the chiefs, and there is no part of the colony where sixty-four acres will be available for each of 1,500 persons. The country is covered with dense forests. I'm sure that even if the British Government allowed them to have their own towns, it would not permit them to set up a form of government. It would be disastrous if these people were induced to go to Africa and find themselves stranded.[3]

It is not without interest that at the very moment Mohammed Ali issued his warning, there was a young man in his office who was at the time acquiring a "keen interest in Africa, its culture, and its administration under colonial rule."[4] Marcus Garvey, who would eventually become Sam's successor as the Pied Piper to the American Negro, had traveled from Jamaica to London in 1912 and was destined to stay there, in association with Mohammed Ali a large part of the time, until the summer of 1914.

The only trusting word for Sam, apart from the unending reiterations of faith by those aboard the *Liberia,* came from F. C. Holmes, manager of Wilson House, who, despite the loss of his boarders, told reporters that from his brief contact with him Sam "appeared to be a very worthy man."[5] Holmes added that some eighty-six persons were expected to arrive shortly from Boston to join the pioneer group, while other Negroes were on their way east from Galveston and Oklahoma.

Sam, too, was expected back in New York at any moment, and his absence had the signal effect of increasing the anticipation of his return. The New York *World* reported, "Thousands of negroes in this city were on tiptoe last night over the expected arrival of Chief Alfred C. Sam.[6]

Now that the movement had invaded its territory, the Brooklyn *Eagle* took full cognizance of Sam and his followers, reporting them as "smugly ensconced" aboard their ship at Pier 2 in the Erie Basin, "marking time and impatiently waiting for the hawsers to be cast off and the voyage to the Promised Land to start."[7]

The *Eagle* reporter, overwhelmed by the excellent opportunity the movement offered him for brushing up on his store of clichés, introduced readers to the background of the movement before trying to explain its *raison d'etre:*

Provided you are a colored person and have the wherewithal to purchase stock in the Akim Trading Company, Ltd., you can soon be sailing over the bounding main to the Gold Coast, West Africa, where Chief Alfred C. Sam, whose ancestors were kings and queens, plans to establish a colony of blacks, on a tract of forty-five square miles he has purchased. Of course, you'll have to hurry like mad to subscribe to the stock because Chief Sam can take only 600 in the first contigent, and inasmuch as fortunes await those who will depart from their native land, it won't be long before the S. R. O. sign will be hung out.

For the first time, however, though the vein was only half-serious, press attention was given to the underlying strains that had provided an impetus to the Sam movement. The *Eagle* reporter noted that

> Chief Sam opines that the negroes in our Southern States get a pretty rough deal, what with lynching bees, burnings at the stake, Jim Crow laws, racial prejudice, social inequality, and what not. Should they stand for it? Not by a jugful when over yonder, right on the Gold Coast of West Africa, he has 45 square miles of fertile soil where the colored people can colonize and, perhaps, form a little republic or empire of their own.

The lynchings in Texas and Oklahoma and "other turbulent regions of the South and West," the *Eagle* noted, "are as common as pink teas on Fifth avenue during the social season."

The reporter was also impressed by the deep religious atmosphere aboard the *Liberia*. The passengers arose each morning at three for prayer, and on Thursdays they fasted all day in sympathy for their associates in the camps at Weleetka and Galveston. There was a Baptist preacher aboard conducting the services, and he explained that he intended to establish a new church as soon as the group arrived in Africa. It would be called the Church of God. The pioneers were also intending to erect a magnificent temple on the highest point of land in Chief Sam's tract. The regime on board ship clearly underlined this prevailing puritan spirit. Smoking and drinking were not allowed. Chief Sam had further shunned the "crap-shooting, roustabout, levee darkies with a propensity for basking in the sun," and had made it known earlier that he was interested only in those recruits who "were full of ambition and were willing to work."

Three o'clock prayers notwithstanding, definite trouble was being vigorously stirred for the pioneers by the British. On February 10, a newspaper reported that "the authorities here are watching Sam's movements closely and the belief prevails that there is 'fake work' in his promise to the blacks, all of whom have disposed of their holdings in America." [8]

Now that Sam was within easy firing distance of the British Embassy, its officials felt that they could personally prod the local law enforcement authorities into tying up the departure of the group with criminal charges against its leader.

Curiously enough, while the investigations by New York authorities were just beginning to get under way, the disparaging view of Sam's back-to-Africa movement, traditionally shown in Oklahoma, was being supplanted by a favorable one. Previous debunkers of the project were forced to adjust to the purchase of the ship, a tangible, unanswerable proof that their original predictions of Sam's motives were incorrect. The *Liberia* was his ship; he had purchased it with the money collected from his followers, and there was no talking around this fact. The Oklahoma City *Times* took time out to review with some admiration the present status of the movement. On February 10, the very day when the New York authorities were publicly voicing their doubts as to the legitimacy of Sam's enterprise, the *Times* stated:

> Beset by many attempts to prove his scheme a fraud, Chief Sam apparently has overcome the prejudice against him and proved the faith of the negroes in his promise to land them in a sunny clime where they can govern themselves.[9]

Chief Sam, the paper continued, had not permitted the opposition to discourage him, and now he had apparently been vindicated:

> So many stories were told about how the negroes would be coaxed away, separated from their money and left broke that the matter has been partially passed off as a joke and if there has really been information obtained to prove Chief Sam's scheme a swindle it is not generally known.

In the absence of their leader, the passengers aboard the *Liberia* found themselves continually visited by reporters from the New York papers, each becoming increasingly fascinated with the details of Sam's plan. Most of the newspapermen must certainly have been expecting to find a bizarre assortment of colorful character types on the ship, since they were often led to point out, as did the *World,* that the passengers were "orderly and neatly dressed." Neither did the group seem to be bothered by Sam's absence; for, to the reporters, "all of the Negroes expressed utmost confidence in their leader." They appeared serene, "well cared for and supplied with funds." [10]

The passengers, of course, had little cause for immediate anxiety. Except for the harassments of the weather, and the all-too-frequent incursions of the reporters, they were comfortably established aboard the ship, and the vessel itself represented presumptively sound warranty of Sam's ultimate return; nothing could happen without it happening knowledgeably to them.

But the campers in Galveston and Weleetka suffered from recurring doubts about the authenticity of the movement, doubts which were being systematically fed by the cynicism of the whites, and by the partially distorted and only occasional news references which were relayed back to Oklahoma and Texas by the wire services.

At Weleetka, for example, news of Chief Sam's absence from the *Liberia* was reported to have "created consternation" among the campers.[11] The Fort Smith *Times-Record* editorialized smugly that it had experienced "no surprise that Sam couldn't be found." [12] The line of communication between the New York group and the campers in the Southwest was perhaps the major source of difficulty. Time-table shifts were particularly distressing, especially when funds were low and anticipation was high. Sam continually said that he would be at a certain place at a certain time, but almost inevitably he was obliged to revise his schedule at the last minute. The Weleetka group, for example, who had been told to be in Galveston February 15, prepared to sail for the Gold Coast five days later. Shortly before that date arrived, however, they were told to postpone their departure; the ship would not reach Galveston for at least another three weeks.

There was also a great deal of confusion about the number of persons who would be transported to the Gold Coast, a confusion both fanned and reflected by the conflicting newspaper reports. Everyone became aware, once he had seen the *Liberia,* of its comparatively limited passenger space. Yet newspaper reports continued to mention numbers from 500 to 3,000 as the prospective passenger total on this initial voyage. Sam was primarily responsible for this confusion, perhaps, in his failure to designate clearly the persons who would make the first trip. His sales inference, as well, had regularly been that all persons who bought shares in the Akim Trading Company, Ltd., would be equally entitled to sail to Africa.

When Sam had still not returned to his group on February 12, the *Age,* always interested in spinning a web of intrigue about the movement which it found improbable, pointed caustically to the overdue departure of the *Liberia* and noted that "mystery surrounds the whereabouts of Chief Sam whose appearance in New York has been anxiously awaited for the past three weeks. Even Chief Sam's trusted lieutenants do not seem to know where he is or what he is doing." [13]

With righteous concern for their brothers, several delegations of New York Negroes had taken the opportunity to visit the colonists in an attempt to dissuade them from accompanying Sam. They had advised the pioneers "to return to Oklahoma and the Southwest, but these appeals have been unavailing." [14]

W. H. Lewis, one of the most zealous of the passengers, was acting as spokesman for the group. A graduate of Fisk University in Nashville, Lewis had gone to Oklahoma as a schoolteacher. The "professor" constantly and adroitly represented the movement in its most favorable light to the newspapers, despite their articulate and unrelenting disbelief in his college degree. Typical of this skepticism was the misspelled comment by an *Age* reporter, presumably a graduate of no university, that Lewis "claims to be a Fiske graduate." [15]

Lewis pointed out that the Negroes had complete faith in Chief Sam; and visitors to the ship, despite their own misgivings about Sam's honesty, were forced to concede that everything seemed to be running smoothly aboard the *Liberia.* "These people believe implicitly in Chief Sam and their one dream is to go to Africa where they can escape Jim Crow laws and other obnoxious measures aimed at the citizenship of the American Negro," the *Age* reported. Another newspaperman, who "expected to find the Back-to-Africa band of Negroes bemoaning their fate and the disappearance of Chief Alfred C. Sam," found instead that the passengers were "happily engaged in a big course dinner." [16]

Lewis expressed some pique at the morbid curiosity of the visitors to the ship. "We are not worrying over the success of the company," he told one of them, "and we are the only ones who should worry at all." Chief Sam, while still out of town, certainly had not fled the country. He would, Lewis was certain, be back in a few days and then the group would be off soon after that. "We have to lay in some provisions before sailing, but that won't take long," Lewis explained.[17]

Lewis also attempted to summarize why the Sam movement would succeed in contrast to earlier schemes that had ultimately failed. He pointed out the singular asset that the present enterprise possessed: it was being led by an African Negro who could furnish land in Africa for the group, a man who intimately knew the country to which they were emigrating:

> No American Negro could raise the money for that boat, but Chief Sam is a real African and he has the land and everything is all right. Of course, we don't expect to find homes all built for us over there. I've had letters from Chief Sam's mother and from friends in Africa and they tell me he's all right. We'll have to fell trees and build our own homes, but we had to do that in Oklahoma and we can do it there too.[18]

Finally, Lewis underscored the inadvertent aid that the newspapers were providing to the colonists' morale by printing stories which were patently untrue. With these inaccuracies in mind, the passengers were able to extend a skeptical attitude toward everything that the press said about their movement. This mental discounting of unfavorable stories was reinforced by the *African Pioneer,* the movement's own newspaper, which printed articles purportedly dictated by the Holy Spirit, each one pointing out the fate of liars, slanderers and "others who utter bad news about the company." [19]

"The Chief was actually here on the boat when articles were printed that he had gone," Lewis told a reporter from the New York *American.* Then he repeated the same words that he had uttered over and over again. "Chief Sam is in Boston and will return soon. We are all well and happy, the boat is well provisioned and we have plenty of money to put through the proposed expedition." [20]

Many Negro intellectuals and political leaders were considerably less confident than Lewis about the success of the back-to-Africa movement, and they seized upon several opportunities to publicize their misgivings. It was the same as it had been in Oklahoma when the burghers of the Negro towns had turned stolid backs on Chief Sam, branding him a charlatan from the moment he had first broached his scheme. In fact, George W. Perry, the fiery editor of the Boley *Progress,* one of Sam's earliest opponents, was still seeking ammunition. He dramatically telegraphed the *Age* on February 12: "Wire me at once at my expense whether Sam has fled." [21] Perry's skepticism, mixed undoubtedly with a good share of wishful thinking, found companionship in at least one New York quarter, as the *Sun,* gleaning its news where it could find it, reported that "the old salts around the Erie Basin chandleries have given up hope of Sam's return." [22]

Two Liberian officials also had dark words of foreboding for the enterprise, words which were echoed by a native African, an alleged prince, who went one step further and claimed that Sam had confided to him that he was not really a chief at all.

Dr. Ernest Lyons, the Liberian consul-general in the United States, though he admitted that he did not know Chief Sam, said that he was nonetheless certain that the *Liberia* "will never sail," and that if "it does, it will never land on the Gold Coast of Africa because the American Negro is *persona non grata* along that western shore." [23]

Dr. Lyons reported that he had received many letters from persons in Oklahoma inquiring about the Chief Sam movement and other repatriation schemes. He had warned the authors of these epistles that the Sam venture was foolhardy. In addition, to add weight to his argument, he had decided to do a little personal investigating and the previous night had visited the *Liberia* in her Brooklyn berth. He had seen nothing to convince him that his original misgivings were not correct.

Except for Liberia, Dr. Lyons asserted, no country in West Africa wanted American Negroes. He went on to explain the impenetrable barriers to possible colonization:

> The whole coast is partitioned among European nations, and if the American black man emigrates there he will find himself at sea. He will not be allowed to enter the territory at all. He will find conditions uncongenial, for the prejudice against him on the west coast is greater than it ever was in this country.

The whole migration scheme, Lyons stressed, was impractical and impossible. Like a man trying to carry off the difficult task of forcefully stressing the obvious to persons who stubbornly refuse to see it, Lyons enumerated some of the roadblocks to the successful completion of the enterprise.

"It is foolhardy," he said, "on the part of the Negro in America to sell his property and go where he does not know." He asserted that the

British authorities were even now turning away whites as undesirable according to the strictures of their rigid exclusion policy.

"Knowing things as I do," he continued, "I am at a loss to know where these people are going." Granting, for the sake of argument, that Sam's pioneers might reach the coast of Africa (which Lyons thought ridiculous, all things considered), he pointed out that acclimatization to the new environment would pose an insurmountable problem. Harsh in the extreme, the coastal lands were asserted to be harsher on Negroes than on whites. "The blacks die faster," Lyons said ominously. "The only reasons why the American black man would stay there would be because he couldn't get away."

The claim by Lewis that Sam's familiarity with the Gold Coast and his status there would prove a passport to colonization success received a rude rebuttal from J. Edmestone Barnes, one-time Minister of Public Works in Liberia:

> There is no longer any chiefdom on the Gold Coast. The feudal system is a thing of the past and the last Ashantee chief was killed when I was there. No one can travel in any part of the country without a permit and to get one you have to show the authorities that you merit it. Why, the British government would not allow them to land. I know they do not encourage American black men to immigrate into the country. The only safe place for them is Liberia. Even the Liberian black man is unwelcome.
>
> Furthermore, no tribe has any land except as reservation under the authorities, and that can't be alienated in any such way as Sam proposes. I don't think the vessel will ever clear this port, but I know it will never land on the Gold Coast for colonization.

Barnes had previously included much of this information in letters to Oklahoma farmers, but he reported that such warnings had had the effect "of water on a duck's back."

Prince Frederick Bouman also joined the anti-Sam forces with an additional stricture against the movement, and issued a strong request that the authorities save Sam and his followers from themselves. Bouman, an outraged stockholder, had angry words about the project in which he felt he had been swindled.

Prince Frederick had been born in Unyora Albert Lake, Manza, British Africa, and reported himself as widely travelled, having visited in England, Japan, Calcutta, Java and the United States. Some three

years before, while touring this last nation, he had been induced to buy
some shares of stock in what was probably the original Akim Trading
Company. Bouman had been victim of the confusion inherent in the
similarity of names as had other people who had come into contact
with Sam. In any event, Bouman neglected to obtain a receipt for the
money which he had given to the business, and had ultimately grown
concerned about the surety of the investment. He accosted Sam on a
number of occasions, but, he reported, "Sam kept putting me off until
one day I cornered him and we had words." It was during this interview that Sam confided to Bouman, according to the latter's word,
that he was not a chief at all, but simply acting for the chiefs of the
Gold Coast. This latter conversation, said Bouman, "was in the African
tongue." [24]

Bouman told Sam that he would assuredly find himself in serious
difficulties if he continued to represent himself in the United States
as an African chief. Sam, however, attempted to assuage the fears of
the Prince by telling him that he had "fixed everything up before he
left for the Gold Coast." Bouman's difficulties with Sam continued:

> A few months later I went to California, sailing for a trip around the
> world. I returned to the United States about a month ago and I heard
> all about Chief Sam and his scheme to take the Negroes of this country
> to Africa. Liberia is the only place that is open to immigration in Af-
> rica and I have asked the British Consul there, as well as the police,
> to investigate Chief Sam's scheme before he is allowed to leave with
> the steamer for Galveston.[25]

Sam's return to the ship the following day, February 14th, stirred
the newspapers to some of their gaudiest outbursts of prose. The event
was treated with the same type of drama that might have been evoked
by the restoration of the prodigal son to his long-waiting parents. A
reporter from the New York *Sun,* on hand soon after the homecom-
ing, described the event in detail:

> Some time between Sunday afternoon and yesterday morning a
> medium-sized, well-built negro, very black indeed, dropped off the
> back of a trolley labelled "Erie Basin" and trudged through the snow
> to the steamship *Curityba* [*Liberia*] at the end of a snow covered
> pier in Beard's yacht basin.
>   Old Cap'n King didn't see him, but remembers hearing about forty

darkie voices shouting "Hail to the Chief" along in the night some time. It was too cold to investigate, but the old man slapped his shin and said to himself, "I'll bet that's him," and poked the fire a bit.

It was, but the captain wasn't sure until he flattened his nose against the frosty portlight yesterday afternoon and saw the adopted sons and daughters of Akim gathered around their chief in a genuine council of war that could not be mistaken. . . .

Then the captain went to collect a bet. The council of war went on until the shivery blasts from the bay blew in and it had to adjourn to the boiler room, where the snow drifts had not piled up.

Chief A. C. Sam had arrived and the patient members of the Akim Trading Company, Ltd., had visions once more of Indian rubber and palm oil along the Gold Coast.[26]

Shortly after Sam arrived aboard the ship, two other Negroes climbed up the gangplank, each carrying a bundle of daily papers, which he spread out before the "boiler room councillors." From his stance at the portlight, the reporter could hear nothing, but he could watch the Chief as a follower read aloud. As Chief Sam listened, "his regal brows contracted, his stubby black mustache bristled with indignation. His tribal pride was wounded beyond repair." The reporter observed that "a stout white man, the only one on board, apparently looked at Sam with an 'I told you so nod,'" and that "the councillors whispered to each other in twos and threes, and sidled nearer the boilers."

The *Sun* reporter went up the gangplank and knocked on the door of the main salon. Glowering, one of Sam's women followers opened the door. Inside the room he found the pioneers, in groups, lounging about, and "another daughter . . . adopted . . . of Akim . . . abusing a perfectly good typewriter every few minutes hitting a key while a companion dictated something."

When the reporter asked for Sam, someone was dispatched to find him, but "just like a real chief, he sent a vice-chief before he came himself, and the visitor never realized that he was in the presence of royalty until a hand shot out to be shaked and its owner said 'I'm Chief Sam.'"

The reporter was apparently not altogether pleased by the results of the interview. Sam related that he was "grieved by all the papers" and that he felt he and his movement had been slandered. When "his grief seemed about to fade his white friend nudged his elbow and revived it."

During the course of the interview, the pioneers from their boiler-room stations had filtered into the salon to join their chief. Apparently bolstered somewhat by his growing contingent, Sam grew annoyed:

"Dat's all, dey hab ruined me," said Sam, his indigation spoiling his English. "I won't say one syllable moe. Who thinkd I'd buy a boat and then flee? I'm not crazy. Dey twisted my facts so I neber knew dem myself. I tell you, man, I'm afraid of reporters, and I won't talk. No sir. I don't know when I'm going to sail, and anyhow I wouldn't say if I did."

The reporter commented:

This left the mystery unexplained. Chief Sam is aboard but the *Curityba* [*Liberia*] has no crew as yet, and no one knows when it will weigh anchor and depart. . . .
A few more bets are being placed at Erie Basin's ship chandleries, this time on the sailing of the *Curityba* [*Liberia*].

A collision of personalities, which threatened to postpone the departure of the *Liberia* even further, occurred almost as soon as Sam had returned. By the time the clash was over, Sam was again on the road in search of money, and Captain Edward Hauck, erstwhile skipper of the vessel, was at the Legal Aid Society in New York, angrily demanding that it help him obtain the money that he claimed was due him from the ship's owner.

Hauck said that he had been engaged, by a colored man whom he met in Kingston, Jamaica, to captain the ship and take it to the Gold Coast. He was told that the man represented a large trading concern which owned three ships and made many regular voyages to Africa. The captain had decided to sign on, was advanced a small sum of money, and was sent on his way to meet the ship at Brooklyn.

The captain had been in command of the ship until the day of Sam's return. A short time after Sam had come aboard, Hauck had been accosted by a messenger from the Chief who stated that the captain's presence on board was no longer wanted. Sam had apparently justified this move by insisting that he knew nothing of Hauck and had not authorized his hiring.

After this affront, Hauck felt called upon to hurl a few verbal slings

at the expressed plans of the group to leave Brooklyn at the end of the week. The amount of money that it would take to fix up the *Liberia,* Hauck said, would be large. Hauck had sailed the African coast for many years; he thought the climate there was "exceedingly dangerous, except to natives," and that the Negroes who were planning to emigrate would encounter "many serious difficulties." [27]
He continued:

> "I have never known white men to go into the country to stay more than a year because malaria is terrible there. These blacks are not acclimated. I do not understand Chief Sam. He says he is going to take his party to an island on the Gold Coast, yet one has only to pick up a map of the continent to see that there are no islands on that coast, and that the only one near it is Ferdinand, P. a Portuguese possession, on which they could not land."
>
> "If the party lands on British territory, there will be trouble, for I do not think that England would permit them with the freedom that Chief Sam says is to be theirs."

Hauck's irritation over his salary and his general reservations about the feasibility of the expedition made little, if any, impression on Sam, his immediate followers, or his supporters. Back in Oklahoma, the *African Pioneer* was still calling Sam "Christ-like," and praising his concern for the poor and humble. "He did not first go to large cities and fix tricks and plans with diamond front and silk hat gentlemen, to take Negroes to Africa," the paper reported, but sought out the disillusioned and ill-treated farmers.[28]

Even as Hauck was taking his troubles to the Legal Aid Society, Sam was off again on a new proselytizing tour, this time to the state of Delaware. As one newspaper put it, "He came right in, turned right around and walked right out again." As he left the ship, "he was heard giving his forty followers, who are suffering greatly from the snow and cold, words of good cheer."[29]

When Sam returned from his mission to Delaware some days later, he was immediately summoned to the British consulate for an interview with Sir Courtenay Walter Bennett, the counsul-general, who was stepping up his efforts to keep the expedition from leaving New York. With Sam to this interview went A. E. Smith and F. H. Kellogg, a New York attorney who had been engaged to handle the legal affairs of the Akim Trading Company, Ltd.

The discussion at the consulate was long and occasionally acrimonious. By the end of it, Bennett was even more convinced that "there is every reason to fear that Sam's operations are a pure swindle . . . even giving him the benefit of the doubt as to his really thinking that he is engaged in philanthropic work." [30]

Bennett, educated for a career in the British civil service, with previous duty in all parts of the world—including a stint as consul-general in San Francisco during the 1906 earthquake—represented the full, trained dignity of the British Empire. He was fifty-nine years old, in his thirty-seventh year as a Foreign Office representative. He had occupied his New York post for some seven years.

Bennett plied Sam and his companions with questions about the operations of the trading company, insinuating again and again that he was aware of its fraudulent nature. The information he elicited from his visitors primarily concerned the financial status of the company, the legitimacy of Sam's claim to land on the Gold Coast, and his alleged position as an African chief.

Bennett was particularly appalled by the fact that the *Liberia*'s ownership was vested exclusively and absolutely in Sam's name. "He is therefore free," Bennett wrote to Sir Cecil Arthur Spring-Rice when reporting on the interview, "at any moment to go to Philadelphia, San Francisco, or Liverpool, with the Bill of Sale in his pocket and sell the ship devoting the proceeds to his own use."

Bennett attempted to emphasize this fact to Kellogg, who replied weakly that an agreement had been entered into between Sam and the Akim Trading Company, Ltd., in which the vessel was considered to be the property of the company, not of Sam.

Bennett then wanted to know if this unwritten agreement was sufficient to prevent Sam from sailing the vessel when and where he chose; and Kellogg, painfully aware of Bennett's point, admitted that it was not.

With regard to the Gold Coast properties which Sam alleged he held, Bennett reported the following to his superior in Washington:

> I have further elicited from Sam the fact that the leases referred to in my previous letter and others are still in existence, but the lands cannot be used for the purpose of colonisation. The originals, he tells me, are with Dorman, and the operation of the leases is dependent upon arrangements which have not yet been made, and which Sam tells me

never will be made, for the development of the land in question by
means of syndicates. They appear to have been deposited with Mr.
Smith with intent to bolster up Sam's case and lead people generally
to believe that these lands were available for his colonisation purposes.

Sam tells me that he has land of his own in Akim consisting of 64
square miles which belongs to his sister Abinabio of Brofu Edru, and
that he had letters from his sister stating that she is prepared to accept
any negroes whom he may take to the Gold Coast as members of the
tribe.

It was with regard to the documentation of Sam's land claims that
Bennett was most cynical. When Sam was asked for the letter "it was
not forthcoming," Bennett reported. It was supposed to be in London
"if it exists at all."

Bennett also felt that he had trapped Sam into the damaging admission that he was not a chief. Sam, he reported, told him that his mother
had wished him to accept the chieftainship of the tribe, but that he
had declined in favor of his sister, Abinabio. Bennett immediately
called to Sam's attention a previous statement in which he described
himself as "Chief of Babianita Villa." According to Bennett's version
of the conversation, Sam then admitted that this was a most misleading
title and that Babianita consisted of a collection of but four persons,
none of whom now resided in this phantom community.

Bennett then inquired more carefully into the present financial condition of the company. The information he elicited from the three
somewhat frightened officials of the concern was certainly not likely
to convince him that the corporation had any ability to remain solvent
for long. Sam reported that he had collected in all about $75,000. The
Liberia had cost him $69,000, but the ship was still far from seaworthy.
It seemed likely, Sam agreed, that it would take about $5,000 to render
it fit for the voyage to the Gold Coast.

Bennett dutifully added these figures and came to the grim conclusion that the cost of the completed vessel being thus approximately
$74,000, only $1,000 would be left to carry 1,200 men to the Gold Coast.
His addition, it is true, was accurate; but Bennett gave no clue as to
where he had received the information that Sam actually planned to
take 1,200 persons with him on his first voyage to Africa.

The interview was closed with a less than veiled threat to the three
men, a threat directed particularly at the two white men who had

associated themselves with Sam, and whose presence in the business gave the entire affair a respectability that Bennett certainly did not want it to have. The consul-general advised both Smith and Kellogg to drop the whole scheme "and not to lend their support to a policy which would very likely land them both in serious trouble."

Certainly most frustrating to Bennett was the fact that the hands of the British authorities were tied insofar as direct action against the movement was concerned. Only Sam was a British subject, and he was conducting his business on alien soil. All of the other participants in the venture were Americans and well out of the reach of British jurisdiction. The most that Bennett could hope to do was to prod the local and federal authorities in New York into a full-scale investigation of Sam's activities. This he determined to do at once.

After reporting to the British Ambassador in Washington, he wrote to both the United States Attorney in New York and to the New York District Attorney, supplying them with the details of Sam's operations as he had discovered them during the interview. He also added a postscript, trying to impress upon the officials the urgent need to detain the *Liberia* in New York until more accurate information, already in the process of being assembled, was available on conditions in the Gold Coast.

> In conclusion it will interest you to learn that I have received telegraphic instructions from His Majesty's Ambassador to inform Sam, Mr. Smith and Mr. Kellogg, and anyone else connected with the enterprise, that the Ambassador has requested the final views of the Governor of the Gold Coast by telegraph, and that until receipt of these final views, His Majesty's Government strongly disapproves of any emigrants sailing from the United States for the Gold Coast.[31]

Bennett's efforts shortly began to bear fruit. "Smith left the consulate in a shaken state, insisting to the Vice Consul that he had had to do only with the 'commercial end of the affair,'" though Kellogg on the surface appeared unperturbed.[32] But it soon proved that it was the latter who had taken the consul-general's admonition to heart, for the following day Bennett received a telegram from Kellogg noting that he had been completely upset by Sam's responses during the interview, and had subsequently determined to withdraw his services from the company. He added the gratuitous comment that he hoped that he might never see Sam again.

Bennett forwarded this information to Washington, where Spring-Rice passed it on to John Bassett Moore, the counsellor and second-in-command to William Jennings Bryan in the State Department. Spring-Rice also had a response to his telegram to the Gold Coast, and he could report that "the Governor of the Gold Coast states that the leases of land which 'Chief Sam' purports to have concluded have not been registered in the Colony." [33]

The State Department elected to pass the buck to the State of Oklahoma; and Moore, as had been his previous wont, forwarded the information from Bennett and Spring-Rice to Governor Cruce in Oklahoma City. Along with this correspondence went a copy, for the Governor's confidential information, of a cable message from the British Foreign Office to Walter Hines Page, the United States Ambassador in London, which served as reinforcement of the work of the British representatives abroad by their home office:

> His Majesty's Government . . . are strongly of the opinion that the immigration of these negroes into that colony should not be encouraged for the reason that the land is almost entirely held communally by the native chiefs and communities, so that a negro from the United States could only obtain land by adoption into a native community—which as the immigrant would presumably be Christian and civilized would no doubt be unacceptable to them—or by lease, which would involve lengthy formalities and uncertain results. In addition to these objections, His Majesty's Government consider that the climate and conditions of the colony are entirely unsuited to natives of the North American continent.
>
> Enquiries have, moreover, been made as to the bona fides of the negro Sam, with the result that it has been ascertained that his transactions are not genuine, nor the Company for which he acts reliable. The Gold Coast Government have denied that they have any authorized immigration agent.[34]

The Foreign Office also noted that the British officials earnestly desired that steps be taken by the United States government to prevent the departure of the immigrants. They were "morally certain that the entire scheme is fraudulent."

Sam, apparently still undismayed, was back on board the *Liberia* on February 21. For the moment, however, the leader was silent about his plans for the future. He continued to maintain that the purchase of the vessel was an "earnest of good faith." [35] But he would make no statement as to when the ship would get under way.

Increased tension soon became evident aboard the ship, however, when the British publicly announced on February 25 that they had requested the American authorities to keep a close check on Sam and his activities with a view to pressing a criminal charge. Bennett told the newspapers that he had learned in his personal interview with Sam that Sam "when cornered and quizzed, admitted that he wasn't a chief at all and that his bailiwick of Babianita Villa contained only four persons besides himself before it ceased to exist altogether." [36] He also related the fact, duly recorded by the newspapers, that "the pseudo chief from the Gold Coast is wanted in that land of rich and unmaterialized promise for obtaining money under false pretenses." [37]

The reaction aboard the *Liberia* was to draw a curtain, though a rather porous one, around some apparently frantic maneuvers to get the ship out of New York and into clearer channels. Guards were posted at every entrance way to the ship, and only select newsmen were allowed to come aboard. Even then, they could not breach the inner sanctum to Sam, who was reported incommunicado, given over to meditating.

To a reporter from the Brooklyn *Eagle,* it seemed that "an air of darkest mystery had been hung about the ship." [38] Negroes were observed scurrying around the docks, heading like impatient ants toward the supply stores soon after these opened for business. By ten o'clock in the morning two trucks with flour and potatoes were observed backing up to the side of the *Liberia* where they unloaded their contents into her hold.

The *Eagle* reporter also ferreted out the news that orders had been issued to an extra crew of mechanics to get to work on the repairs of the engine. The machinists had been told, it was said, to work day and night until the job was finished. The rumor was afoot that Sam had abandoned plans for his proposed visit to Galveston, and was going to head straight for the Gold Coast.

The *Times,* with an ear, perhaps, for more precise details on the frenetic activity aboard the *Liberia,* added additional information to the plot. The *Liberia,* it told its readers, had been scheduled to sail that very evening. In the excitement, twenty-three of its "dusky pioneers" had abandoned ship, to be replaced by thirty-seven new passengers. Indeed, it was reported that the emigrants had been coming and going at the rate of ten to fifteen a day, subsisting on board the ship "until they could stand it no longer" on canned provisions.[39]

But the major block to a quick getaway was a competent crew to handle the ship. Fourteen Portuguese sailors who had been engaged to serve as part of the crew had left the *Liberia.* One Pedros Senagros, their spokesman, said that they did not intend to return until the money due them for several weeks past was paid in full.

The *Times* reporter, diligent in his pursuit, finally penetrated to the innards of the ship where he "essayed to find Sam." Venturing into a stateroom, he met a heavy-set mustached Negro who said that he was Sam's secretary. The suspicious reporter asked him whether he himself was not the Chief.

"That's none of your business whether I'm Sam or not," replied the man. "This is my boat and when it is ready to sail it will sail— probably in a couple of days."

A representative of the *Sun* also paid a visit to the *Liberia* after Bennett's suspicions had been made public. He noted that there apparently would be a further prolongation of Sam's exodus to the Gold Coast where he planned to take—"for a consideration"—1,200 American Negroes. He appended a botanical note to his story, describing the goal of the group, that happy place where they were to settle:

> On the mossy banks of the rivers of milk and honey in this land— according to Chief Sam, the flora include the 'harita' or butter bush, and the 'hata' or "flour vine," not to mention the "boba" or cheese tree which doubtless comes under the head of fauna. . . . Cheese is chained to the trees and a leisure class can be quite leisurely.[40]

The newsman, with little compassion, felt that the unfavorable press reports and the prolonged delay were finally beginning to tell on the prospective emigrants:

> It was evident that very little is needed to disillusion the forty negro men and women who have waited patiently for three months for the ship to sail. Murmurs of dissatisfaction were heard, and deep below the religious veneer which glosses life on board could be felt rumblings of trouble that will make the *Curityba* [*Liberia*] a hot place for Chief Sam if he does not "make good."

The reporter went into the salon which he found "warm and roomy."

A number of "drooping, quiet figures" sat about. One elderly lady, he wrote, "sat facing the wall in an attitude of utter dejection," while the reporter transmitted the British press release to Lewis. Another old woman, simply eavesdropping, said, "Oh, dear, oh, dear," while outside the cabin the reporter heard one man utter an oath which "emphasized a belief that they wouldn't ever reach the Gold Coast no how."

Sam, meanwhile, had again left the ship, leaving behind him a "puzzled group and a benediction." [41]

It became evident, however, that the investigations, partly out of inertia but largely out of the lack of adequate information, would come to nothing. None of the American agencies seemed inclined to do the dirty work of the British and interfere with a movement that concerned them only vaguely and incidentally. In Oklahoma, the Governor had finally made up his mind that he was "thoroughly convinced" that Sam was a fraud and that "the people who had been lead into the scheme he has on foot will be robbed of the money put into the proposition." But nothing could be done at this late date. Sam was in New York and the largest group of his followers had already left Weleetka for Galveston, where they were patiently awaiting Sam's arrival. The Governor reported that local investigations by county attorneys had shown that it was "impossible to get evidence upon which to maintain a successful prosecution." Certainly, the Governor bemoaned, "there should be a law somewhere to reach him." [42]

In New York, the authorities also reported an inability to deal judicially with Sam. District Attorney Cropsey of Kings County had referred Bennett's request for action back to the British, asking them to make some specific charges against Sam. Cropsey found, however, that outside of the British assertion that title searches on the Gold Coast had shown Sam not to be the holder of any real estate in his own name, the District Attorney's office had no evidence upon which to make a charge. Cropsey considered it futile to proceed against Sam in the absence of any direct accusation by the British that Sam had obtained money under false pretenses, and decided to turn his share in the matter over to federal authorities.

These officers had no better fortune in establishing a base for criminal proceedings. United States District Attorney Marshall announced that he was searching for proof, though to date without success, that Sam had used the mails to defraud. He had referred the matter to his assistant, Harry Content, but Content soon announced that his department "had done nothing and would probably not proceed against Chief Sam since there seemed to be no crime." [43] Content summarized the state of affairs clearly on February 28: "No matter how impractical his scheme is we have nothing on which to proceed. He told the people in Oklahoma that he had a boat. We have confirmed the purchase of one and know that the money he collected was put into it." [44]

Inspector C. E. Booth of the Post Office Department could do no better than Content. He reported that he had investigated everything connected with the case and found that Sam had made his solicitations in person and had not used the mails at all. "Unless it can be absolutely proved that Sam cannot do what he plans we have no case," Booth said.[45]

Sam had told Booth that he had been severely browbeaten during his interview with Sir Courtenay and that he had been driven to utter things which he never meant to say. Sam had further stated that he not only had the land on the Gold Coast, as advertised, but that his deeds were legally and properly filed in Africa.

On board the *Liberia* a new atmosphere of relaxation was perfectly evident. The hurried preparations for departure had come to a halt. There was a new crew on board, too, headed by a Captain McKenzie. The captain had three white assistants. Sam was in better spirits than he had been for some time, and he summarized his position in more philosophical terms when a reporter from the *World* came to see him. "This is a great race movement and God is back of it," Sam told him. "It is like the exodus of the children of Israel from Egypt." [46]

In a more relaxed mood itself, the *World* editorialized mellowly about Chief Sam and his Gold Coast visions.

We find it hard to go back on "Chief Sam"—even though the government of Great Britain batters at our faith.

If Sam is not really the supreme lord of sixty-four square miles of African territory, and if the "Curityba" [*Liberia*] does not sail proudly forth from the Erie Basin to collect some hundreds of negroes in the south and take them overseas to the promised land where the "butter bush" blooms and the "flour vine" flourishes, we shall feel that the world is indeed flat and prosaic.

Here is a son of Akim with enough imagination and get up to buy a real ship and paint the glories of old Africa in colors that set a thousand dark-skinned Americans hankering to get back to the home of their ancestors. The Gold Coast—magic destination, admirably chosen! And that touch about nobody being expected to work on Saturdays and Sundays on the voyage! Have many land pirates had these flashes? [47]

Other newspapers had looked somewhat less kindly at this particular phase of the movement, as is obvious from the sarcastic note in the *Sun* on whether it was Sam's intention "to permit the ship to float around and around on these two days of each week." [48]

The *World* continued:

If Sam is not all that he says he is, all we can say is that he deserves to have been. Lawyers may quit and great governments may scowl at him, but we shall keep our eye on Sam's star as long as there is a twinkle left in it. [49]

The same sympathetic paper gave Sam a prominent write-up in its Sunday edition, calling the passengers on the *Liberia* "the strangest party . . . that ever contemplated sailing from the harbor of New York." [50]

Sam had received the *World* reporter in his cabin, with a group of men and women sitting about him. He had a Bible in front of him, open to the section telling of the exodus of the Jews from Egypt. To the reporter, he looked younger than forty years. His face seemed "round and pleasant." He talked volubly, explaining in detail his own background and the history and dreams of his back-to-Africa movement. The reporter apparently tried to reproduce the material in fairly verbatim fashion to retain much of its original flavor:

This movement for a migration back to Africa, whence they had been taken by force years ago and brought here without their consent, has been inherent in the negro race in America for generations. There have been many attempts. Take the Liberia emigration, for instance. Telling my cousin, Asai Kwani, that when I came back it would be with a shipload of these people, with a trading company organized and with money back of us to continue the immigration . . . I went to Southampton December 31, 1913 . . . and on May 11 last reached Oklahoma.

Sam then went on to tell in brief the story of the organization of the clubs, a tale which was by now well known to the entire country.

"Everywhere," said Sam, "tremendous excitement was aroused. The meetings all had a religious trend." He claimed a missionary purpose: "I am a Christian myself, though not all of my people are. The 'Black Home' movement has for its goal not only the development of the Gold Coast, but the Christianizing of all those who do not love the Lord."

Sam recalled that on many occasions the number of people who gathered at his meetings, scheduled most often in churches, was so great that "we had to go out under the sky." He reiterated that all of the money raised by personal solicitation by local treasurers had ultimately reached his hands and had been promptly transmitted to New York. "Everything was done above board and honorably."

Sam was obviously pleased with the failure of the authorities to find grounds for criminal proceedings against him:

> The Postoffice Department and the United States District Attorney in New York have been unable to find anything wrong, because there was nothing wrong. Every dollar of stock is held by colored people and it's a colored-man and colored-woman movement. I bought the ship . . . there isn't a mortgage on it.

Sam talked on of the spiritual tenor of the movement. The women, he said, in the western states have been deeply moved by the project and have organized a federation of women's clubs devoted primarily to intensive prayer for the success of the exodus and "to raise money."

> It is a wonderful country we are going to. It was my childhood home and the land of my young manhood. It is rich in rubber, lumber, grazing, tropical fruits, corn, cattle, and many other things which American Negroes know how to cultivate. The cocoa bean is perhaps the most easily raised and the most profitable. We are to locate so far inland—over a hundred and twenty miles . . . that there is no danger from malarial fever and other sickness.

Sam, now moved by the sentimental recollections of his homeland, told of schools and native courts, of laws administered by chiefs, subchiefs and elders of the various tribes. The colony, though under the protection of Great Britain, was still, he felt, a predominantly African colony:

> The vessel we have bought has a Boston crew of colored men, with four white officers and four white engineers. There are about thirty

on board now in all, but when we reach Galveston we shall take on more and then sail for Africa.

After we land the boat will continue to make trips between the Gold Coast and New York bringing African merchandise here and carrying back negroes who want to get to the fatherland. I have myself sixty-one square miles of land besides the tribal lands of my people.

Sam also speculated on the reasons for the violent opposition of the British to the movement. He felt that they feared a diversion of trade to America. This was the chief explanation for their antagonism. In addition, Sam believed that the British might be afraid "that American colored people will bring in ideas that disturb the peace of the colony." But he thought this was not likely. To the contrary, he said, "our American negroes will develop the resources of the country and make it more prosperous."

His concluding remark summarized his faith and his position succinctly, "I am an African negro, a free chief in my own country, and I know that these people will be welcome there."

Soon after this interview, the *Liberia* cleared the Port of New York. The departure took place at five o'clock, Friday afternoon, March 6. The ship was still flying a Cuban flag, its legacy from the Munson Lines, and was reportedly en route to Portland, Maine, for additional repairs and outfitting.

Shortly before the sailing, Sam had gone aboard the ship to hold a final conference on her destination. He called together the shareholders who had made the ship their floating hotel for so many weeks and told them of his plans. His group, according to the *Times,* included seventy men and twenty women.

Shortly after the conference, Sam ordered the women to pack their belongings and leave the ship. Despite what the newspaper described as "loud lamentations" from the women, Sam remained adamant. The women finally obeyed his order and left the ship since, as the *Times* observed, Sam had "successfully assumed a prophetic as well as a tribal leadership of his followers." [51]

Sam's next order was to Captain McKenzie and Engineer Benford. They were told to get up steam for an immediate sailing to Portland. Seventy-five tons of coal had been put aboard the previous Tuesday, and Sam was confident that his ship could make its destination on that amount.

Having settled the affairs of the sailing, Sam and a number of male passengers debarked, and the hawsers were cast off. As the gangplank was drawn up, the crowd of dispossessed women "sat on their piles of chattel on the pier and set up ulalations and sang hymns. . . ."[52] In their midst were Sam and the Baptist minister who had undertaken the spiritual guidance of the pioneers during their long seclusion on the *Liberia*. As the ship backed away from the pier, the women expressed their apprehension over their destinies, considering, after all, the latest move of the vessel without them. Sam, however, reassured them and told them that he had arranged to pay their railroad fares to Portland.

When the *Liberia* had finally cleared the Erie Basin, Chief Sam ordered his followers to assemble their luggage and come with him. The weeping women "walked slowly out of the ship yard and boarded trolley cars for Manhattan. . . . Despite the assurances of the men folk . . . the majority of the women continued to cry out and sob until the cars were reached."

It was reported that a meeting of the remaining stockholders was to be held at the 125th Street offices of the trading company in an effort to clarify the next move which the emigrants would make. The following day, a reporter found the offices of the company closed, "and it was said in the building that A. E. Smith . . . had gone to Boston and Portland and would not be back for a week or ten days." [54]

"After the vessel sailed Sam disappeared," the *Times* reported, noting that he had not been seen recently in his South Brooklyn haunts, and that the *Liberia* had dropped from sight like its owner shortly after it passed City Island on the night it sailed.[55]

6

"He Patched His Ark With Hick'ry Bark"

It's a mighty rocky road,
I'm almost done traveling,
It's a mighty rocky road,
I'm almost done traveling.
I'm bound to go where Jesus is.
(From "I'm Almost Done Traveling")

FROM NEW YORK to Portland, Maine, is a distance of some four hundred miles by sea. But the distance was more than enough to allow time for the spinning of additional intrigue about the *Liberia* and Sam's movement. The information which ultimately reached the residents of that Maine seaport was as distorted as any had previously been during the movement's now relatively lengthy history. From the first, the Portland newspapers chose to enshroud the back-to-Africa move with an aura of deep mystery, and they approached the Negro pioneers with a cabalism better suited to an international espionage plot than a well-publicized migration program.

On the very day the *Liberia* sailed out of New York Harbor, the Portland *Sunday Telegram* whispered to its readers that the "air of deepest mystery" surrounding the coming of the ship had "sharpened last night." "All sorts of rumors were in circulation," the paper noted, "and men said to be interested in the coming of the ship to Portland refused to give any definite information regarding the ship." These men were said to have told the *Telegram* reporter with a confidence which was certainly vapid, that "the matter would undoubtedly be fully explained Monday or Tuesday." [1]

127

The one fact which seemed unassailable was that the *Liberia* was being brought to Portland for additional repairs. This, the *Telegram* confidently reported, was the observation of the Associated Press, "the most reliable news gathering organization in the world." Smith, by now almost notorious in his affiliation with the movement, had written to a number of local business men, and the *Telegram* asserted that he had advised them he would call upon these merchants in order to make arrangements for supplies and coal.

Portland provided the suitable historic backdrop against which to paint the Sam movement colorfully and enigmatically. Residents of the city were well acquainted with the erratic career of the Holy Ghost and Us Society, a revivalist, fundamentalist religious sect which had wound its way through the recent life history of the city, providing Portland with some of its most exciting and interesting events.

When it was prematurely guessed that there might be some connection between the society and Sam's group, the African movement suddenly had new import, and it could be worked easily into the same pattern that had been woven for the perplexing biography of the Holy Ghost and Us Society.

Under the guidance of Frank W. Sandford, the Holy Ghost group, founded in 1893 in the Androscoggin Valley of Maine, had experienced a phenomenal growth. By 1914, the sect owned possessions throughout the world, valued at more than three million dollars. Its Maine temple alone was worth more than a quarter of a million, and it possessed a fleet of ships, model farms, printing establishments, shoe factories, and other industrial concerns of note, to say nothing of a huge and staunch flock of converted members.

The society and its leader were nearly synonymous. Sandford, born at Bowdoin, Maine, in 1862, had attended Bates College at Lewiston, and later studied at the Cobb Divinity School. By the time he was sixteen, Sandford had begun to communicate regularly with the spirit that was to lead him through his quixotic religious career. For a while, he was the star pitcher on the college baseball team, and later played professionally. But he soon abandoned these physical involvements and determined to try divinity school.

At school, the orthodox faculty was more appalled than impressed with Sandford's strange ways and his alleged conversations with God. The school refused to graduate him, and later unsuccessfully attempted to block his appointment to a church at Topsham, New Hampshire. Soon he moved on to Great Falls, where, to quote a chronicler of Sandford's career, "his imagination ran riot; varying creeds jangled on his nerves; voices were talking to him, and his congregation fled and left him alone." [2]

A short while later, Sandford began a pilgrimage around the world, during which he was shipwrecked off Joppa, on the coast of Palestine. He attributed the ship's accident to the bad character of its passengers, and his own rescue to his faith. He revisited the Holy Land in 1898, 1905, and 1907, and succeeded in converting the Syrian boatman who had saved his life. The tour impressed upon Sandford the fact that there were two hundred million more heathen in the world than at the time of the birth of Christianity. Appalled, he took to the woods, fasting, praying, and listening to voices. The voices told him that he had been selected to change the religious map of the world; and Sandford, never one to question his revelations, assumed his new character.

"I am Elijah, I am David the Prince, I am Tsemech the Branch, a priest forever after the order of Melchisedec," he told people after his period of communion with the spirits. Converts were quick in flocking to the sand hill where Sandford said God had commanded him to build a temple. Samuel M. Shaw, for example, an early convert from Aroostook, came and gave Sandford $8,000.

"Is there no more?" asked Sandford. He stood on top of the hill that he had named Shiloh, a small, wiry man, his clothes in tatters, his brown hair and mustache flowing, his beard unkempt and knotted, his cheeks hollow.

Shaw, awed and impressed, said that he had $4,000 in life insurance and that he also owned some hogs.

"Life insurance is sinful. Swine are unclean," Sandford told him. Shaw listened, and then went away to turn in the insurance policy and to drive the hogs into a swamp where they were soon buried.

Shiloh blossomed, and its property was registered in the name of God Almighty, "to have and to hold for His works." A rehabilitated brigantine was purchased to carry the Word by sea to the heathen and the unbeliever. The ship cruised off the coast of Maine, putting in at various towns, though once the fishermen off Drain Island rejected the Word and stoned the ship until it put out to sea again. Soon, Sandford began to claim that he had effected miraculous cures among his followers, though he once had to fight through three court hearings before he was freed of a charge of manslaughter, lodged against him after the death, by diphtheria, of a child in his colony.

It became Sandford's dream to establish a kingdom in the Holy Land, and to make it the center of his scheme of world evangelization. He hastened to acquire ships, and soon had three of them, operating collectively under the sportive name of the "Kingdom Yacht Club." Two of the ships, the *Coronet* and the *Kingdom,* made a trip to the Holy Land with seventy of Sandford's followers; and when the frail craft returned safely through storm-tossed seas, Sandford took this as another token of divine indulgence.

But when the Shiloh colony flourished and began to exert political influence throughout the state, Maine authorities moved to put an end to Sandford's activities. Since the manslaughter charges had failed, Governor William T. Cobb ordered an investigation of affairs at Shiloh. This led to nothing, however. Investigators found the religious colony running smoothly, and all of its affairs apparently in good order.

The next step taken proved to be more effective. The federal government was called upon to look into Sandford's financial affairs; and on the basis of evidence which it collected, Sandford was convicted in late 1913 of using the mails to defraud. He was sentenced to the federal penitentiary at Atlanta for ten years. Shiloh went into a decline with his departure, though Sandford exercised considerable administrative control over its affairs from his cell.

The similarity between the Sandford movement and Sam's program was, in some respect, a striking one. An interpreter of Shiloh inadvertently drew the parallel when he attempted to explain the underlying appeal of Sandford's sect: "The psychology of the contagion of faith that met him is not difficult of analysis," the writer said. "It is a state of mind common in country communities, similar, though more advanced, to the hysteria of a Georgia negro camp meeting. The French describe it as a 'Folie à Dieux,' a term for which we have no equivalent." [3]

The more direct relationship between the two movements was established at once by the Portland newspapers on the basis of several strongly suggestive and persistent rumors, and some weak evidence. The day before the arrival of the *Liberia,* the Portland *Sunday Telegram* went so far as to claim that the ship "has been secured either by purchase or charter by the followers of Rev. Frank Sandford . . . for the purpose of re-establishing the Shiloh colony on the west coast of Africa." [4]

This story, the newspaper continued, came to it from a person with "excellent foundations" for supplying the information. It was particularly reasonable, it seemed, that the ship had come to Portland "to transport the remaining members of the Holy Ghost and Us colony from Shiloh to Africa . . . carrying out the long cherished plan of the leader of the sect," since Sandford had earlier attempted such a colonization. In 1911, Sandford had sailed with a group of colonists and had reached the African continent aboard the *Kingdom,* though the ship had been wrecked off Sangomar.

The best support for the rumor came from McKenzie's position as captain of the *Liberia.* A man bearing the same name, the Portland papers pointed out, had been the captain of the *Barracouta,* the third ship of the Kingdom Yacht Club.

Despite the apparent strength of these arguments, from Shiloh came an emphatic denial of any connection between the two movements. N. E. Coolidge, of Lisbon Falls, Maine, the Shiloh Colony lawyer, said that he knew of no relationship whatever between Sandford's followers and what the newspapers had persistently been calling the "mystery ship," due to arrive at any moment in Portland; and, Coolidge added tartly, if anybody would know of a connection, he would certainly be that person.

Other news preceding the *Liberia's* arrival came from a local supply agent, who reported that he had received a letter from New York informing him that the *Liberia* was to be equipped in Portland to carry a thousand passengers. Smith would also soon appear in Portland, the local agent said, to negotiate for the purchase of fuel.

The *Sunday Telegram,* already so far out on its speculative limb that fact mattered very little, decided to embrace all rumors indiscriminately, and added another one to its list:

The story that the coming of the *Curityba* [*Liberia*] from New York would serve to open a fruit line between this port and the West Indies and the mystery surrounding the Negro colony to be established on the African coast has set local steamship and business circles afire and only the authorized representative of the Akim Company will serve to set their minds at rest. [5]

The *Liberia* arrived in Portland on Monday, March 9, but though the newspapers cleared up the mystery surrounding the coming of the steamer to their own satisfaction, they had, in their deductive flights of imagination, created many more puzzles than they claimed to have solved.

Chief Sam, the Portland afternoon daily asserted flatly, was "a convert to the Holy Ghost and Us Society, having been converted some years ago when the Rev. Frank W. Sandford visited the African Gold Coast." The stockholders of the Akim Trading Company, Ltd., were claimed to be "religiously affiliated" with the Holy Ghosters, though by an inscrutable logic, the paper reported in the same sentence that "the followers of Sandford are not interested financially in 'Chief Sam's' movement." [6]

Whatever the details of the connection between the two movements, there was concrete evidence soon after the arrival of the *Liberia* that the members of the two groups were at least mildly interested in each other. Shortly after the ship dropped her mud hook off the Eastern Promenade in Portland Harbor, two small boats skipped out of the Holy Ghost and Us Society anchorage in the upper harbor and proceeded down to the *Liberia*. The men from Sandford's yachts were seen boarding Sam's ship, and later the Holy Ghost power launch carried McKenzie to the Customs House.

There was a new policy of restraint evident aboard the *Liberia* when it came to supplying information for public consumption and interpretation. Captain McKenzie curtly informed the Portland customs officials of his arrival, and said that the "ship had come to Portland light and would not take out any cargo from here." Beyond that, he refused to answer questions directed to him by the officials and curious hangers-on in the Customs House.

Failing with McKenzie, a reporter swept down on the hapless boatswain of the power launch, but found him, too, reticent. The man "refused to give out any information and would not even admit that he had brought the captain ashore."

Nor were the passengers on the ship more communicative. A reporter was refused permission to board the *Liberia,* and when he attempted to solicit information from a group of Negroes leaning over the deck rail he was told that any questions would have to be asked directly of the captain. McKenzie had, it seemed apparent to the eager newsman, "left instructions to those on board to 'keep their mouths shut.'"

This policy of silence—new to the Sam movement—was not unique to the Portland reporter. It reminded him of the press relations which had existed between his paper and the Holy Ghost and Us Society. "At any rate," he commented, "all those on board the *Curityba* [*Liberia*] have cultivated the Holy Ghoster's ability to retain a Sphinx-like silence when asked for information."

The Portland papers, deprived of a direct pipeline to the ship, sought out their information elsewhere and found a "prominent official of the consular service" who was able to shed considerable light on the Sam group and its recent voyage from New York to Portland. He, too, was convinced that Sam was a convert to the religion of the Holy Ghost group, and that his ultimate mission was the founding of a religious colony on the West Coast of Africa.

Sam had left New York, the official explained, because "persecution and extortionate prices" in that city had made it impossible for him to complete work on the ship. He had been told by someone whose name would "no doubt be divulged in good time" that he would be "well received and fairly treated" in Portland.

The official also explained the curious move on Sam's part in debarking the women before he sailed from the Erie Basin:

"The *Curityba* [*Liberia*] is here," he said, "to renew her license which has expired. On that account she was not allowed to carry passengers coastwise and for this reason the Negroes were sent to their homes, some to Oklahoma and others to Boston, temporarily. Unless something that I do not know of at present happens, it is likely that when the vessel is repaired and fitted out, has her license and other papers, her people will come to Portland to sail."

"Chief Sam is not in Portland at present," the informant added. "I know him personally. He is a quiet mannered and earnest man and the trading company he heads is formed under the laws of New York for the purpose of dealing in mahogany and other products that make up a strictly legitimate business. He will probably found his colony there and trade between it and this country."

The official was somewhat shocked at the unnecessary mystery which had "been woven around the movements of the ship," and reaffirmed that he had every reason to believe the statements as he had made them to be correct in each detail. Chief Sam, he added with caution, might change his plans, however, either upon arrival in Portland or subsequently.

In New York, meanwhile, the lengthy series of investigations which had characterized Sam's stay in that city were beginning to come to a head. In a sixteen-page typewritten document, beautifully conceived and exquisitely argued, Postal Inspector C. E. Booth outlined and evaluated the Sam movement to his superior.

The report, Booth began, related to "an alleged fraudulent use of the mails by A. E. Smith and Alfred C. Sam," and was "jacketed upon a complaint made by Arthur Cranston, County Attorney, Oswego, Labette County, Kansas." [7] Cranston's complaint had originally been lodged with the District Attorney in New York, but the latter had promptly turned it over to the Post Office Department.

Booth had been assigned the difficult task of sifting through the materials relating to the movement, and of removing the now massive body of rumor from the slim facts which could be brought to light by interviewing and other investigation.

After working his way through the materials he had assembled, Booth summarized the principal claims made by Sam in connection with the movement: (1) that he had organized the trading company for the purpose of dealing in products from the Gold Coast, and that he had averred to purchasers of stock that they would be entitled to free transportation to West Africa; (2) that he was a chief in the Akim tribe of the Gold Coast; and (3) that certain native chiefs of Africa had agreed to allot to American Negroes as much land as they could reasonably cultivate.

Booth concluded on the first point that the company had in fact been organized and that such monies as had been paid into its treasury were expended, in proper fashion, for the purchase of a ship which, Booth found it reasonable to assume, would ultimately be employed to transport the colonists to Africa. On the second point, Booth only repeated what Sam had told him of his noble connections. On the third point, the inspector quoted Sam's statement that a deed for the lands in question had been registered at Accra, Gold Coast, on November 4, 1912, and that Sam had expended thirty pounds to have the deed properly legalized. Given the fact that Sam was prepared even to name the witnesses to the filing, Booth doubted that the story was fabricated.

Getting to the point of the investigation, Booth noted that the use of the mails, either by Sam or any of the other individuals who occupied various administrative posts in the local clubs, had been comparatively small. Postal service had been primarily employed for Liddell's correspondence with local club presidents, for the forwarding of money from those clubs to Smith in New York, and for Smith's acknowledgments of the money.

Booth summarized his own feelings about the movement:

It occurs to me that if Sam is a Chief of a tribe on the Gold Coast, as he claims, and if the other Chiefs in that country . . . agreed to receive these negroes into tribal relations, and if Sam has title to these sixty-four square miles of land he claims that however unfortunate the conditions may be there and however badly disappointed these negroes may be after their arrival, that the case does not involve a fraudulent use of the mails, and before any action can be taken here we will have to have some definite information to disprove the claims of Sam.[8]

Booth concluded by suggesting that additional investigations be made in Oklahoma, and hinted that Sam might be trapped in connection with the mailings of the *African Pioneer,* the movement's paper, which had on most occasions been less than modest in its claims about the scheme. Booth also suggested that the matter be taken up anew with the British Ambassador in order to determine with greater exactness the status both of Sam's rank and his land deeds.

The Post Office report in essence stalemated the attempts of opponents to sidetrack the Sam movement. But now the apparent connection between Sam's group and the Holy Ghosters led to renewed hope that the African pioneers might prove as vulnerable to criminal charges as Sandford had been shown to be. Federal eyes kept close watch as visiting between the *Liberia* and the Holy Ghost and Us Society anchorage continued apace. Speculations began to spread that the *Liberia* would be accompanied to the Gold Coast by the two remaining Holy Ghost ships, the *Coronet* and the *Barracouta*. Both ships had been in Portland since the previous fall, undergoing what seemed to be extensive repairs. They had been fitted with new riggings, new topmasts, and a new bowsprit, all the work having been done by members of the society who, it now appeared, would also undertake the necessary repairs on the *Liberia*.

Certainly there was a good deal of evident friendship between the two groups, as boats were seen drifting back and forth between the various harbor sites. It was even reported that the Negroes and a few whites would act as Holy Ghost missionaries on the East Coast while the *Barracouta* and *Coronet* would continue on a tour of "evangelization" to other parts of the world.

The *Liberia*'s passengers remained mute and unapproachable. None of them seemed anxious to come ashore. Portland's business world, which had been reported as nearly "afire" about the movement at an earlier date, now only smouldered. The *Evening Express* stated ruefully that none of those "on board are evidently . . . hurrying matters as none of the local shipbuilders have been approached or asked to submit bids for repair work." [9]

Sam appeared in Portland on Tuesday, the day after the arrival of the *Liberia*. As usual, he was besieged with questions which he answered patiently and clearly. He was reported to have admitted his conversion to the Holy Ghost and Us Society and added that McKenzie and six other crew members—all white men—were also followers of Sandford. They had come to New York from Portland to assist in getting the ship to the Maine harbor. It was not certain, said Sam, that McKenzie would remain in command of the vessel for the African voyage.

Sam had been accompanied to Portland by nine Negroes, including four women, two of whom had been with their husbands. He said that those persons who had made the sea trip to Portland—twenty-nine persons in all—had been registered as crew members. Sam said further that the trip to Africa would be in the nature of an investigating party, and the passengers would include those now on board the ship as well as thirty additional persons from the Galveston camps. They would view the land claimed to be owned by Sam and report to the other shareholders about its promise as a colonization site.

The Portland paper surveyed the pioneers and found that each, with the exception of the women, was "either a mechanic or a professional man," that among them were four clergymen. It reported that all were "American citizens and of the Christian faith, . . . inclined toward the faith of the Holy Ghost and Us Society," with several "now preparing to visit Shiloh to be baptized."[10]

Sam bore out the consular official's earlier report that the ship had left New York because of the unfair treatment he had received. He denied the statements printed by the New York press that the persons removed from the ship the day of its sailing had been left foodless and destitute, dependent upon charity for subsistence. Sam insisted that all of the persons aboard the *Liberia* during her prolonged stay in Brooklyn were now in Portland and being cared for.

For the first time, however, Sam deviated from the story which he told of the lands in Africa. He abandoned the statement that the lands were grants from Akim chiefs, and said instead that the Akim Trading Company was organized to develop sixty-four square miles of territory in Aburi, some sixty miles inland on the Gold Coast. This land was rich in mahogany, rubber, gold, and fertile soil. He said that he had purchased this tract himself with the proceeds of some ten years' trading in cocoa beans and rubber. He had acquired the land originally with the intention of developing it with the aid of the people of his tribe; but as a result of the plan advanced by Dr. Dorman, he had decided to attempt the colonization of American Negroes instead.

No sooner had Sam appeared in Portland than a telegram, again raising the monotonous doubts about the scheme, appeared as well. It came addressed to the Portland Board of Trade from the Galveston Commercial Association, asking about the *Liberia*. "Is there such a ship now in Portland?" the Texans wanted to know. "We will appreciate any information you can give us, as these Negroes [in Galveston] are liable to become public charges in the event of the failure of their proposition and our inquiry is made with a view to their best interests."[11]

The Galveston telegram was only a pinprick, but the official bodies which had been on Sam's trail since the beginning of his recruitment program in Oklahoma still had not given up their harassment tactics. Each time that Sam emerged from one of these official encounters with a clean bill of health, the agencies involved twisted their minds to a new avenue calculated to frustrate his migration program.

On March 12, several days after Sam arrived in Portland, the British government appeared to have hit upon a policy which would hamstring the expedition nicely.

Sir Cecil Spring-Rice explained the move with care to the U.S. State Department, which in turn sent a copy of the letter to Governor Cruce of Oklahoma. Spring-Rice first avowed the purity of his motives and those of his government:

> I have explained that there is no prospect whatever that Chief Sam would be able to fulfill his promises as regards the acquisition of land in the Colony; that the climatic conditions are highly unsuitable for American negroes; and that enquiry here has thrown grave doubt on Sam's bona fides; and that therefore His Majesty's Government desires to do all in their power to discourage the movement.[12]

Then Spring-Rice detailed precisely what the British indended to do:

> I have now received a telegram from Sir Edward Grey instructing me to inform the United States Government that it is intended to pass an Ordinance compelling every individual immigrant into the Gold Coast, not being a native of West Africa, to deposit security for his repatriation if required to do so by local authorities. The amount of the security will be 25 pounds per head and the period during which it will become forfeit, if the immigrant becomes destitute, twelve months. The captain or owner of the ship will be obliged to carry back the immigrants who cannot give such security.
>
> I have the honor to request that you will be good enough to bring this information to the knowledge of the competent authorities.

Unsolicited but useless support came for Sam from an apparent world traveller, writing from Luzon, but with a permanent address in London, who wrote the Secretary of State. This traveller, J. O. Sanders, remarked that he had been making a study of "What is popularly termed the Negro Problem in the South for a period of eight years," and that he felt that Chief Sam's scheme, which he had read about in a Philippine newspaper, "may have something worth looking into." [13]

Four days later, Spring-Rice relentlessly tightened the British net about Sam a bit further. He informed the U.S. Secretary of State that "the British Vice Consul at Portland, Maine, had been instructed not to issue British papers to the steamer *Curityba* [*Liberia*] which I understand has been purchased by 'Chief Sam' and is the property of the Akim Trading Company of South Dakota." [14]

Although the report was made from so distant a place as Manila that "the state department takes the position that it has no right to interfere with the immigration of negroes," [15] the Guthrie *Daily Leader* howled happily once more that "federal investigation of the proposed pilgrimage to Africa . . . was begun today in response to instructions from Washington." [16]

Sam was called to an hour-long conference in the office of Collector of the Port Willis T. Emmons, where the African leader was confronted by Emmons, Assistant District Attorney Arthur Chapman, and Deputy United States Marshal W. S. Hasty. McKenzie accompanied Sam to this meeting, just as Smith and Kellogg had accompanied him when he was confronted in New York with Courtenay Bennett.

Sam repeated his assurances of good faith, routine by now, and described again the financial structure of the Akim Trading Company. He stressed that while many of his followers were converts to the teachings of the Holy Ghost Society, his proposed trip to Africa was in no way connected with the Sandfordites at Shiloh or those on board the Sandford yachts in Portland harbor.

At the end of the interview, Emmons cagily declined to discuss his conclusions or the full details of the discussion, though he asserted that "the matter would not be dropped at this point" and that "further investigation will probably be made of 'Chief Sam' and his remarkable enterprise." [17]

After the interview, a Portland *Evening Express* reporter fell upon Sam and McKenzie, and was rebuffed in his efforts to get information from the chief. The captain "acted as a sort of body guard for the Negro 'chieftain' . . . and when a reporter asked 'Chief Sam' for information . . . McKenzie brushed the 'chief' to one side and stood between him and the reporter." [18]

"He hasn't a thing to say," McKenzie quickly interposed. "He has had trouble getting the wireless equipment for the ship, and it is not certain when the ship will sail."

Sam, meanwhile, wore what the reporter interpreted as a "sort of worried expression," and made no move to join the conversation.

"Will you go to Galveston and pick up the Negroes waiting for the ship there?" continued the persistent newsman.

"That is the plan now," replied McKenzie. Then he took Sam by the elbow and led him down the Custom House stairs and along Commercial Street at a brisk clip, hoping to outdistance the reporter. The newsman, however, proved up to the race.

At the public landing on the west side of the pier, McKenzie and Sam were delayed in getting out to the *Liberia.* Part of the boat crew had left the launch. The reporter noted that the Negroes from the ship "wore old overcoats and were thinly clad. They asked if they might enter the stores on the pier and get warm, saying that they had not been so far north in their lives, and that they were suffering from the chilly atmosphere."

Sam and McKenzie also came in for comment. Sam, the reporter noted, wore a heavy overcoat with a fur collar, but "he can never be accused of being a fashion plate or a 'loud dresser' as his trousers were not of the modern cut and his slouch hat was evidently a relic of styles worn some years ago." McKenzie, the newsman continued, "was well dressed and appears more like a business man than the captain of a steamer which will carry 250 or more Negroes to Africa. . . ."

The reporter supplied further details on the wireless equipment causing Sam so much difficulty. He noted the existence of a regulation to the effect that if more than fifty persons were to be carried aboard any ship, it would be necessary for the vessel to be equipped with a wireless apparatus and inspected by United States officials. Sam was negotiating at the time with a Boston electrical concern for the wireless, and would not be allowed to sail until it had been installed and approved.

On April Fool's Day, British Vice Consul John B. Keating, for some reason feeling called upon to comment, asserted that current reports in the Portland newspapers to the effect that the *Liberia* would transport over two hundred Negroes to the Gold Coast were absurd. Keating alleged that "the law will not permit the Curityba [*Liberia*] to carry, nor has she accommodations for, more than 56 passengers." [19]

On the same day, the Portland morning daily carried a story stating that Assistant District Attorney Arthur Chapman had given "a word of praise for 'Chief Sam's' expedition and that he believed the movement worthy of success." [20] This unique approval was more than the movement could possibly have hoped for; and indeed, by the time the *Evening Express* was on the streets, Chapman, either really misquoted or annoyed at having an off-hand comment put into print, had denied the entire story. Chapman said that he had not "said anything of that sort but that he had said nothing had been found that would indicate that . . . Sam had violated any laws." [21]

While the British and American governments were somewhat desultorily looking for ways to tie up the movement, there was a revival of criticism from Oklahoma on the feasibility of the program. From that state came word that "many of Chief Sam's disciples has come back to the fleshy pots of Oklahoma. They are now hunting places to live." [22]

"Oh Lord," the *Guide* Mosaically intoned, "How long will we be fools." [23]

The United States government also released a report from one of its representatives abroad in a further effort to undermine the faith of Sam's followers. All last-ditch methods were now being used.

From Freetown, Sierra Leone, Consul Yerby filed a straight-forward warning of the dangers of settlement in Africa which the State Department now felt it was time to release. Negroes were not wanted in the colonial possessions of European governments in Africa, Yerby cautioned, and, with the exception of Liberia, "there is no glad hand of welcome extended towards American Negroes." [24] Liberia, in fact, invited only those Negroes to colonize who were well educated and suitably equipped with money. Yerby underscored his warnings:

> Of the few American Negroes who have found their way to West Africa, 99 percent are unprepared to meet the economic conditions and express regret at having left America. These, excepting a few who cannot secure passage money, return to the United States.
>
> My advice [to Chief Sam's followers] is to select some well informed person to make a thorough investigation, visiting the particular section in which they intend settling before they pay any part of their passage money to West Africa. It is quite evident that some of these schemes are in every sense fraudulent.

In the event the logical approach did not affect its audience, Yerby grew ominous:

> Those who have come to West Africa suffer untold misery, are for the most part illiterate farmers who have, through a long struggle, managed to save enough passage money for themselves and family, with barely enough to live on through their first certain attack of African malaria. Many have expressed the choice of prison life in America to freedom here. In addition to the above, now and then a misguided independent missionary comes, suffers and dies.

While the official agencies were hopping about from one tactic to another, the members of Sam's colony had made some progress toward departure. By May 16, the ship had taken on a quantity of coal and some provisions, and the wireless telegraph had finally been installed. One curiosity was the recent replacement of McKenzie by W. F. Caneca, who had come to Portland from New Bedford, Massachusetts.

The British, meanwhile, continued to hold the ship in port by their stubborn refusal to grant registry papers. Worse than this was the reported dissension aboard the *Liberia* between the Shilohites and those who had not accepted the Holy Ghost creed, a dissension made even worse by McKenzie's summary replacement. The *Evening Express* noted that since both factions were stockholders in the company, both had equal rights to an expression of their opinions on the captaincy of the vessel. Both Caneca and McKenzie remained aboard the steamer by day, though "it was learned that Captain Caneca had not remained on board the ship nights and that he came ashore every afternoon." [25] McKenzie, on the other hand, regularly attended the nightly religious services on the ship.

Two days later, both the problem of registry and a captain had been resolved. Though no reason was forthcoming to explain the British reversal of earlier orders not to issue registry papers, the *Liberia* was suddenly granted those papers on May 20 by Vice Consul Keating, and in a brief ceremony the Cuban flag was hauled down and replaced by the Union Jack. The newspapers reported this event without passion, and none seemed at all curious about the unusual change of British mind.

The outcome of the dispute over captains was also settled, with the terse announcement that "Captain L. S. McKenzie, the Shilohite who brought the steamer to Portland from New York will be in command on the trip to Africa instead of Captain Caneca who came here . . . to assume command some weeks ago." [26] Despite this change, Caneca was nonetheless named as the master of the vessel on the official copy of the registry papers, a condition, perhaps, laid down by the British for the issuance of the documents.

The *Liberia* was in readiness to leave port; her hull and boilers had "been inspected by the local U. S. Steamboat Inspectors Thompson and Trevett." [27] She was reported to be destined once more for New York where she would pick up "knock-down" berths which would provide accommodations aboard for another 250 persons. She would then stop at Newport News for bunker coal, and thence sail to Galveston.

Finally, on June 1, the *Evening Express,* sticking to the end to its contrivances, announced that Sam's "so-called mystery ship . . . will undoubtedly leave Portland harbor on her long delayed voyage to the Gold Coast . . . within a few hours. . . . It is believed that the *Liberia* will leave port tonight." [28]

On this day, Captain McKenzie, accompanied by Captain Austin K. Perry, another Shilohite who was making the trip, appeared at the Customs House to obtain clearance for the *Liberia.* The clearance papers listed Saltpond, Gold Coast, as the destination of the ship. Aboard were sixty-two persons, including several women.

On June 1, a group of fourteen persons had been put ashore and had left Portland for Boston. This aroused some interest, since many women had been included in the group, and it appeared that the last minute abandonment act of New York might be repeated in Portland. The *Evening Express,* still guessing, said that the people might be returning to Oklahoma, though it admitted that they might just as well be planning to go to Galveston to join the ship there. It had no explanation for their taking so circuitous a path to rejoin the ship they had just left.

But on the next day, reported the *Express,* unusual "activity has been noticed on the *Liberia* . . . and that she is preparing to leave port soon is evident. Smoke issues from her funnel and a quantity of supplies has been taken aboard." [29] Sam had, for the past few days, kept the Shiloh launch *Doris* under contract, and had been dashing back and forth between the *Liberia* and the shore, collecting provisions and making what appeared to be final arrangements.

Catastrophe almost caught up with the *Liberia* before she could get out of Portland. A barge, swinging at anchor near the ship, struck her in the side, and jammed. Immediately, a power boat from the Kingdom Yacht Club anchorage swept out to the rescue. The launch carried a line from the side of the barge to another barge, some one hundred yards away, and the *Liberia's* nemesis was towed from her side by steam winches. On inspection, it was determined that fortunately no damage had been done to the *Liberia.*

Finally, on June 3, at 4:30 A.M., the *Liberia* belched out a torrent of black smoke, cast off from her buoy, and steamed eastward from the harbor. She ran out as far as Green Island, where she abruptly came about and headed back. A power launch rushed to her side, and remained there while the *Liberia* floated about near Spring Point Light. Finally, the launch retired, and the *Liberia* vainly attempted to negotiate a turn near the light. This failing, she headed toward the lower harbor and passed through the middle of the fleet, then, abruptly, came about again and headed out to sea.

At 7 A.M., after engaging in a series of dizzy antics that left the witnesses at the harbor astounded, the ship passed the Portland light and headed out to sea, the British flag fluttering from her stern.[30]

7

"But the One More River to Cross"

But we have but the one more river to cross,
And then we'll sing hosanna,
But we have but the one more river to cross,
And then we'll sing hosanna.
(From "One More River")

THE LONG, COLD, and despairing months during which the *Liberia* lay at anchor both at Brooklyn and Portland saw hardship piled upon hardship in the Weleetka camps. Though spasmodic reports about the activities of Sam's east coast contingent filtered slowly back to Oklahoma both by word of mouth and over the wire services, the campers received only the most barren versions of the affairs of their fellows.

Already desperate in the extreme, and in the full throes of disease and cold, the Weleetka colonists sickened emotionally with each new onslaught and with each apparent setback that the movement suffered.

The Oklahoma City *Times,* for example, predicted knowingly the downfall of the movement:

> It is only a matter of time when the scheme of Chief Sam, self-styled chief of the Ashantee tribe of Africans, will collapse, and leave scores of negroes more helpless than they were before he met them. Some of them may be left far from the only homes they have ever known with little prospect of getting back.[1]

The Tulsa *Star,* grown more hostile in its attitude toward the movement by the apparent lack of success which its exhortations were having in halting the exodus, undertook a critical examination of Sam's geographical knowledge for the benefit of its readers and the Weleetka campers:

> The followers of Chief Bogus Sam say he is a smart man. He is not smart in geography, however. But geography is not a necessity to his line of coin lifting. In his speeches Chief Bogus Sam says: "The Gold Coast wheat fields are watered by the Nile River." . . . The only ways for the Nile river water to reach the Gold Coast is to fetch it in buckets, or from rain clouds to carry it all across Africa and drop it there. When Sam's followers reach Africa and start before breakfast to go down to the Nile River for a bucket of water, they will merely have a walk of about 7000 miles, and will be "mos pow'ful hongry" when they get back.[2]

But the Oklahoma Negroes remained doggedly faithful to both the movement and the low, brown man with the "bright" skin and the unfamiliar British accent. "Slick Sam" had offered them what no other man had ever been able to, and they were prepared to stand behind him and run the risk, if need be, of the crop of "African fever, coffins, and tombstones" which the *Star* predicted for them.[3]

On February 5, forty-one Negro families left Logan County in Oklahoma for Galveston to await the arrival of the *Liberia*. This group, comprising part of an alleged three hundred families who had recently departed, took a special Santa Fe train from Seward, where they had been congregating for several weeks. Plagued to the last, the Negroes found a local grocer running frantically about among them as they began to board the train. The grocer was helplessly attempting to attach the few belongings the group possessed in order to realize payment on merchandise he had dispensed on credit. But the tradesman was totally unsuccessful, for "the stuff was shipped in the name of 'Chief Sam,'" and apparently could not be identified with particular delinquent individuals.[4]

Meanwhile, other Negro families and lone individuals who could raise the money necessary for the trip made their own way to Galveston. By February 19, some 109 men, women and children, "poor misguided fools," were in the Gulf port city.[5]

In Galveston, O. L. Parker, one of Sam's local agents, was sorely pressed to make the necessary assurances, both to the press and the growing complement of waiting colonists, that the movement still had not only a viable existence, but that it also possessed a set of plans in terms of which it was operating. Parker, of course, knew no more than the Weleetka campers about events in the East. But in response to reporters who tirelessly baited him with the gloomy news dispatches from New York, dispatches stating that Sam had deserted both the city and the movement, Parker asserted that he was confident that Sam was away only on a brief business trip, and that he would return in due time. News reports like these, Parker said peevishly, were deplorable.

The citizens of Galveston, with some justice, were beginning to feel apprehensive about the part their city seemed scheduled to play in the back-to-Africa movement. Local newspaper stories had reached new statistical heights in estimating that nearly forty thousand Negroes had signed up for the journey to Africa, and they implied that the bulk of these people would soon converge on Galveston and take up at least temporary residence until the *Liberia* appeared. The *Tribune* reported:

> From . . . reliable sources it has been learned that about 2,000 negroes, eager to sail for Africa, are quartered at Weleetka, Okla., where they are waiting the word to start for Galveston. These negroes, like those already in Galveston, have secured passage on the ship said to have been purchased for the expedition and are taking the matter of securing rates to Galveston up with railroad officials.[6]

The bulk of the colonists were waiting at Weleetka, the *Tribune* carefully explained, because that portion of Oklahoma was populated largely by Negroes, and it was thought more advisable to "quarter them there than here." They were, however, the paper added without much comfort, but one day's ride from the city, and could come to Galveston on extremely short notice.

In Oklahoma, Governor Cruce was still receiving his usual quota of mail from impoverished supporters of Chief Sam. On February 20, the Governor was solicited by W. H. Harris of Depew, for a loan of $55 to transport himself and his family to Africa. Harris, arguing with unassailable logic, pointed out that he had been paying taxes in Oklahoma since before statehood, and felt that he was now entitled to certain considerations for his faithful fiscal outlay. Weary Governor Cruce, bedeviled with a bad situation which now was drifting happily out of his legal domain, replied that he could offer little encouragement for the prospects of such a loan.

The Oklahoma *Guide,* too lazy to dig up the news in its own journalistic backyard at Weleetka, reproduced instead a prattling interview with a "white lady" in Galveston from one of the Texas newspapers. She, it was reported, had "a whole lots of information [on the Gold Coast] as she has not long been from Africa at this writing." She warned the colonists to beware their enterprise, for she knew the "West coast Africa" and stated that conditions "are unfavorable for colored people, and they should not leave this country for there." [7]

By mid-February, North and South Gold Coast camps at Weleetka had been glutted, with more than six hundred persons spilling over the boundaries of the tent colonies. The prospective pioneers had been recently advised from New York that they should prepare themselves for the trek to Galveston. A tentative sailing date of February 15 had been wrenched from one of the officials on the East coast. But shortly thereafter, a countermanding order was sent which pushed the sailing date back another several weeks.

Having made their plans to sail too often, only to have them abruptly and impersonally altered, the Weleetka campers took matters into their own hands early in March. The directives from the East had been vague and contradictory. Too often their source was unknown. Now weary of the constant and disparaging attention which they were receiving from the white citizens of Weleetka, and of the abominable conditions under which they were living, many of the campers made their own decision to move to Galveston and take up residence at the port of embarkation, even though the *Liberia* still languished without promise in Brooklyn.

On March 5, early in the morning, 180 of the African pioneers walked smartly down Gold Coast Avenue, the main thoroughfare of South Gold Coast camp, and made their way to the railroad station. Many of their friends, some five hundred of them, would be left behind this first trip; but unembittered, they followed along behind to wish the travellers well. Those who were leaving had gathered together all of their belongings the evening before. Depleted by a long encampment, some were shoddy, but others were able to dress appropriately for the occasion. They had, to a man, withdrawn their remaining money from the local banks, and were now preparing to leave for the last time this area which had once promised them so much.

Two glee clubs had assembled at the station to see them off, and each man in the crowd had a flag to wave. The excitement was high. Finally, "with black faces peering from every window," the train drew slowly away from the platform.[8] At the exact moment of departure, the glee clubs burst jubilantly into song:

> Old Noah once he built de ark,
> Dar's one more ribber for to cross,
> He patched it up wid hick'ry bark,
> Dar's one more ribber for to cross.

The train reached Galveston late that same day. R. A. Burt, Parker's co-agent in Texas, met the group and conducted them to MacGuire's Park in the Negro section of the city. The reporters could scarcely contain their eagerness. By early morning, a number of them had descended on Burt, demanding an interview. This was, after all, the first installment of the forty thousand Negroes who would soon come boiling out of Oklahoma to meet the *Liberia* in Galveston.

Burt, like many of his colleagues who were connected with the movement in vague administrative positions, had grown extremely cautious. He indicated, as Parker had earlier, that he could scarcely overstate his bitterness and disappointment with the "sensational reports that have been circulated from time to time regarding Chief Sam."[9] He said that he was unwilling, because of the press's irresponsibility, to provide any information on the whereabouts of Chief Sam. It turned out, however, that his withholding of information to punish the press was somewhat expedient. He did not know where Sam was. He finally covered this lack of information with a blanket endorsement of Sam's activities, whatever they might be.

"Sam has never been any place where he could not be found," Burt stated flatly. "His going from place to place was always on business."

Burt ended the interview on an optimistic note. "It is but a matter of a few days until the ship will put in at Galveston to take on her first load of colonists," he said. He did not know how many persons would be able to make the initial voyage, though he stated confidently that "the ship would be loaded to capacity." This proved a rather specious remark when he was unable to state what the ship's capacity was. When pressed for an estimate of the number of persons who might be expected to descend on Galveston before the affair had ended, Burt simply declined to comment.

The *Tribune* reporter was amazed to find that the colonists, busily bivouacking in the park, were "seemingly in high spirits and in good condition physically." They were, he discovered, a well-organized group, and all actions of the party were "done through channels presided over by some member of the body." [10]

In the afternoon, on March 24, another trainload of Negroes left Weleetka. Loaded into four special coaches, and Jim Crowed to the last, these two hundred persons were on their way to Galveston to join the others. The coaches were attached to the Katy's train Number 7 until it reached Durant, where they were removed and sent on through Texas as a special train.

The group arrived in Galveston at 12:55 in the afternoon of the following day. Burt met the contingent this time, and took them to Cotton Jammer's Park, again in the Negro section. Though Burt and his assistants claimed that fewer than 120 persons had arrived with this group, the *Tribune* quoted a porter who had joined the train at Smithville, Texas, as saying that "there [were] fully 300, as each of the four coaches was filled to capacity." [11] In addition, more Negroes were expected shortly. The members of this second trainload reported that their fellows at Weleetka were now preparing to leave the camps *en masse* within the next few days.

Though the relatively recent arrivals were in good spirits, many of those who had earlier come to Galveston had by now lost much of their enthusiasm. For them, the Galveston wait had been dismal and enervating. Prospects of the ship's arrival seemed vaguer each day. There was also a rash of unpleasant incidents to mar the initial holiday mood. A twelve-year-old girl had drowned while exploring the Galveston piers, and the life-saving stations had dragged the waters unsuccessfully trying to locate her body. Several members of the encampment also turned out to be fugitives from justice in Oklahoma who were attempting to use the anonymity and mobility of the back-to-Africa movement to avoid apprehension. The nightly rallies at Cotton Jammer's Park, combination carnivals and revival meetings, were exciting and novel at first, but with regular repetition the excitement had begun to wear thin. Some of the campers were dejectedly returning to Oklahoma.

The Tulsa *Star* chortled at this development:

News comes from Boley and Weleetka that followers of "Chief Sam" are going back to the soil. They are busy now looking for land to farm and places to live . . . a wiser and better people. The "Chief" is perambulating, is up north enjoying the comforts from his easily gotten coin from the fanatics of Oklahoma.[12]

But, overall, the "wiser and better people" were in a minority. Most of the campers were digging in with all of the hope they could muster and with every intention of waiting out the ship.

The *Tribune* was drawn to run a human interest story on the fantastic camp-out, and on April 1 sent a reporter to interview a number of the people residing at MacGuire's Park.[13] The reporter found the scene "striking." The park presented a colorful and chaotic picture. The big hall in the center, which had been used for dancing and to house a refreshment stand, had been partitioned off into sleeping quarters; and the court surrounding the hall was filled solidly with tents. Children played in front of the tents; and household goods, too bulky for the interior of the canvas houses, were strewn on the cluttered lawn.

The reporter, particularly impressed with the new estimate of "90,-000 negroes from six states of the Union" who were enrolled in the movement, could not resist asking, not without considerable rhetorical awe: "Was history being made here?"

The first Negro approached for an interview was returning to the camp from downtown Galveston. He had been a farmer near Dallas and had worked for a time as a cook. He had recently sold all of his property and joined the Weleetka campers. He was vague about what the group would do when it reached Africa and was reticent to discuss the matter, arguing that "it was the newspapers which were causing Chief Sam so much trouble." He and the other Negroes in his vicinity who had joined the movement had chartered a special car to carry their household effects—"shack plunder" he called it—to Galveston. The car had been on the road for seven days now, and the distance was only five hundred miles, but they had so far had no word on its whereabouts. He had only enough money to admit him to the ship; prolonged residence in Galveston would render him destitute. "He would have nothing to eat unless the car came soon, nor would his family."

This man's account of the founding of the movement is interesting, for it adds additional documentation to show the appallingly poor lines of communication within the movement. He believed that members of the Church of God, "a negro church of general extent and large membership," had dispatched a number of delegates to the Gold Coast in an effort to determine whether lands suitable for colonization could be found. The reports of these delegates had been encouraging; and bolstered by the outcome of interviews with British and American diplomatic officials, the movement had been launched.

The reporter was then taken to the tent of O. L. Parker. Parker was "nearly white, evidently without mannerisms of embarrassment, and of a fair education." He spoke "plainly and without grammatical mistakes."

After the usual recitation of slogans about Sam's complete honesty and integrity, and the ritual assurance that Sam's frequent absences from the ship were connected with the business of the exodus, Parker offered a more intellectualized account of the movement's origin. He believed the dissatisfaction of the Negroes with the treatment accorded them in the southern states to be of vital significance.

"We had no rights," he said. "We were disenfranchised and annoyed. We wanted to go to a place where we could have similar privileges and not have to take our orders from a dominant and unfriendly race."

A large group of Negroes had surrounded Parker and the reporter by this time.

"That's right," chimed in a husky Negro who was standing in the ring. "We want to go where we get a square show." The reporter watched "the circle of dusky faces and shining teeth" nod emphatic assent.

Parker denied that any religious organization was involved in the movement. He denied also that delegates had been sent to Africa, but asserted instead that American Negroes had received letters from tribal chiefs proffering invitations to return to the fatherland and gain freedom there.

Parker also outlined his understanding of the British attitude. He said that the British had been seen since their first statement denying the Negroes permission to sail. They had been forced to admit that the land was under the control of the chiefs and that any one could go to Africa who was invited by the chiefs.

The reporter queried Parker about the financial background of the movement. The usual account was forthcoming, though the figures were again swollen considerably. Parker detailed the economic opportunities awaiting the migrants on the Gold Coast, and described the method of operation which would be used to exploit these:

> The strip of land where we are going extends 5,000 miles along the sea coast and 3,000 miles into the interior of the country. It abounds in all kinds of natural resources and there is a chain of great lakes which will aid in transporting products of the coast. A line of railroad is already started to the interior . . . we have already arranged a market for the lumber. We have the money to buy saw mills and other tools necessary. The lumber will be sent to the United States on the *Liberia,* and on the return trip she will carry back more negroes. . . . the mines which are in the interior will also be developed.

Parker also spoke of money which had been deposited in a bank in the Gold Coast, "which will be owned by the subscribers and which will be administered for the common good."

There was no apparent limit to the agent's optimism.

"We expect to take seven or eight hundred on the first trip, and I hope we can keep on carrying negroes away from here until every one in the United States is gone."

"Yes sir, we're going to work," another member of the audience added. "We're goin' to buckle down to it like we did when we came to this country. Got to begin all over again."

But whatever the optimism shown by the campers toward the success of their movement, the Galveston telegraph office, on the following day, transmitted this message to William Jennings Bryan:

> Approximately five hundred negroes here and en route from other points awaiting arrival of boat to take them to South African gold fields under character of agreement with one Captain Sam. Think whole scheme a fake as are proposing to transport whole families for twenty-five dollars. No prospect of boat arriving here for several months and doubtful if English Government will permit landing in Africa if boat ever sails there. These negroes are practically without funds and congregated here a menace to public health and they will become a charge upon this or any other community. Cannot this Gov-

153

ernment have these people return to their homes and prevent others from coming here? [14]

The wire was signed by Lewis Fisher, Mayor of Galveston, who had obviously become gravely concerned with the concentration of landless Negroes in his city, and was clearly prepared to take major steps to disperse them.

On the day he sent the wire, Fisher had met with Chief of Police Perrett and members of the city health commission. Following the conference, the Mayor issued an order to the campers that their temporary sites must be abandoned, and that they should quit the city of Galveston with all possible haste. Fisher gave as his reason for the demand his fear that the camps were unsanitary and that the spread of disease was an all-too-imminent possibility. The campers had been described as living in acute squalor. The situation was much aggravated, in addition, by the inability of Sam's local agents to give Galveston authorities any reasonable estimates as to when the group proposed to leave for the Gold Coast.

"Captain" Sam's agents approached the Mayor on the following day, telling him of their new plan to house the campers in the city, and received his support. He felt that such an arrangement would meet with the spirit of his earlier decree, and would therefore be satisfactory to the city officials.

Spurred on by the threat of dispossession, most of the campers did find lodging in the city without much difficulty. The Negro community offered many temporary quarters, doubling up the pioneers in apartments and small houses in the dock area. Wealthier campers were able to rent places in other parts of the city. Some of the Negroes had by now obtained employment in Galveston to bolster their finances. One, for instance, worked as an attendant at John Seeley Hospital, another had a job pouring concrete for a construction project, and a third worked in a cotton warehouse. Still others acquired odd jobs along the Galveston waterfront, which was bustling with nervous activity as the prospect of imminent warfare with Mexico permeated the air.

Some days after Fisher's wire to Bryan, the Secretary of State replied. His response, lengthy and redundant, contained no information that Fisher could not easily have culled from local newspapers. Bryan recited the restrictions on land tenure which had been originally furnished him by the British Colonial Office, and predicted once more that any emigrants who reached the African coast, would find themselves in the direst of straits.

To Fisher's specific request for aid in the removal of the Negroes from Galveston, Bryan had little to offer. He wrote:

> The Department presents these statements and regrets to say that federal government has been unable to take action to frustrate Sam's plans. Should these American Negroes migrate to Africa there is no appropriation at the disposal of this government to pay their return passage to America.[15]

The Galveston Commercial Association, better advised on the entire plan than was Fisher, also directed a query to Secretary Bryan. But once again, little constructive advice was forthcoming. From the office of the Third Assistant Secretary, to whom the inquiry eventually devolved, came an instruction to one Mr. Cooke to "draft reply to this letter . . . along the same lines as the telegram which we recently sent to the Mayor of that city." [16]

At Weleetka, the situation continued to grow darker. It was reported that although many of those in the camps "still have faith in the colored Moses and believe that he will eventually take them to Africa," provisions had grown desperately short, and many of the campers were avoiding starvation only by finding sporadic employment in the little town and through the benevolence of Negro farmers in the vicinity who worked incessantly to attempt to feed the campers.[17]

O. H. Douglas, a white man in Weleetka, underscored the faith of the colonists in Sam despite their aggrieved plight. His cook, Douglas said, had recently told him that Sam was "the greatest in de world, he don't even pray like the rest of us black folks. When he prays he jest tells God what he wants." [18]

The Boley *Progress* continued to drone out its dire statistics on the discouraged returnees. Sam's followers, it said in sweeping fashion, "are deserting and many of those who went to Galveston have returned." [19]

Even the parochial Clearview *Patriarch,* a newspaper which had heretofore systematically ignored the African movement, saw fit to take stock of things toward the end of May, and moralized at length:

Strange, strange it is, that the Negro will go headlong into every scheme that comes along. This African move has financially ruined many negroes.

The poor deluded people who joined this Chief Sam move, sold all they had at a sacrifice last fall. "Going to Africa at once," and they have consumed most of what they have, lost a year's work and are still here.

The man who has nothing can go nowhere and the man who has accumulated very little is very simple to sacrifice what he has to follow any scheme that he don't understand. This African move is impracticable as has been shown by the Liberian move. No real help can come from a move to Africa.[20]

On May 23, the atmosphere changed with news that the *Liberia* was at last preparing to leave Portland for Galveston. The news electrified the Galveston colony. The *Daily News* observed that the "care-free, happy-go-lucky negroes of Louisiana, who were depicted by the lyricist in the popular song as 'Waiting on the levee—waiting for the Robert E. Lee'—have nothing in point of enthusiasm or optimism on the colony of four hundred negroes who are waiting" for the arrival of the *Liberia.*[21] Of the 550 persons who had come to Galveston to join the ship, barely a hundred had become discouraged enough during the long wait to return to their homes in Oklahoma.

In the camp there were constant reiterations of faith in Chief Sam from families interviewed by local reporters. One woman, a graduate of Tuskegee Institute, said that the "Shepherds," the name given to Sam's local agents, had repeatedly warned the Galveston colonists that only a limited number would be taken on the first voyage. Many would have to wait additional weeks to go to Africa, she said, but they all understood this when they decided to come to Galveston.

The *Liberia,* all agreed, would arrive in port by June 10. On June 11, with the *Liberia* still somewhere at sea, the Okemah *Ledger* obtained a first-hand report of the ship's movements from D. B. Garrett, the man who had earlier interviewed the British Ambassador on behalf of the Chief Sam group. Garrett had left the *Liberia* in Portland and made his way back to Oklahoma, presumably to visit with relatives before departing for Africa. En route he dropped in at the newspaper to give his account of the interview with the British, and to refute some of the charges made by local Negroes against Sam's project. The ship had been unjustly detained in New York and Portland, Garrett claimed, mostly because of "our own people of Boley filling the papers with lies." [22]

Garrett also threw a new light on his visit to the authorities. Governor Cruce's letter of introduction to the British Ambassador was reinterpreted as "papers of recommendation." Garrett told how he had let the Governor and the British know that "they were misinformed about the matter, and that I thought I could give a better light on the subject." To this end, he had told Cruce and the British that the chiefs of Akim had invited them to settle there because "it was from their tribe that we were stolen nearly 300 years ago, and it would only be their children that would be returning home, and would receive the blessing back that we were taken from."

The British, Garrett thought, were thoroughly taken with this line of reasoning, for as he recalled the remainder of the interview, it went somewhat as follows: "The British Ambassador said that the English did not own the land, but only held a protectorate, that he wished us God speed." Garrett confidently predicted that he "would leave for Africa Thursday."

On the 17th of June, the *Liberia* was still somewhere at sea. Though now equipped with wireless, she certainly did not employ it to communicate with Galveston where the local Negroes, residents as well as prospective immigrants, were making preparations to celebrate the forty-ninth anniversary of Juneteenth. It was on June 19, 1865, that the slaves had finally been freed in Texas, two and one-half years after Lincoln's Emancipation Proclamation. Preparations were already underway for a general Negro celebration:

> . . . a holiday from all labor, a wearing of the best and most attractive clothes in the wardrobe and a happy-go-lucky attitude of good will for all men and all creatures. There will be many chickens in the pot, and the oven; there will be special watermelons of a rare flavor in the ice box . . . and if not the ice box, then the gunny sack with its maximum of sawdust and its minimum of ice.[23]

The commentators on the festivities could not but point to the appealing coincidence that the arrival of the *Liberia* in Texas might very likely mesh with the celebration of the Negro's freedom in the state. The *Liberia* did not disappoint those looking for significant historical omens. At an early hour on June 18, the day before Juneteenth, the *Liberia* hove into sight of Galveston. News of the ship's arrival spread throughout the city, and "at once the wharves of the east end of the island began to fill with eager colored faces who strained their eyes to catch first sight of the ship of their hopes and to see the leader."[24]

The setting for Juneteenth was now complete:

> Great times are planned for tomorrow and just a bit more than is customary . . . it is understood and talked about among the colored population of the city that the *Liberia* will be christened by her new name tomorrow, and that the ceremony will be performed by a dusky damsel from Weleetka, Oklahoma, who will break over the prow of the ship the historic bottle of champagne.[25]

With the ship in port and the prospect of a mass depletion of the Negroes who had congregated in Galveston, the tone of the press changed abruptly to one of great amiability. The *Tribune,* for instance, paid tribute to the name *Liberia,* finding it an appropriate one for the mission on which the ship was engaged. This is the ship, it mused, which

> is to carry so many of the tribe of Ham out of the land of oppression to the shores of their ancestors where joy and peace will reign, where they will be the equals of their fellow men and where they and their descendants will build homes and enlighten the minds of their black brothers who have not had the advantages of the liberal training of America.[26]

The Wichita Falls daily, under a Galveston dateline, also paid some high compliments to the colonists, commenting on the "remarkable demonstration of their racial patience and optimism which has been given by the 500 negroes most from Oklahoma, who came more than five months ago expecting to be taken to the Gold Coast of Africa by Chief Sam."[27]

The paper elaborated on the extent of the patience which had won its approval:

> Though Sam's scheme has been publicly denounced in the press, though months ago these negroes paid their passage and hold nothing but a slip of paper as security that they will ever get any returns, less than one hundred of the original "bound for Africa" colony have deserted the long watch and returned to Oklahoma. The rest of them

are living here, some single, some "just married" and some married and with good-sized families, scattered in small groups through the negro colony. These negroes say they realize they cannot all go on the first sailing of the steamer *Liberia* . . .

Disappointingly for the many who jammed the docks, the *Liberia* could not immediately come into the pier. A pipeline had been laid across the channel and was blocking all traffic. But later in the afternoon the ship would be able to steam up the channel to Pier 41 to find berth during what all hoped would be her short stay in Galveston.

By five o'clock, the *Liberia* had made her berth. The *Daily News* described the docking:

A large, black negro, gaudily dressed, leaned over the rail of the steamship as she swung alongside Pier 41 yesterday and with arms uplifted to the sun dramatically proclaimed to an audience below on the dock: "We are here, my brothers. We are here. We are on our way to our own land. Are you ready to go with us?" [28]

The man was, of course, Chief Sam. The crowd went nearly wild with cries of, "We shore are."

The ship came slowly to a halt, the hawsers were thrown out and secured, and the gangplank was lowered. "Negroes of every size, shape and description, who have been waiting in Galveston for months, swarmed aboard and literally threw themselves upon the leader in an ecstacy of delight."

With the milling crowd was the ubiquitous reporter. While Sam's reception was in full swing, the newsman walked up the gangplank and asked to speak with the Chief.

A six-foot major domo of the vessel, with all of the officiousness of a subway guard, grabbed the reporter and impressed upon him that white folks were not then welcome on the ship, hustled him unceremoniously down the gangplank. The crowd of negroes cheered gleefully.

But Sam, witnessing the unorthodox departure of the reporter, stepped dramatically from the center of the group that had been lionizing him, and with upraised hand silenced the crowd of Negroes and the boat's watchman. He began to speak.

"My brethren, we welcome investigation. We have nothing to hide. We are here for a week or ten days. Then we are off to the west coast

159

of Africa. We go to prepare a place that the people of our race may establish themselves in self-sustaining condition. Our purpose and plans have been falsely displayed in the North by the newspapers. They have told untruths about us. We have never been given the opportunity to put ourselves right with any but our own people. Do you doubt that my people are anxious to go back to a land they can call their own?"

With that, the *News* dramatically continued, "he swept a diamond bespecked hand in the direction of the crowd that was eating 'free lunch' on the boat."

Sam, eloquent but restrained on matters of fact, continued.

"This trip to Africa is mainly for the purpose of locating our colony. . . . We have no land yet, but have been assured that we can readily secure all that we will need on the west coast of Africa from the native tribes. If we can purchase lumber and cement at reasonable prices in Galveston we will take a quantity along to build the nucleus of our colony, which will probably be a dormitory, a chapel and a store. Our people are not homeless. They are not idlers or drones. Our plan is to establish a government in which our race will be supreme. When our colony is established and the people of our race see that we are successful, this boat will be crowded on every trip that she makes to Africa."

Sam had, it was apparent, considerably modified his public statements on the exodus. It was no longer the mass movement it had once been painted, nor was Sam prepared to continue to assert his claims to land in the Gold Coast Colony. The British, hacking monotonously away at this latter point, had by now convinced the bulk of Sam's followers, and perhaps Sam as well, that whatever lands he might have conceived himself to have held, the necessary and legal registration of such lands had not been accomplished to the satisfaction of the colonial government.

Sam was pressed for details "as to the . . . problems of tenancy and capital." He indicated that details had not yet been completed, though he declined to address this point further. Both Sam and his followers, the *News* remarked, appeared to be in good circumstances. Passengers were well-dressed, the ship was "clean throughout and the ship's crew was dressed in spotless white." To the certain amazement of many, Galveston port officials had reported that the ship and passengers had stood a more than satisfactory inspection.

The reporters, however, were clearly shocked by the relationship which existed between Sam and his partially white crew, who, "from the captain down, 'stepped about' in obedience to his gestures of command, as readily as did his followers."

Negroes from all over the city thronged the waterfront to see and board the ship. They shook hands with one another and with members of the crew. Those who could get aboard sat about in deck chairs and "touched the ship's brasses lovingly. 'Our ship,' they called the *Liberia*." So great was the crush of people that "later in the evening it was necessary for Chief Sam to receive his visitors in installments."

The *News* epitomized with a shipboard vignette the passionate involvement which the Negroes felt in this old ship:

> An old mammy, evidently a washer woman, stood by the deck rail . . . partaking in a hearty fashion of the free lunch offered all visitors. "Sister, are you with us?" inquired Chief Sam as he stretched out his hand in welcome and beamed a wide come-all-ye smile. She made an old fashioned courtesy to the leader. "I shorely am on my way back home," she replied confidently, with a look of smiling gratitude for having been recognized, "and that's the truth."

Despite the previous plans, the *Liberia* was not christened on Juneteenth day. But this made little real difference to the celebrants, and the occasion could not have been a better one. Early in the morning, a band formed at the head of one of the main streets in the Negro section and a large crowd gathered behind it. To the brassy strains of "Come on Mandy, Get Your Glad Rags On," "the gay procession . . . went to MacGuire's Park in the West end, where there were things to eat and diversions galore." [29]

In the days that followed, reported the San Antonio *Express,* "Sam set up a sort of African court, holding receptions and giving almost daily entertainments with the deck and cabin of the ship as the theater of action." A fee of twenty-five cents was charged to board the ship and "to exchange a few words with the chief called for an additional 25 cents." [30] Though the "free lunch" was an institution during the first few days of the *Liberia*'s stay in Galveston, the financial affairs of the movement could scarcely bear such extravagance for long. Every visitor might eat in the dining salon, but each was soon made to pay for his meal.

The skeptical *Express* reported that in booths set up around the deck of the ship, refreshments were offered for sale to those who chose not to eat the full meal. On certain days of the week, it was alleged, Sam would serve crocodile sandwiches and tiger stew, "the carnal ingredients of the delicacies, it was claimed, were brought across the ocean for the delectation of Sam's followers in Texas." [31]

On July 5, after weeks of tiresome visits to the ship and little in the way of definite plans, the christening was announced. It was to be held on the following Thursday, and the elaborate program was released to the press. The festivities, which were to begin at 3 P.M., included a variety of speeches and reassurances by prominent members of the movement.

The program read:

Devotional exercises ....Rev. A. Davis
Address of welcome to Galveston
Response ....Chief Alfred C. Sam
Address, selected ....Professor W. H. Lewis
Address, "What the Colored Women are Doing" ....Mrs. Hall,
    President of the Woman's Club aboard the *Liberia*
Address, "Africa, the Black Man's Home" ....Rev. O. Faduma,
    of Sierra Leone, West Africa
Address, "The Akim Trading Company and the Business Side of The
    Movement" ....Judge M. A. Sorrell
Address, "The Results of Immigration and Colonization" ...Dr. J. A.
    Edmundson, Seattle, Washington.[32]

Sam was not in the city at the moment. He and a number of his followers were touring Texas in an attempt to raise additional money for the enterprise. Though he had anticipated his absence as being only for a few days, his tour had proved more extensive than planned. To cope with some of the difficulties arising in Weleetka, Sam had ultimately hired a special car to take him briefly to that town. He returned to Galveston, though, on the morning of July 9, the day scheduled for the christening.

But the delays, which had by now become so characteristic of every phase of the exodus, plagued the christening, too. Late Thursday afternoon, well after the hour advertised for the beginning of the ceremony, Sam was forced to report that in response to many requests from Negroes in the interior that they be given opportunities to witness the ceremony, the christening would be postponed.[33]

Hundreds of people, however, had already paid their fifty cents admission to the ceremony before this tardy announcement was made, and each felt he should have some satisfaction for his expenditure. Always ready for an emergency, Sam made a compromise, and determined to carry out at least a portion of the ceremony for the crowd which had assembled.

Sam had originally been scheduled to deliver his address from the upper deck of the ship, a point where the greatest number of people might see him. But when he reached his position, after pushing desperately through the crowd, he noticed a fumbling motion-picture camera operator attempting to obtain a proper focus. Sam became enraged, and immediately hastened off to his "Holy room." He insisted that he would not emerge until the operator had been removed from the premises.

But, as the *News* observed, removal of the cameraman was impossible, so Sam "consented to speak to those on board the ship out of range of the camera."

Through a drizzling rain which eventually drenched both the crew and the spectators, Sam talked on of the African trip:

"My brethren, you have gathered here to witness the christening of a vessel, the first ship which the negro has owned, and to give thanks to Almighty God for things he has done for the black race. This ship has come to take you to the land of your forefathers. You have served the white man 250 years, and now it is time for you to begin life for yourselves. Our conditions here are bad; there is a free land waiting for you on the other side of the water."

Sam grew whimsical.

"Primarily the races are opposed to each other," he said. "In most places the white man hates the negro and the negro hates the white man. Under these conditions you can never go to heaven, for the Bible teaches that one must love his neighbor."

The crowd laughed appreciatively.

"No matter what you do in this country, some white man will jim crow you; on the train, in business, on the farm, you are jim crowed. Do you think a white man could take anything from you on this ship?"

He paused to wait for the applause to subside. Sam and his colonists knew full well that they still had a long way to go, and the bravado was soon tempered. Sam leaned against the rail and talked easily, "his countenance frequently lighting up with the effect of his remarks."

"But after all the white man has been our best friend in getting the movement started. The greatest trouble has been with our own people. It has been hard to get them to join our movement, but in the end we will be successful, and before many years have passed we will have a fleet of ships plying between America and the Gold Coast of Africa."

Davis then spoke briefly. At "short intervals, he paused and sang a snatch of song." The audience joined in antiphonal chorus. With this, the quasi-christening ended. Sam, when approached after the event, was still unable to give an estimate as to when the ship would sail.

The second christening was set for Saturday, July 11. Shortly after noon, new throngs of people began to collect on the deck of the *Liberia* and soon overflowed onto the pier.

Though the crowd assembled at the ship, the first portion of the ceremony was scheduled at the Southern Pacific cotton shed. Sam's lieutenants and members of the ship's crew were having difficulty in redirecting the many observers. Despite a special train which had been arranged to bring Negroes from Houston to the ceremony, the crowd was smaller than it had been on Thursday.

Once the group had been assembled in the cotton shed, the ceremony began.[34] Several of the scheduled addresses were deleted, owing to the confusion which had eaten up much of the allotted time. The program started with an address by J. P. Liddell, president of Sam's federation of clubs throughout the country. Rev. Orishatukey Faduma followed Liddell with a song and a prayer.

The principal feature of the program was the address by Sorrell, in which the "business side of the movement" was described. Sorrell provided an account of the origin of the company, and continued with a sketch of Sam's life. Sorrell reviled the eastern newspapers and Negro churches for their attacks on Sam.

"One man," said Sorrell, "declared that he had been in the penitentiary with Chief Sam. Others knew him as a boy in Alabama; people have said all manner of things about him and many have tried to brand him as a fake and the Akim Trading Company as pure fraud."

The speaker assured the crowd that Sam's status was an entirely *bona fide* one. His citizenship, Sorrell added, "had been investigated and established beyond question by the English legation at Washington before he was permitted to sail under the British flag, and further that he formerly was a chief of a native African tribe." The Judge concluded with an urgent appeal to the crowd to purchase additional stock in the company, in order that this movement might continue, now that its fruition was so clearly in sight.

As the address ended, a band struck up the "National Emblem March," and the audience was led double file from the cotton shed back to the ship to witness the formal christening of the vessel. The spectators climbed "to every point of vantage on the ship from crow's nest to bridge" in order to watch the event.

Sam addressed the group once more, delivering essentially the same text that he had given on the preceding Thursday. He emphasized "humbleness before God, without which . . . nothing could ever be done." He spoke again of the significance of the movement for his race. He reminisced about his boyhood in Africa, and recalled "that on many nights while he was in his native land . . . God came and told him to come to America and lead the black race back there." He declared that finally "he could no longer disregard the call and started out to accomplish the task."

"And if I can take one black man with me," he said, "I will feel that a part of my contract has been fulfilled."

Like Sorrell, Sam concluded with a strong appeal for additional financial support.

"If you have money," he said, "don't keep it, but give it to us. Many of you smoke good cigars when you could as well do without them and give the money to this God-sent plan of restoring the black race to its own. 'Liberia,' the name that has been given this ship, means freedom."

Sam then presented Lucille Garrett, the plump, light-skinned girl who had been chosen to christen the ship. She was dressed in an evening gown. Miss Garrett had been selected, Sam said, in recognition of the important role which the Oklahoma Negroes had played in the movement and the extent to which its financing was due largely to their efforts.

The child, prompted now by Sam, forced her way through the

crowd toward the prow of the ship. When she reached her station, "she barely had room to stand." She slowly climbed the rail, and breaking the almost religious silence which had fallen over the spectators, she pronounced: "I christen thee *Liberia* . . . ship sent by God to take the black man back to the land of his forefathers." As the girl finished speaking, she slowly poured a bottle of palm oil over the bow of the ship, and "as it draped itself slowly down the ship's sides a salvo of lusty hurrahs from hundreds of throats broke the stillness."

Before the noise had ceased, Sam quickly ran through the throng into his prayer room. The crowd on the pier poured over the ship, congratulating one another. It was after six o'clock when the three-hour ceremony ended. Despite the delays and early confusion, the ceremony had been a wonderful success. The effect it had on the colonists at Galveston was awesome. Once again, their faith in the movement had been validated, and they conceived themselves one more step closer to Africa.

In Oklahoma, the Guthrie *Leader* took begrudging note of the event, remarking that "speech making and the breaking of a bottle of gin over the bow by an Oklahoma girl, formed the christening."[35]

Though the christening had given the colonists new hope, they were no closer than before to sailing. No date had yet been fixed, and Sam's assistants were routinely evasive. Members of the colony, doubtlessly predicting on what scanty information they had, alleged dates ranging from several days to several months. The Galveston colonists had no choice but to return to their temporary abodes and await their instructions. The physical presence of the ship was certainly a comfort to them, and would sustain their faith for additional months if need be.

At Weleetka, however, the situation was grim. Despite the depletion of the two camps some months earlier when a number of people had decided to wait out the ship in Galveston, some five hundred persons were gathered in tents by the end of July. Both camps, the one south of town along the Frisco right-of-way, and the other to the north on Alabama Creek, were still very much in operation. Constant delays in the sailing had emotionally debilitated the colonists, and the situation was now being defined by them as almost hopeless. With no homes to which they could return, they languished pointlessly in the camps, hoping against hope that a call from Sam might come.

Even the christening had been prosaic for them. Distant from the ship, and still suffering the lack of adequate communication with Sam and the officials of the movement, they learned only that the grand event consisted merely of speech-making and the breaking of "gin" over the bow of their ship. In dry Oklahoma, and among a group whose religious devoutness had earlier been objected to by Weleetka citizens, this must have seemed a vulgar touch.

The townspeople of Weleetka, with probably valid concern for the public safety, had finally called upon County Physician H. A. May to investigate the condition of the African camps. There was great alarm expressed over the high death rate, and the Weleetka people once again feared an outbreak of disease. A committee of citizens, accompanied by Dr. May, determined to make an inspection of the Negro burial grounds. To their horror, they found that more than fifty-six persons had been interred during the past two months, twenty of whom were positively known to have been associated with the Gold Coast camps. Three Negroes, alleged one of the campers who was questioned, had died the very night before the investigation.

At just about the time that the committee resolved to take action to eliminate the camps, Chief Sam happened into Weleetka on one of his frequent visits to the camp, visits during which, according to one of the newspapers, he would work his colonists up "to a semi-religious frenzy," with shouting, singing, and praying "until nearly morning, making sleep or quiet impossible to the people of the town." [36]

"Forbearance having ceased to be a virtue," the citizen's committee called a meeting and asked Sam to be present.[37] The Chief could not come, however, and sent one of his assistants. Dr. May advised the representative of the movement that he would shortly issue an order for the campers to disperse. He would give them five days to comply with this directive. The agent begged for more time, pointing out the extreme difficulty of moving more than five hundred persons, some of whom had been ensconced on the site for nearly eight months, in five days. May agreed to extend the time to ten days. Following the meeting, a group of whites visited Chief Sam and reported the committee's decision. Sam promised that he would supervise the breaking up of the camp himself, and that he would have all of his followers off the site by the deadline.

It was by now obvious to all, including the campers, that the small vessel in port at Galveston could not by any means transport all the Negroes collected in the camps at Weleetka and scattered about the city of Galveston. Despite the fact that the Galveston *Daily News* had earlier remarked that the "accommodations aboard are ample for a large crowd," Sam's determined followers constituted something more than a mere "crowd." [38] Sam's plan had been so magnetic that he was now overwhelmed by the response to it. Somehow he had to cope with the people he had promised to take to Africa if they purchased stock. Somehow he had to see that they survived until he could reach the African coast, debark his first contingent, and return for additional passengers. But even assuming that his passenger load was as high as one hundred persons per trip, it would take him many years to accommodate all those who had bought stock from him.

Despite the serious problem posed by the sheer arithmetic of his success, Sam was still in desperate need of more money, and without it even the first step of his program could not get under way. He pushed aside consideration of the dilemma posed by additional recruits and canvassed the countryside to enroll stockholders in the Akim Trading Company, Ltd. He was reported in Berwyn and Humby, small towns in Carter County, soliciting funds and promising "complete emancipation of the Negro race." [39] A few days earlier, he had been in the vicinity of Ardmore, where, according to the local paper, "inspired by that familiar ragtime air 'Every Nation Has a Flag but the Coon,' Sam had little difficulty in working up sufficient interest to charter or buy a vessel and now vast hordes are awaiting the sailing of that vessel." [40]

Meanwhile, as Sam feverishly searched for funds, further blocks were put in the way of the *Liberia,* when the sailing procedures for all merchant vessels leaving the United States under foreign flags were changed, and port clearance was made more difficult to obtain.

As a direct result of the European war and the desire of the United States to protect its neutrality, the collectors of the various American ports were directed to obtain full and complete manifests from all alien steamships before clearance papers were issued. Previously, the procedure was considerably more haphazard; and a merchantman could file a summary manifest on sailing, providing that the more detailed document was entered into the record within four days after clearance. In the face of the new regulation, Sam's assistants aboard the *Liberia* were forced to draw up a detailed statement on the ship's cargo.

Sam returned to Galveston by August 12, and arranged with the port authorities to have his ship shifted out into the Bolivar Roads section of the harbor.

At Weleetka, the painful and complicated business of breaking camp was underway. Some of the campers drifted back to their homes. A number of them—150 in all—boarded a special three-coach Frisco train for Galveston, determined to try their luck in that city despite the discouraging news that the number of colonists on the first voyage would be severely limited. The Weleetka *American,* reported that the "Frisco sold $1,114 worth of transportation to the pioneers," and that "between six and seven hundred dollars were distributed among the negroes to leave on." [41] The source of this money was not disclosed, though it was certainly Sam who had provided it. The Chief himself accompanied the last contingent of pioneers.

Sam's latest arrival in Galveston went unheralded. Though it seemed obvious by now that the ship would sail and that there was nothing to be done to stop it, the British made one last feverish atttempt to discourage the departure. S. W. Barnes, acting British consul at Galveston, on instruction from the Ambassador in Washington, issued a stern warning several days after Sam arrived in Galveston. Barnes recited the plaguing objections which his government had to the movement. He stressed that the passengers on the ship would be considered only as members of a committee of inspection, and not as immigrants to the Gold Coast. He warned that even the question of their landing on the Gold Coast was entirely in the hands of the Governor of the colony, who would reach a decision on the matter only when the ship arrived in port.

Since the ship was sailing under the British flag, "provisional permission having been granted for the privilege," his government felt called upon to issue this last warning in the interest of the "delegates." [42] Barnes said that "he understood some of the passengers were planning to take their furniture and other household effects" and that in view of this fact he felt it necessary to "make the conditions as plain as possible, so there can be no misunderstanding." [43]

But Sam had long been prepared for the "delegate" system. As early as November of the previous year, vague reports of "delegates" had been made by Sam's assistants. Sam, himself, sometimes referred to certain of his people by that term.

The exact method employed for the selection of those to sail on the *Liberia* is obscure. There was a blanket ban against children under the age of thirteen, and no single woman made the trip. Sam absolved himself of the heavy responsibility of selecting delegates by appointing a committee of three which weighed the qualifications of the mass of applicants. There is no question but that financial status was one of the most telling assets for inclusion in this first passenger list. One young man, of a wealthy family, was asked to make the trip with the group, but eventually had to decline because his parents objected, though he himself felt that he was a "strong, robusted fellow, used to the plow" and capable of caring for himself.

On August 20, with sixty delegates having been weeded out of the mass of persons desperately anxious to be included in this first voyage, the almost unbelievable occurred. An obscure line under the heading, "Shipping News," in the Galveston morning paper, reported the departure of the *Liberia* in terse, abbreviated form: "Cleared Ss *Liberia* (Br.) McKenzie, Master, for Gold Coast, Africa, via Pensacola." [44]

The announcement told fully that the "mystery ship," with its improbable passengers and their unthinkable scheme, had left the North American continent, sailing off into the Atlantic, heading for the promised land.

Compared to the flamboyance which characterized less important events, the sailing of the vessel was a prosaic affair. On the Sunday preceding the departure, many of the men who had been living aboard the ship during her stay in Galveston collected their belongings and quit the vessel. One young boy who had served as a waiter remembers sadly gathering up his few clothes, and being taken ashore in a launch.

The ship left early in the morning. Many of the colonists, living at considerable distances from the pier, had to awaken in predawn darkness and ride rapidly on bicycles in order to be on hand for the sailing. Despite the hour, however, the departure was the "occasion of the gathering of a large number of the members of the colony on the docks. Ribbons and badges were seen everywhere. There was a waving of flags and many tears and wailings mingled with shouts of good-luck and well-wishes for a happy and prosperous voyage." [45]

The manifest, filed several days before the clearance papers were issued, declared that the *Liberia* would first stop at Pensacola to take on coal. From there, she was to proceed across the Atlantic, stopping at various points on the African coast, "among them being Gold Coast, Liberia, Akim and Sam City." [46]

The cargo of the ship consisted mainly of "cement, flour, lumber, hardware, breadstuffs, some arms and ammunition and household goods, each particular commodity being itemized and accredited to one or more of the individuals who are members of the company chartering the vessel." [47] The length of time it would take for the *Liberia* to reach the African coast was not known, though the *Daily News* predicted that it would certainly require in excess of forty days, the *Liberia* being a slow ship.

Newspapers throughout the country took only limited notice of the *Liberia*'s sailing. This was not the kind of news which had previously been associated with a scheme that had almost universally been declared a swindle and a fraud. The mere report of the sailing would have belied almost a year of "accurate reporting and predicting." The San Antonio *Express* was one of the few exceptions to the press blackout. It ran a small and condescending notice on the *Liberia*'s departure, as well as a photograph of Sam and the ship. "The biggest house-boat party ever held by the colored race in the South is now on its way across the Atlantic," the newspaper reported. "The steamship *Liberia*, on which Chief Sam of the Akim Trading Company plans to inaugurate the back to Africa movement of his race . . . sailed yesterday." [48]

The *Express* was amazed at the bravado displayed by Sam in sailing into the Gulf of Mexico, while other British merchantmen, fearing the rumors of German cruisers in the Gulf, cowered at Galveston. The *Express* concluded:

> In the meantime, the passenger list of over a hundred negro colonists, culled from Oklahoma and Texas communities, was enjoying a record siesta. The Liberia's decks form a delightful lounging place. Over the rail the family washing of the black mammies on board flies in the breeze. Fishing lines overside kept the "hot cat"supply of the commissariat up to the maximum. At nightfall, the sound of old plantation melodies floated out. . . .

The exodus was underway. Whatever torment the Negroes might have had in the United States was now behind them. Whatever apprehensions about the possibility of sailing they might have had were now irrelevant. The ship was committed to its course. The bright new world of Africa lay across that "one more river."

8

"Across the Sea It Flies"

> The Lord a glorious work begun,
> And thro' America it run,
> Across the sea it flies;
> This work is now to us come near,
> And many are converted here,
> We see it with our eyes.
>
> The little cloud increases still
> That first arose upon Mow Hill,
> It spreads along the plains,
> Tho' men attempt to stop its course,
> It flies in spite of all their force,
> And proves their efforts vain.
>
> (From an untitled hymn
> attributed to Hugh Bourne)

THE LIBERIA COULD hardly have chosen a more inopportune time to venture out from Galveston into the Gulf of Mexico and from there to attempt the perilous crossing of the Atlantic under the provocative colors of the British Empire. On August 20, the day that the *Liberia* departed from Galveston, the German cavalry captured Brussels and was pushing on toward Antwerp. American refugees were pouring back into the United States by sea, relieved at having escaped from the European war zone. From the Vatican, the news of the Pope's death was taken by a few optimists to indicate the renewed possibility of an end to the war, but the dispatches from the fighting zones belied the reality of such a prospect.

Two items, particularly, were significant to the Negro pioneers pushing out into the open, war-threatened seas. The first was a seven-column, bold-type headline in the New York *Herald* which inaccurately reported that the entire English fleet had been destroyed, some of it in battles, the rest by zeppelins bombarding the dreadnaughts in port. In addition, there was a brief notice of the invasion of Nairobi in East Africa by German troops crossing over the border for a quick thrust at the British protectorate. In West Africa, the *Liberia*'s destination, the British, Germans, and French lived in unhappy proximity; and the possibility of war in the Gold Coast was not an unlikely one.

Despite the ominous world situation, however, and the appalling wartime conditions on the high seas, the voyage of the *Liberia* was hardly a tense or frightening experience for its passengers. In fact, the trip had tremendous attractiveness. The Negro migrants aboard were at last free from the incessant, unpredictable harassment of government officials, from the prodding, sarcastic questions of newspaper reporters, from the condescending stares of tourists, and from the chatter and nervous tension of the other Negroes who hoped that they might be among this first group. Most important, the period of waiting had come to an end; the ship was pointing toward Africa and the resolution of their project.

In many ways, the ship was a refreshing and cozy racial island. This was physical and psychological isolation carried to its very ultimate. This was self-government in its most unfettered form. It was the freest of freedoms, here on the seas, untouchable by white rules and white decisions. In the *Liberia,* the Negroes had found a piece of property that was uniquely theirs. It might have struck them, as their ship rode the seas in inviolate majesty, that this ark represented, for the length of their voyage, the most exciting possible resolution of their search for self-fulfillment and racial integrity.

The voyage, despite periodic harassments, and despite the uncertainty of its outcome, provided the passengers with moments of inordinate pleasure, with episodes that they would remember when their days were almost completed as the happiest times of their lives. For most of the passengers, the most unfortunate fact was that the *Liberia,* like a modern-day *Flying Dutchman,* could not have sailed on and on, endlessly unbothered by the realities of racial existence.

Each passenger had taken with him his Bible, and he had an opportunity to make use of it during the prayer meetings which were held without fail every evening and on Sunday. The services were inter-denominational, and they were often followed by a discussion meeting in which the passengers would prod Sam about Africa. He seemed to enjoy these sessions immensely; and sooner or later, he would begin to tell stories about his boyhood in the Gold Coast, and about the beauty of the land. He was, they noticed, reticent about discussing his family. His father, Sam said, was dead, and he would add no more details. But he carried a picture of his mother which he would show, if asked.

There was no dancing on the ship, but the previous rules against drinking were relaxed completely, more by default than by edict. Sam simply ignored the stern prohibition that had governed shipboard conduct while the *Liberia* was tied up in New York, Portland and Galveston, under the critical eyes of the press.

Sam, in fact, seemed less concerned with the details of the voyage than he had been previously. He appeared to be preoccupied with something and was moody a good deal of the time. Often, he would retreat to his cabin for long periods, and he routinely fluttered about the ship, probably the least relaxed person on board. Only when he had the group before him, when he had their rapt attention as he told his stories, did he appear to be as dedicated and certain of himself as he had been during the crusading days in Oklahoma.

The ship offered a floating palace for relaxation and amusement that had rarely been a part of the life of these passengers, especially in such concentrated and prolonged doses. There were few chores, food was plentiful and—despite earlier reports—free. Soon, an elaborate social life became part of the shipboard routine. There were parties of all sorts, tea parties every afternoon, late evening get-togethers, and most memorable, birthday parties for those who were fortunate enough to have a birthday during the three months that the *Liberia* took to churn her way slowly toward the coast of Africa.

The thirteen women on board—"half-grown" Lucille Garrett, plus a dozen married women—would each bake a cake in honor of the birthday. The cakes were then given to the mate of the person who was celebrating the occasion, and it became his duty to hide the cake. It was child's play, searching for suitable hiding places on the strange byways of the ship, and it provided great fun.

At the parties, the games were simple but enjoyable. The celebrants would spin a plate around and around, and the person who had been designated as "it" would have to dive and catch the plate before it stopped spinning and collapsed to the deck. There was another game with coins, and the person designated had to guess who had hidden the coins.

But the pleasures of those aboard the *Liberia*, the select few from the many thousands who had wanted to make this voyage, were in sharp contrast to the fortunes of the remainder of the prospective colonists who had been left behind. In Galveston, the Negroes who had earlier flocked to the coast slowly started their journeys homeward. Their earlier plans to remain near the *Liberia*'s home port seemed, with the absence of the ship, too unreal and illusory to implement; and most of them were in serious financial difficulty. Many wrote pleading letters to relatives, asking that they send money to pay the transportation home for them and their families; and when they did return home with this money, they found themselves faced with the knowing comments of those who had, they said, known all along that Chief Sam was no Moses, and that the trip to Africa was but one part of his fraudulent scheme.

With untiring persistence, despite the passage of the ship beyond its jurisdiction, the Post Office Department carried on its investigation of the activities of the Akim Trading Company, Ltd. Inspector Booth's almost definitive report on the movement was soon supplemented by an investigation conducted by Inspector W. G. Swain.

Swain merely reviewed Booth's material, though he did add some additional comments of his own that had resulted from interviews with complainants and participants in the Sam movement. In addition, the Post Office Department file on the activities of Sam had grown even more voluminous since Booth's report five months before.

Swain reiterated Booth's conclusion that Sam had not thus far engaged in any activity which was clearly fraudulent. Sam's principal claim had been that he would use the funds collected to purchase a ship on which to transport his stockholders to Africa. He had obviously purchased such a ship; and Swain, reviewing the group's finances, was forced to conclude that he had used virtually all of the money he had gathered to buy the ship.

Somewhat unapprised of recent developments, Swain asserted that the ship was now lying at anchor in the Port of Galveston, and that it seemed "likely that the ship will remain there indefinitely." Sadly, he said, "if such proves the case, Sam and his associates will have a very good excuse on account of the war now raging in Europe." [1] "I recommend," concluded the Inspector, "that this case be closed without further action."

On September 5, the Tulsa *Star,* usually unreliable in matters concerning the African movement, and often deliberately deceptive, reported that the

> latest now from the audacious Chief is that he landed at Key West and telegraphed back that each club would have to send him $100 before he could continue the journey. The Chief has fifty clubs in Texas and Oklahoma. If they comply with the Chief's demands, Chief Sam will leave Key West with another additional $5,000 in his slush fund.[2]

The truth of this report is certainly open to question. While Sam undoubtedly needed the money, as always, this method of raising it seems unlikely to have offered much hope.

The *Liberia* put in at St. Andrews, Florida, on September 10. Whatever else she may have done there, she changed her engineer. Ira Benford, the white engineer who had come aboard at New York and had remained with the ship through Portland and Galveston, was replaced by Will Hurt, one of the pioneers who had been serving as "acting fireman" on the ship. Hurt was one of the most highly regarded members of the expedition. At Galveston, he had been one of the crew members questioned by the ship inspectors on his knowledge of damage control. The inspectors wanted to know what Hurt would do if the ship caught fire and developed a leak. All of the persons they questioned fumbled around unsuccessfully for a solution, but Hurt responded quickly. He told them that he would take a hose, put it against the point at which the leak had developed, and turn on the water with as much pressure as he could command, presumably battering the incoming water back into the sea. According to a witness to this incident, the inspectors seemed pleased with his response, and his status among the pioneers was firmly established.

After leaving St. Andrews, the first definite word of the *Liberia* came from Bridgetown on the British Island of Barbados, where the ship stopped to obtain final registration papers. She had sailed from

Galveston with only the provisional certificate of registration which had been issued at Portland on May 20. This certificate needed final validation, and Barbados seemed the most likely place to obtain such a registry.

The ship remained at Bridgetown for about two weeks, while the papers were put in order. Though the women stayed aboard the ship most of the time, the men went ashore, fascinated by the variety of tropical trees, by the abundance of fruits which were strange to them, and by the people. They never tired of bringing fruit back to the ship for the women who, in their turn, exclaimed a good deal at their wonder.

On October 13, under a registry paper on which was neatly inscribed, "First British Registry," the *Liberia* came officially under the jurisdiction and protection of the British government. The registration listed in detail the measurements of the ship, and the equipment she carried. Her call letters, it recorded, were S. Q. P. T. Sam was listed as the ship's owner, holding all sixty-four shares in the ship. He was listed as a "merchant, temporarily residing at Portland, Maine, U. S. A., though his permanent abode was given as Apassu, Gold Coast.[3]

It is quite possible that the final acquiescence on the question of issuing a provisional British certificate of registry to Sam was in some way contingent upon a legal clarification of Sam's exact relationship with his company, and the precise status of the ship.

The *Liberia* left Bridgetown shortly after October 16, and sailed off into silence. It was not until mid-December that additional news of her was received.

The Guthrie *Daily Leader,* quoting from the *National Baptist Union Review,* carried a shocking story:

> Three weeks before she met her own fate, the German cruiser Emden in the Indian Ocean sank the Libeira [sic], Chief Sam's ship, which was carrying negroes from the United States, many of them from Oklahoma, to a brighter home on the Gold Coast of Africa.[4]

"The sinking of Chief Sam's steamship," the paper continued, "ends the chapter of many hopeful and noble-hearted pioneers who sought the fatherland, Africa, to help civilize their racial brothers." In a masterful bit of understandment, the article jogged the memories of those to whom the news story might not have had immediate meaning:

"The public knows Chief Sam about whom the papers have said so much while in this country gathering pioneers." And finally, in dreadful dirge, the statement ended: "All on board perished."

What the *Liberia* might conceivably be doing in the Indian Ocean was explained neither by the Baptist paper nor the Guthrie daily. The *Daily Leader,* however, was not altogether willing to swallow the entire account of the *Liberia*'s demise. With careful skepticism and no little condescension, it noted that "this is the belief of negroes who get their information from an editorial paragraph" in the *National Baptist Union Review.*

Other persons were also concerned about the fate of the ship. From Cushing, Oklahoma, came a letter from Rev. W. F. Taylor to the Secretary of State, "Mr. James William Bryan," asking:

Sir it aford me no Small Degree of Plecher then to write to you at this time in regard of a words of information about the Akim Trading Company, LTD of Gold Coust W. africa and what wanted to know is that company still in operation or is it now . . . if so please Kinly let me know at once and also is Aford C. Sam the President is he in the united States or he is in Africa if you know will you kindly let me know at once.[5]

Taylor reported that he had attempted to write to the secretary of the company and had failed to get an answer.

Ten days later, Bryan responded through John E. Osborne. The reply, bereft of information as usual, stated that the department "is not informed whether or not the compnay is now in existence or of the present whereabouts of Mr. Sam."[6] Osborne repeated the routine paragraphs on the understanding which his department had regarding the movement and the falsity of the statements reportedly made by Sam. From here, he swept into the more comforting clichés of the bureaucratic correspondence which had characterized most of the mail emanating from Washington regarding the back-to-Africa movement.

The last months of the *Liberia*'s voyage, as she approached her destination, were filled with untoward events. There was a strange episode in which the *Liberia* met a British ship on the seas, and the almost paranoid sensitivity of the Negro pioneers blew the incident up out of all proportion.

The *Liberia,* spotting the British ship, immediately prepared to salute it. The mutual recognition of vessels on the seas, according to the impersonal codes of ocean transportation, was always one of the most satisfying experiences to the *Liberia* passengers. But this time the British ship hesitated in returning the salute; the Negroes watched anxiously, peering across the water at the British flag boy. The *Liberia* dipped her flag in recognition three different times, but the British ship acted as if "they'd taken a notion not to salute." Once, their flag dipped imperceptibly, but that was all. As they sailed off, the passengers on the *Liberia* all agreed that the British were "acting uncivilized." Sam and the others aboard took the incident as a personal affront, and it upset them badly.

Shortly after the saluting incident, the *Liberia* ran into the only stormy weather she encountered on the entire voyage. One night the waves began running high, and many of them washed over the bow and sides of the ship. McKenzie feared that his vessel might founder, and he quickly ordered all the passengers to take up their positions in the lifeboats. The Negroes complied, with some few exceptions who argued that they would "be safer on the deck than in them little boats." The wary and frightened passengers remained in the boats until dawn, when McKenzie finally released them from their emergency posts and they returned sleepily to their cabins.

Though rough weather did not plague the passengers, sea-sickness did. The Negroes, almost to a man from landlocked areas of the Southwest, had not counted upon this peculiar and debilitating ailment when they had anticipated their flight across the Atlantic. One passenger recalls that nearly all on board suffered horribly from sea-sickness at one time or another. She said proudly, though, that she did not become sick during the voyage except on one occasion, when she brought it on herself. Sam had apparently tied a dory to the stern of the ship and was towing it across the ocean. One evening, a rumor spread that the dory was leaking, and the passengers rushed to the stern to watch it sink. The lady in question, choosing to remain in her cabin, peered out the port hole in her room and for several minutes, craned her neck to catch a glimpse of the stricken boat. During this time, she recalled, she became "quite ill" and had to retire. So immune to sea-sickness was she, that the seamen aboard gave her "some kind of stout name." Throughout the entire trip, she related, "I was just as healthy as an alligator."

Sam was among the most sensitive aboard to the invidious rolling of the ship. On several nights, he collapsed in his cabin, and the men would hasten in to surround him and bring him gently out on the deck to get some air.

The voyage was also disturbed by a death aboard as the ship neared the end of her trip. The pioneers, quiet and anxious about the death, gathered together on the deck for the funeral service. When the body was prepared for burial, the steward told the captain to stop the ship, and the *Liberia's* screws reversed. The ship came to an eerie standstill in mid-ocean. Then, "when all the talk was talked that wanted to be talked," the captain tapped a bell, the signal that the passengers could pay their last respects to the body. Then the bell was tapped again and the enshrouded body, which had been balanced on the rail on three long planks, was tipped into the sea. The body had been weighted down with lead around the neck, knees, and feet; and it bubbled out of sight at once.

The ship sailed quietly on again. Since Sam had not put aboard any supply of salt at Galveston, and since he was planning to trade salt when he reached the Gold Coast, he ordered McKenzie to put in at Mayo Island, in the Cape Verde group, to put aboard a supply.

The ship tied up at the island, some six hundred miles off the Senegalese coast, and the passengers had another opportunity to go ashore and view parts of the world that were incredibly strange to them. As before, the women stayed aboard the ship, but Sam and the men went ashore every day. To pass away the time, some of the women fished over the side of the vessel. One passenger, apparently no fisher-woman, had collected the materials necessary for an attempt at the sport. Someone had tied a hook and sinker to her line, and she tossed it over the side of the ship one day, just as the men had gone off to the beach. She fished for most of the afternoon before she had a strike. As she struggled with the fish, the men returned to the ship in a launch, and as they rounded the stern, one of them yelled at her, "Pull him, pull him, you got him."

In mild panic, the woman hauled in on her line and the fish flashed into sight. He was a monster, with "great big eyes and little, bitty ears." Frightened, she threw it on the deck and retreated to her cabin. Several of the men cleaned the fish somewhat later, and it was served for dinner that night, but the woman refused to eat it. "After that," she recalled with amusement, "I didn't fish no more."

Shortly before the *Liberia* was scheduled to leave Mayo Island on the last leg of its trip, it was set upon by a British man-of-war, the *HMS Victorian*. If Sam had been disturbed by the earlier incident with a British ship, he was terrified by this encounter. Though all of the passengers were dismayed by the British attitude, Sam was described as "the scairdest man aboard." During the time the British searched the *Liberia,* Sam ran back and forth from cabin to cabin, went up on deck to look around, and then went hastily below again.

The reasons for the British boarding of the *Liberia* are somewhat obscure, though Captain Somerville, of the *Victorian,* is alleged to have said that he had reason to believe that the Negro ark was illicitly employing its wireless to communicate with the enemy and, perhaps, to relay information to the Germans. This clearly improbable accusation was doubtless a cover-up for continued British concern over the landing of the Negroes on the Gold Coast, and may simply have been a last minute attempt to prevent the ship from ever reaching that colony. In any event, the *Liberia* was boarded, and an inspection party searched her from stem to stern.[7]

Dr. Dorman, who described himself in a letter to the "Dalis Morning News" as the "Author and head promotor of the African Emigration Association and the organizer," remarked in explanation of the boarding that the British believed the wireless "to be built by the Germans, though it was built in the City of Boston."

"After they examined our papers," continued Dorman, "they call our ship a suspicious one and put on a crew called a prize crew."

Captain Somerville dealt only summarily with McKenzie, and turned his attentions to Sam, of whom "he asked a lot of questions." Sam was frightened, but was nonetheless able to provide the answers which Somerville demanded. The British commander apparently questioned the other passengers as well; but they, according to an elderly survivor, "frustrated the British minds," and were left alone.

Finally, Somerville ordered his prize crew to take control of the ship and take her to Freetown, Sierra Leone, where a more detailed investigation of the ship's papers and general status would be conducted.

This delay proved disastrous for the *Liberia.* Though food had been plentiful during the voyage, the delay caused by the seizure began a series of hardships which the passengers would endure for the remainder of their stay in Africa. One passenger recalls that prior to the landing at Mayo Island, food had become a little scarce, and that by the time the ship reached the "suburbs of Africa," presumably after the British seizure, food was quite limited.

The *Liberia* upped anchor and was taken to Freetown, where she arrived on November 23. Three days later, Sam was arraigned before the "Supreme Court" at the Sierra Leone capital, and was there examined on the question of his ownership of the vessel. He swore it was registered under his own name, and he attempted to explain the purpose of his voyage. But the court was not convinced, and the inquiry continued for nearly forty-five days.

During this tragic and inert period, the ship's crew and passengers were becoming increasingly desperate. The British would not assist them in their quest for supplies; and Sam's money, planned to the last penny before he ever left the United States, had entirely run out.

The passengers finally began to go ashore when they could, and found that they were well treated by the natives. Many of them came to depend heavily upon local gifts of food for sustenance. Sam avoided the British as much as possible during the stay, telling the colonists that he "didn't think much of the English," and that their activities thus far had failed to impress him.

After the nearly one and a half months during which the ship lay idly at Freetown, the vessel was released from British custody. Though Sam and his pioneers petitioned for some restitution for having been obliged to remain in the British port, the authorities were unwilling to grant such.

Dorman, in his letter to the Dallas paper, likened the event to the tribulations of the Israelites in Egypt. "When we look back in Genesis," he said, "there Pharoah treated the poor very hard, but God being Almighty he defeated Pharoah and the Isrealight were at peace."

Finally, on January 13, 1915, the *Liberia* completed her interrupted voyage to the promised land, returning the emigrants to the land their ancestors had left some 300 years before. The Gold Coast *Leader,* under the by-line of Orishatukey Faduma, grandly announced the "REMARKABLE RECEPTION OF CHIEF SAM AND AMERICAN NEGRO DELEGATES IN SALTPOND." [8]

The *Liberia* was in the Gold Coast.

9

"Ye Trav'lers to Canaan's Shore"

> Ye weary, heavy laden souls,
>   Who are oppress'd and sore,
> Ye trav'lers thru the wilderness,
>   To Canaan's peaceful shore,
> Though chilling winds and beating rains,
>   And water deep and cold,
> And enemies surrounding us,
>   Take courage and be bold.
>   (From "Weary Souls")

JANUARY IS ONE of the few agreeable months of the year on the Gold Coast. The torrential rains which fall from April until July, and the less violent downpours of late autumn have passed; and January settles down to a period of relative climatic quiet. The coastal areas escape even the severe dry season that plagues the interior during the late fall and winter period, when the harmatan, the northeast trade wind, sweeps down from the Sahara and parches the air, settling choking red dust everywhere.

The weather at Saltpond could not have been more favorable when the *Liberia* arrived. The Rev. Orishatukey Faduma, reporting on the occasion in the Gold Coast *Leader,* described the day in glowing terms: "The reflection of the sun on the sand beach seemed to change every grain of sand into gold," he wrote, "and it was in harmony with the bright colours of the native costumes." [1]

The ship had reached the coastal city of Saltpond on Wednesday evening, January 13. The passengers, crammed along the deck rail, first spotted the old castles, surrounded by their fetid moats. It was from here that the numerous slave ships had once set sail, taking their live cargoes across the infamous "middle passage" to slavery in the New World. But less philosophically inclined were the colonists' thoughts as they watched the ship move laboriously into the harbor. The major emotion which they felt was curiosity, a curiosity tinged with a strong element of uncertainty as their voyage was coming to an end. "I just felt sort of strange," one passenger recalls. "It was an awful strange place there, and I know I must have looked curious to them."

The reception of the ship by the natives was overwhelmingly friendly and enthusiastic. The British, except for the minor formalities of port entry, paid no attention to the visitors. But the natives gathered on the shore when the *Liberia* first came into sight, and they remained in the vicinity until the following morning when the first landing was made from the ship by Sam and Judge Sorrell. The two were immediately surrounded by well-wishers. The paramount chief of Saltpond and his official followers were on hand, as was the chief of the Hausas, the local militia. The natives stood about in their "long silk capes and their flowing gowns." To the passengers on the *Liberia,* they looked a bit odd and unusual, but they were nonetheless "beautiful." Even a group of khaki-clad Boy Scouts and the native police were on hand, all in their best attire, to add their bit to the welcome.

Though there was considerable disappointment that the bulk of the pioneers could not come ashore, there was nonetheless cause for festivities; and the passengers, drifting remotely out in the harbor, could hear most of the celebration even though they had difficulty in seeing it.

"The variegated native costumes and the beating of native drums made the occasion peculiarly native," commented Mr. Faduma somewhat redundantly. "The ringing of church bells gave an air of sanctity to the gathering and was in keeping with the idea of the West African Movement, namely that it is a Divine and therefore Sacred movement."

The Rev. Mr. Reynolds, a native minister, welcomed Sam on behalf of the entire town, and Sam responded for himself and his delegates. Arrangements were made for the formal reception on the following day, and finally, after "handshakings, genuflexions, and embraces," Sam and Sorrell returned to the ship.

The reception the next day, though less spectacular, was more a "feast of reason."

No drum was beaten, no church bells were rung. The rolling waters of the Atlantic bore the party in surf boats which galloped along and above them and finally landed them safely on the shore. Instead of armed men as escorts, peaceful natives and children of both sexes greeted us, and embraced us during the march from the beach to the park. Excepting in dress and language, American Negroes bare striking resemblance. The lost chord in the African's native life was found, the family severed for over 300 years by European greed began to be united in this meeting.

At 3:30 in the afternoon, the landing party from the *Liberia* met with the chief of Saltpond and his representatives in the park, "shook thrice hands and were seated."

Reynolds again delivered the address of welcome, this time on behalf of Kurantsir III, Ohin of Saltpond. It was a hospitable greeting, yet it was tempered with much advice that must have seemed somewhat superfluous to the colonists unless conditions on the Gold Coast were not as Chief Sam had alleged.

Welcome home is the salutation from the townspeople, Ohin Kurantsir III, and Elders and Representatives of all the religious denominations in town to you, new arrivals from America:

About four months ago we heard of your embarkation for our shores . . . which according to tradition appears to be your fatherland, for we are of the same blood and colour.

Our anticipation has been a reality as we see you face to face here to-day. Because of the great and terrible war, there was some apprehension on our part of some dangers that might befall you during your voyage, but we are thankful to God for His providential care of you, as He has directed your cause hitherto.

Your emigration to our shores at this juncture is providential, for besides a recognition of brotherhood we shall learn from each other what may tend to mutual advantages. Here is a great chance for you. "The field is already ripe for the harvest." Remember that there are difficulties and temptations before you in the transaction of your business, but we persuade you to have a full confidence in God, for "He shall keep them in perfect peace whose mind is stayed on Him."

Reynolds must have utterly confused the colonists with his next lines; for they had, of course, had nothing but trouble with the British:

> Depend upon it that you will have the favour of the Government by whose permission you are come to sojourn here, of all the religious bodies, and all of the Fantee Kings and Chiefs. We therefore welcome you home with open arms and a kind heart.

Chief Sam replied to the welcome in Twi, his own native language. His response was translated into English for the benefit of the delegates. He began by thanking the kings, the chiefs, and the people of the Gold Coast for the warm reception given to him and to "their relatives who for more than three centuries were absent from their African home through no fault of theirs." Sam felt that he had accomplished a "divine mission," despite the extreme difficulties he had encountered. He credited God, rather than his "frail self" with the success of the mission.

He had been hunted down in America, he said, as a fraud; and the newspapers had printed the most incredible lies about him. The American and British governments, misled by the press and other influences that "were hidden," had put all sorts of obstacles in his way "to frustrate God's plan."

Sam made the most, too, of the fact that here, at last, he could present proof that he was legitimately a chief, and he wished that the British and American people might now be on hand to see the people of the Gold Coast recognize him as such. "He hoped the American press as well as others would take back the assertion that he is not a Chief."

In his supreme moment, Sam grew magnanimous toward his persecutors: "He was willing to pardon all offenders against him and the truth, if only in the future they will reform in their ways. If they deserved punishment, God, not he, would see about it."

Sam stressed the fact that his followers were "intelligent farmers and mechanics who will put into practice all they have learnt in the tilling of the soil and in handicrafts. They are used to soil and are not city dandies. . . ." They did not come to foment trouble and dispute British rule, but to introduce "higher and newer" methods of farming and civilization.

Sam could not resist lashing out against the £25 levy which the British had raised against every immigrant. He called it prohibitive, and asked that "the Chiefs and the country at large will see that a reform be made so that what is drastic in it will be struck out, and the best of our lost kinsmen will be encouraged to return and develop the land of their ancestors."

"These Negroes are not strangers," called out Sam, growing more emotional, "and should not be considered strangers. They and their forbears were taken away by force from home and are now, some of them, anxious to return home. The land is as much theirs as yours. God has preserved you to take care of the land till their return."

Sam was interrupted "all along with cheers and pleasant remarks." Sorrell and several of the women followed Sam as speakers, outlining in more detail their own interpretation of the aims of the movement, and their own aspirations with regard to it.

Sorrell devoted much of his speech to laudatory comments on the British rule in the Gold Coast. He praised the British for a long list of good things, including peaceful government, mutual goodwill, progress in native government, and justice. On this last point, the judge betrayed himself by saying too much when he asserted that the pioneers had "great confidence in British justice even though they were seized by a British man-of-war." They had, he continued, no "fears that all will right at last."

The colonists, Sorrell went on, had not left the United States for the purpose of "undoing the work England had started" in the Gold Coast, since they were "sympathizers and had come to contribute their share in the work of civilizing the native."

Taking his lead from the somewhat immodest statements which Sam had earlier made, Sorrell then set the pace for the later speakers. He continued to say that he and the other pioneers had co-operated to purchase the ship *Liberia* in order to help develop the country industrially and materially. "They stand for law and order as well as hard work," he insisted. "They are ready to open schools in which all kinds of industrial work will be taught, and in which the head, the hand, and the heart will cooperate."

Two of the pioneer women followed Sorrell. Mrs. Hall "electrified the audience by her patriotic speech." She moralized that "woman was intended by God to be man's helper and home maker." She and the women of the movement were intent upon following this precept, and they had come to Africa to "contribute toward elevating the social

189

and moral condition of the native African women who are like other women in other parts of the world." Thus elevated, Mrs. Hall continued, the "influence of the women in native society would be gentle, sympathetic and silent, but they would nevertheless have an upper tendency." After an absence of three hundred years, Mrs. Hall was more than glad to be home.

Mrs. Lewis also dwelt lengthily upon the contributions which she felt the migrants could make to African life, and she herself volunteered that "if she was not returning to the States, she would be glad to commence her work of teaching African girls." In addition, Mrs. Lewis made some general comments along the same line as had Mrs. Hall, a line that would have served well as a keynote address at any meeting of a Woman's Emancipation Club:

> She was glad that by this African Movement a larger impetus would be given to the development of the social life of native women. There is much for the modern woman to know and do in the home for the perfection of family life. There can be no true progress which leaves out the uplift of women. The women of the African Movement stand shoulder to shoulder with all other agencies already at work for the uplift of the family life of the native Africa.

Not one of the speakers mentioned the benefits which members of the movement might derive from their stay in Africa, nor the degree to which an acquaintance with African tradition and custom might conceivably assist them. No syllable touched on the possibility of African custom intruding on their way of life. It was a significant omission, and certainly betrayed a sudden awareness on the part of the Americans that their fatherland was historically a long way behind them, and that what emotional ties they fancied they had with it were somewhat vapid. Despite their obvious delight at being on the continent of their origin, they reacted as would have any European on being confronted with barefooted, gaudily dressed men and women of tribes little distant from outright savagery. The psychological disassociation of the emigrants from their brethren was almost immediate.

The meeting was closed with repeated thanks from Chief Sam. The delegates were all invited to various African houses to partake of native hospitality.

The receptions in the houses were beyond all expectations. The newcomers were served quantities of palm wine and fruits of many kinds that were strange to them. Plantains came in abundance, and at least one of the ship's passengers found them to taste like sweet potatoes, "only better."

The first weeks of the emigrants' stay on the Gold Coast were spent in complete dalliance. They visited daily among the natives and revelled in the sudden acquisition of prestige which they experienced. The Gold Coast people were lavish in their traditional hospitality. "They were the loveliest folk I ever met in the world," said one passenger.

They insisted that the visitors come to their homes, and once inside, "they would pull our shoes off, wash our feet, and then rub them with towels." Members of the family would disappear and return with calabashes of fruit on their head. The choicest bits were always given to the visitors.

"They was always willing to do anything for us, get anything for us, rub us, pat us."

"They was making merry of us," one survivor said, "because we'd been gone so long."

Sam became increasingly nervous as the *Liberia* remained anchored at a point midway between Saltpond and Anamabou. He arose early each morning, and ordered the landing boat. He would then disappear for long periods of time. To the passengers, it seemed as if he had "suddenly gone wild." They could "hardly do nothing with him." After some weeks of this unorthodox behavior, they began to suspect that Sam's activities were in some way connected with a discrepancy between the promises made to the group in the United States and the reality of their situation as they floated somewhat aimlessly off the African coast. Though the passengers spent much time in visiting their new friends in town, their lives lacked direction; and many of them were eager to see the land upon which they were to settle.

Though nothing came to an immediate head, the anxieties which the passengers felt were increased by the disquieting rumors which they had begun to hear.

"Sam is no chief; you shouldn't call him a chief," one woman was told while visiting in Saltpond.

The woman quickly relayed this bit of information to the rest of the pioneers, and they discussed it nervously. Sam had certainly been treated as a chief during the Saltpond reception; now one of his kind

191

had claimed that he did not have that status. Unfamiliar with the channels of information, and never quite certain of the precise meanings of various things which befell them in this alien environment, the pioneers became suspicious and confused. But they could not yet confront Sam with their suspicions and demand an explanation. The precisely correct opportunity had a way of not presenting itself for this showdown. More important, they had put their implicit faith in Sam, and to bring any loss of faith in his leadership out into the cold light of day would be to admit openly their own gullibility and the accuracy of critics' charges against their movement. They elected to remain silent.

But the general malaise of the Americans, as they lingered on the Gold Coast, was soon transmitted back to the United States where it was given the widest possible circulation by those who rejoiced that Sam's followers had "repented their action and [were] now appealing to home folks to help them come back."

By February 25, 1915, just six weeks after the *Liberia* had arrived in port, Engineer Will Hurt was writing angrily to a friend in Wewoka, denouncing Sam as a total fraud.[2] Hurt's letter unleashed a violent torrent of criticism on Sam:

"Dear Sir and Brother in Christ," Hurt began:

> It affords me great pleasure to write you a few lines in regard to my people who have been carried away from their happy homes and little children, now looking for those fathers to return back home.
>
> We'll, I am sorry to say, that this Negro, our so-called leader, Chief Alfred C. Sam, has only lied and frauded the people out here. I find he never owned sixty-four square miles of land. He is hardly known in Gold Coast by the people. I found out he is a trader on the race.

Hurt grew specific:

> I learn from the Chiefs that Alfred C. Sam never was a Chief in Gold Coast. I learn that he had no place here at all; he fooled our people; he said the cattle here were eight feet high. I learned there isn't a cow in the place—this was fraud. He said you could get horses here; there isn't a horse here—this was fraud. I further learn not one word of truth in what he told our people.

In somewhat interrupted narrative, Hurt described the events of the Sierra Leone seizure. He described as well the British notice that a levy of £25 would be made on each person intending to land in the colony. Then he came back to Sam:

He moved some [people] over in Salt Pond until he got his next trick fixed up. Then came, on the evening of Feb. 1, and fooled the rest he could off next morning out in the bushes. Then after they were gone he got automobiles and ran off with the men's wives. Now, this leaves a stain on us. They have been gone for three weeks and we can't hear a word from them.

By now so impassioned that he was nearly inarticulate, Hurt described the abandonment of various of the colonists whom he alleged had been lured into the bush by Sam. Hurt was told, he said, by one of the natives, that "Mr. Holly and his wife got sick on the road and they were left in the hands of God to starve."

"This is one of the dirtiest things our race has ever gotten into since the world began," he concluded. "We are here . . . starving sometimes, no bread on board, no water; our people are crying for help to come back home, and if the people don't help us we are lost forever. . . . you all can see from that death is at our doors."

Hurt ended his pathetic letter with a plea for help from home. He said that if they could get the money, they would be able to return with the vessel. "I am yet in possession of the engine room," he dramatically declared, "I will try to stay until I can hear from you all."

Though supplies may well have been short, and the general morale of the colonists low, the situation was certainly not as bad as Hurt had indicated. After they had accepted as much as they felt was decent from the Saltpond natives, they began to trade their salt for food.

But rebellion was nonetheless brewing. When Sam finally returned from one of his absences and settled down somewhat, the disturbance among the passengers diminished. There was a heated discussion at a meeting one night during which Sam accused his followers of deserting him, and of joining the wicked forces which had attempted to defeat his purpose. He explained in detail the use of the money he had collected, and he again threaded through the harassments of the British. He said that he would sell the ship if the colonists insisted, and return to them whatever money he could obtain in this way. Apparently contrite, the Americans finally agreed that they would follow Sam's instructions to the letter from then on, and that they would follow him without question wherever he chose to lead them. Sam, in turn, agreed to conduct them to the lands he had promised to make available.

The group, after making the necessary preparations on the coast, began the trek inland to Akim Swedru, the land of Sam's birth and the promised site of the new African cities. Akim Swedru lay about thirty miles from Saltpond over an extremely rough trail. It was one of the leading divisions of the Akim nation, which itself was divided into three sections: the Akim Abuakwa, the Akim Kokotu, and the Akim Bosome.

The Akim, unlike the Fante who lived in the coastal towns, had not confederated, but were instead only a group of loosely integrated tribal units. Though they periodically allied one with another for defensive purposes, they had as often fought on different sides, as they did during the prolonged wars that ripped the Gold Coast before the British finally managed to subjugate the Ashanti in 1901.

The Akim tribes had long been buffers between the Ashanti in the interior, and the coastal Fante, a group erratically supported by the British. At a quite early date, the Akim had been decisively beaten by the Ashanti and were thereafter reduced to a feudal state and required to pay a burdensome war indemnity. Their fortunes varied with the fortunes of their oppressors; and Akim Swedru, situated precariously on the southern boundary of the Ashanti-Akim line, rarely managed to escape the conflagrations that raged periodically through the Gold Coast.

The history of the tribe provides several clues to the history of Sam's family. After the Akim were reduced before the Ashanti, some time around 1700, they failed to pay their indemnity. The Ashanti invaded Akim again, but fell back in terror when the Akim managed to kill the Ashanti king, Osai Tutu, and then fell upon the disorganized Ashanti army. Encouraged by the almost accidental success of the Akim, other tribes began to revolt against the Ashanti; and that nation was finally forced to invade the entire territory to the south and quell the rebellion. This was accomplished during the period 1731 to 1803.

It was at the end of this time that the missionaries first successfully began to penetrate the Gold Coast. The Basel Mission, under whose tutelage Sam had been for a number of years, first sent out missionaries in 1827; but these succumbed to the killing climate, and it was really not until 1843 that their work began. The Basel group concentrated in the Akim region, hoping to be able to use this route to penetrate to the Ashanti who were one of their principal "conversion targets." It was during this campaign that the missionaries set up the station at Kibi, where Sam was sent to school.

The best clue to Sam's forebears is found in a few scattered references in an encyclopedic history of the Gold Coast. Claridge mentions a "Mr. W. E. Sam" as an agent for Messrs. F. and A. Swanzy, an English trading company that typically played the natives against the British, selling supplies to both and inciting discontent to maintain a demand for war materiel. Mr. Sam is credited with having "made every effort" to quell a native uprising at Dixcove around 1870.[3] In 1881, there is another note that Messrs. Swanzy discovered a rich gold reef at Abosso, and took up concessions there. "Abosso" might well be a transliteration of "Apassu," where Sam claimed to have been born; and it is not inconceivable that W. E. Sam was among the Swanzy merchants who were moved to the gold concession. At least, from all available data, 1881 is the approximate year that Sam was born.

The remaining history of the Akim hardly reflects to their credit. The British, to keep the constant quarreling among the natives to a minimum, resettled the Adansi tribe in Akim territory about 1885; but the Adansi induced the Chief of Akim Swedru to espouse their case against the Ashanti. This maneuver aborted, and Akim had a final chance to make a contribution to Gold Coast peace during the British invasion of the Ashanti capital at Kumasi in 1900. Though they provided some men for the British campaign, they failed miserably as soldiers. According to Claridge, "the Akims were arrant cowards now as they had been when serving previously. . . ." Captain Benson, leader of the British action, "had the greatest difficulty in getting them to obey his orders or advance in the direction of the enemy; indeed, so serious a quarrel took place between different factions that he was compelled to disarm and dismiss some of them."[4]

Whatever the historical vagaries of Sam's African progenitors, his American followers were received with great warmth when they finally reached Akim Swedru, after days of gruelling foot travel. The town, though, was a disappointment to them. It was only a small village, and it offered no exciting possibilities. There was, however, some land available for their settlement. The natives did all of their farming with primitive hoes; and to the migrants, accustomed to the more advanced methods used in the United States, the prospect of settling down to a dull existence in the interior of the Gold Coast was not attractive. The colonists were hardly in tune with the native customs and thought, much of which they had now decided to "uplift"; and the "fur bush" of the interior was indeed prosaic.

One passenger described the condition of the territory surrounding Akim Swedru, remarking that farming would have been almost impossible. The brush was so thick, she said, "that you had to stoop down and squint to see only a few feet." She felt out of touch with the native materials, too, and "couldn't think of building a house with gopher wood."

Life became terribly monotonous for the settlers. Sometimes, they would wander down to the Birrim River, which bounded the small village, but their constant feeling that watchful British eyes were always on them made them uncomfortable. The colonists believed the British to be interested in making certain that they did not prospect for gold in the river, gold which abounded so heavily that flecks of it could be seen as they flashed by in the water. (Oddly enough, the Birrim became the site of the first discovery of diamonds in the Gold Coast in 1919, a discovery which led ultimately to a major export industry.)

For the pioneers now in Akim Swedru, Sam's description of the town came into even greater conflict with the realities of its existence. The land certainly was not what Sam had promised them, particularly if Sam's promises were taken at all literally. But even worse, it was not what the pioneers had made of these promises in their own imaginations. They were much too used to living conditions in the United States; and despite their voluntary segregation there, they were unwilling to settle for the standards of the Gold Coast, however much their own Jim Crow status might be alleviated. They did not want to be Americans; but now they found that they did not want to be Africans either.

The land that Sam had promised was not exactly theirs, for that matter, nor did it altogether belong to Sam. All land, the migrants found—and this fact must have brought the British warnings tumbling back into their memories—belonged either to the tribe or to separate families. The Africans practiced a shifting agriculture, allowing some land to lie fallow for several years to recover its vitality. After this period, it was reoccupied. The chief of the tribe, with the consent of his numerous counsellors, was allowed to make use-grants of land to the new arrivals; but the feeling that the land was still tribal was strong, and the pioneers did not fit into the complex kinship system in which the people of Akim Swedru were involved. They could not, in short, ever really own their own farms.

Though the pioneers were still fascinated by the exotica of the Gold Coast, life was eminently weary. They passed away time in collecting large seeds, borne on weedy grasses, and strung these in complicated strands. They bagged anteaters and made purses from their hides. They sampled food and found much of it to their liking. But this was a desultory existence, and they were still plagued by the toll taken by disease.

Mr. Holly, for example, the man whose father Sam had reportedly left in the bush to die, described the difficult straits of the group in a painful note home:

> W. H. Lewis is dead; . . . Garret of near Boley is sick and two women delegates are sick. I wish I was in America and be sure to tell my brothers that twenty years will not be long to get ready to come to Africa. I am not feeling well for I have been awful busy waiting on those who are sick.[5]

In addition, the colonists were by now so destitute financially that it was becoming increasingly difficult for them to obtain even the necessities of life.

The native chief had also imposed certain restrictions on the Americans, which seemed irrational and tedious. After assigning them to houses, he warned that they were not to shift about. They were to remain with their hosts until they chose to leave Akim Swedru for good. Sam's uncle made life a bit more difficult, too, by belittling Sam's status as a chief.

"Don't call him chief," he kept saying. He "made fun" of the colonists for their dedication to Sam. "He ain't no more a chief than I am," he chided.

Most serious for the morale was the death of Clearview Garrett, the father of the girl who had christened the ship. His wife had not made the debilitating trip on foot to Akim Swedru because of her own illness, and she had to be brought up later to her husband's bedside by bearers. "They toted her in a hammock," which was no easy task as she was a "stout woman." She remained with Garrett until he died, and then buried him at Apoli, the area adjacent to Akim Swedru. In short order, three more of the Americans joined him in Gold Coast graves.

The pioneers remained in Akim Swedru for almost eight months. They were discouraged not only by their own restlessness, but by irksome British restrictions. The colony government, for example, levied a daily tax of one shilling on each of the visiting aliens. They also established stern rules in regard to the manner in which the Americans might utilize the lands near Akim Swedru, disapproving in particular the Americans' attempts to make sugar locally.[6]

In addition, the disenchantment with Sam was by now complete. He had talked incessantly aboard the ship about the "angels" who lived in the Gold Coast, who would not steal a thing from the colonists. "You could put a bucket of gold outside your door and nobody would steal it," he had claimed. But in Akim Swedru, one of the Americans, sleeping in a tent, rose to find that all of his possessions had been taken during the night, including his precious food. He had to wear his wife's housecoat to town to complain about the theft. The natives, appalled by the immorality of some one of their number, good-naturedly reimbursed the visitor with money, since they could not reproduce the things he had lost. But another of Sam's myths about Africa had been shattered.

Soon after, many of the Americans began to drift back to the coastal areas where the opportunities seemed more promising. But they were still plagued by the lack of work and the sharp feeling of unreality associated with their presence in this alien land, where they blended racially but diverged culturally. Mrs. Garrett soon died of malaria in Saltpond, and several other persons succumbed to various lethal tropical disorders.

In the United States, the remaining delegates, still hoping to migrate to Africa, listened with trepidation and some disbelief as the woes of the migrants continued to filter back to local papers. Sam insisted that it was the British who were undermining his plans. They had hurt the movement initially by passing the immigration ordinance, and they now refused to sell coal and supplies to the *Liberia*'s owners so that the ship could begin the return voyage.

In Weleetka, Liddell, Sam's treasurer, held a rally in an attempt to raise the $3,000 which Sam claimed he needed, and managed to gather at least some portion of it, though it was apparently never dispatched to Africa.

The United States government, involved in the almost hopeless task of maintaining its neutrality, soon found the Sam migration cropping up again to demand its attention. From Coweta, Oklahoma, came a letter to Secretary of State Bryan, conveying a copy of Hurt's description of conditions on the Gold Coast. "It appears that these people are now stranded, are in a destitute condition, and have been robbed, deceived and deserted by Chief Sam," wrote C. W. Joshua to Bryan. "Is it possible for your department, through our consuls in that country, to aid these people to return to this country?" [7]

The State Department replied quickly that there were "no funds at the disposal of the Department for the return to the United States of such destitute citizens" as Joshua had described, and then launched into a "we-told-you-so" justification of the department's previous efforts to halt the migration:

> From the investigations made by the Department and from reports received from the British Government as to the actual conditions on the Gold Coast, it was feared that the expedition of "Chief Sam" would be doomed to disappoinment, and every possible means was used to dissuade American negroes from being deluded into accompanying this man to Africa.[8]

Reports of the tortured condition of the African migrants was given at least some comic relief by the New York *Times,* which had been so interested in the pioneers during their sojourn in New York, but which had lost contact with them when they left for Portland. The *Times,* attempting to write a further chapter to the story that had earlier occupied its columns, carried the highly erroneous report in June of 1915—almost six months to the day that the pioneers had landed at Saltpond—that the "Chief Sam Party [Is] Missing." [9]

The information came from Rev. Isaiah B. Scott, a Negro bishop of the Methodist Episcopal Diocese of Liberia, who had recently arrived in New York aboard the liner *Buenos Aires.* It was Bishop Scott's regular biennial visit to the United States, and he reported that "the recent expedition of Chief Sam with a shipload of American Negroes to settle in the land of their forefathers was still afloat on the ocean, but he did not know just where it was." [10]

Word had been received in Monrovia, Scott reported, that the *Liberia* had been captured by a British cruiser off Dakar, and afterward released. Since Dakar was within six hundred miles of Mayo Island, Scott's information on this point was nearly correct. The *Times,* using interpretative journalism to jog its reader's memories, presented some background on the Sam movement, along with the wild note that "previous to the departure of the vessel advices were received from Africa stating that the land he claimed to own in Liberia could not be found."

Meanwhile, George W. Perry, who had been the most violent of Sam's opponents among the Negro people, gloated regularly as the misfortunes of the pioneers increased. All of the news from Africa explained clearly "what we have predicted in time past concerning the robbing scheme that left so many people homeless and penniless in the United States," wrote Perry. Then he quoted from letters, and crowed: "Oh, they are up against it now and want to come home. Where is your Moses, Mr. Delegate." [11]

"Some of the delegates will be back soon and tell us all about it," Perry predicted hopefully, and invoked various powers to support his prognostication of dire results for the expedition:

Let the heathens rage and the poor execrable followers of Sam imagine vain things, but in due time all of the followers of Sam will know that they have been robbed to a finish of their homes and everything they owned in this world. Our last appeal to the poor folks is to go to the woods, get down close to some stump or tree, and ask God to forgive them their folly.

Perry's fervid proclamations did not, however, undercut completely the recruiting program now going on in Oklahoma under the expert supervision of Liddell; and for once the white press refused to support the critics of Sam, though it now had excellent reason to do so. The Okemah *Ledger* made mild fun of Sam's detractors, pointing out that "they have as faithfully killed that enterprise every few weeks as some people have been killing Bryan politically for the past twenty years." [12]

In fact, the *Ledger* seemed to believe that Sam was doing well, despite some slight inconveniences which had inevitably beset his program:

> The African Pioneer has increased its size from a two page paper to a four page paper. They acknowledge that the enterprise is getting along slowly because of the hardships imposed upon Africa in the way of scarcity of supplies, but assert that the plan is working out splendidly. Sam's ship is said to be at Salt Pond, Gold Coast, but because of the scarcity of coal, [has] been unable to obtain coal for a return trip to this country.

The difficulty with coal apparently dragged on and on. Little was heard of Sam's group for months, and the papers in the United States simply discontinued their comments. Even Perry soon ran out of ammunition, since correspondence had dwindled to nothing.

But late in 1915, the crew of the *Liberia* finally found its way back to the United States, and its arrival was duly chronicled by the press as a "dramatic chapter" in the colonization scheme.[13] The sailors, arriving in New York on October 5, aboard the steamer *Norseman* from Liverpool, reported that they had been stricken with fever and removed to a hospital at Anamabou soon after the *Liberia* reached the Gold Coast. They were cared for by the British until they recovered and then, as "distressed seamen," were conveyed to England and ultimately returned to the United States as consular passengers.

They had little to say of the enterprise itself but dwelt instead at some length upon the adventures of the *Liberia* during the crossing. The earlier vague reports of the ship's contact with the German cruiser *Emden* were now transformed into a wild chase across the Atlantic by a German submarine. What had become of the other members of the mission was not touched upon by the seamen.

But within two weeks of the return of the *Liberia*'s crew, thirteen of the pioneers—their condition becoming more aggravated each day—petitioned the British government to return them to the United States. Though the British took the petition under advisement, they for some reason did not bring it to the attention of the U.S. State Department until May 1917—almost a year and a half after its writing.

Addressed to "His Excellency, Alexander Ransford Slater, Esquire, Acting Governor and Commander-in-Chief of the Gold Coast Colony in Council," and titled, "The HUMBLE PETITION of the Afro-

American delegates to the Gold Coast for themselves and on behalf of their fellow immigrants," the petition outlined briefly the history of the movement and the present plight of the petitioners. They begged that the Acting Governor "graciously consider their destitute condition and grant them free passages to their homes in Galveston, Texas, United States of America, as the said Alfred C. Sam has refused to return to the United States of America with the *S. S. Liberia* which is now lying at anchor in Anamaboe Port." [14]

The complaints of the pioneers were stated in the most formal language they could muster. They had, they noted, come to the Gold Coast "to see if they could, according to the promises and assurances held out to them by the said Alfred C. Sam, repatriate to the home of their ancestors." They were to return to the United States, they believed, in October 1914. But since their arrival, they had discovered that "the said Alfred C. Sam could not make good his promises and assurances to them as to free and quiet settlement on the land of their ancestors."

In addition, the petitioners claimed that Sam had induced them to part with all of their money during the voyage, with the promise that he would refund it to them immediately on arrival. But he had failed to accomplish this despite their repeated demands.

Hurt had earlier touched on this same point in his letter to the Wewoka attorney. He had said that one man in the crew had asked Sam for some of his money back, and that Sam had told him that if "he fooled with him he would have them tied down and whipped." [15]

The petitioners claimed further that each man had deposited £25 under the colony's immigration ordinance on their arrival, and that Sam had withdrawn this money without their knowledge or consent. Because of this final act of misappropriation, they were "practically starving and in great distress and want in this country."

The British, after considering the request, apparently chose to ignore it; and the new settlers attempted to get along in the best way they could. The original corps of people had begun to break up with the return of the crew, and Sam's virtual disappearance had left the remaining group leaderless and disorganized.

For the next year, the colonists spent their time in making decisions and then changing their minds. Some of them found employment in Saltpond and Anamabou, while others went into the interior and worked on farms. Some determined to migrate to Liberia, where the

"American" atmosphere might be more easily found. Still others refused to give up their hopes of returning home, and worked incessantly at getting the requisite passage money. The distrust of Sam had become paranoid. Even though he was nowhere to be found, the settlers often imagined that he would suddenly appear to take their money if they were so fortunate as to obtain some. One delegate wrote home to his wife, saying: "Don't send me any money; I won't be able to get it. Send me a ticket by cable so I can get home." Another warned his wife not to send any money for fear it would fall into greedy hands. He said vaguely that he would "try and get home some time." [16]

Sam did, in fact, appear irregularly in Saltpond, trying time and again to obtain coal. Debts against the ship were mounting rapidly, and Sam saw absolutely no way out but to dispose of the vessel and abandon for good his grandiose plans of bringing more colonists to Africa. But by mid-April of 1916, Sam lost control of the situation altogether. The outstanding claims against the *Liberia* amounted to £6000, and it was seized by the court and ordered sold. On September 5, at 10 A.M., according to a note later posted on the official registry of the vessel, "there was registered a Bill of Sale dated 19th April, 1916, by which all 64/64 shares in the vessel were transferred from the ownership of Alfred Charles Sam to Universal Transportation Company Limited of Toronto, Canada." [17]

The company arranged to have one of her vessels, the *Zealandia,* tow the *Liberia* back to the United States. When the *Zealandia* arrived in Cape Coast, its captain had to hire a number of Negroes to get the *Liberia* in shape for the 6,000 mile tow to New York. He later shipped some eighteen of the West Africans for the voyage and had his quartermasters teach them to steer the ship.

On December 4, the New York *Times* reported the return of the *Liberia* to the United States. She was towed by the *Zealandia* on an 1,800 foot hawser from the Gold Coast, a completely vapid symbol of a now discredited movement. A typographical error in the *Times* in many respects epitomized the fate of Sam's mission: "It was," the *Times* noted, "an ill-starved colonization scheme." [18]

During the early months of 1917, the condition of the migrants began to receive stepped-up attention from the British and American governments. On May 8, Spring-Rice formally forwarded the petition of the colonists to the U.S. State Department along with a background note, pointing out that it appeared to His Majesty's Government that "Sam grossly misled the immigrants and finally deserted the expedition leaving his companions in a state of destitution." Spring-Rice was not, however, much concerned with the present status of the migrants, but he expressed his hope that the United States authorities "would do what they can to discourage any further attempts on the part of negroes to commit themselves to similar adventures." [19]

Robert Lansing, acting for the State Department, rose to Spring-Rice's suggestion. Lansing reported that he had given a statement to the press "regarding the disastrous ending of the expedition in question for the purpose of discouraging any further attempts on the part of negroes to commit themselves to similar adventures." [20] That both governments were now aiming their propaganda at undermining the mushrooming effects of Marcus Garvey, a latter-day Sam, to transport additional Negroes to Africa, seems quite evident.

The State Department's press release stirred activity from a surprising and recently latent source. A somewhat incoherent letter to the department arrived almost immediately from J. P. Liddell, who had seen its propaganda in the Kansas City *Journal*. Liddell wrote:

> I am gratefully thanking you for detail information as to the matter, as I have been constant inquired. I am in position to further say the "Journal" has been misinformed on the contract in agreement between "Sam" and petitioners.
>
> If, your honor, Sir, you will furnish me with the applicants names, encluding their protest, I assure you to make right information and to give you needful ones in your discretion.[21]

Liddell was still living in Weleetka, despite the assertions of some that he had dashed off to California with the funds the movement had entrusted to him, and might well have been trying to keep interest in the movement alive.

The State Department also employed the petition as a response to J. W. Stevens of Warrenton, Virginia, who wrote on May 3, asking how he "might gain correspondence" with his father, who had sailed with Chief Sam.[22] The second assistant secretary, apparently with more important things on his mind, reported brightly that from the only information he had at hand it would appear that the address of Chief Sam's party, at least on October 26, 1915, was "Cape Coast, Anamaboe,

Saltpond, Gold Coast." [23] For the second assistant secretary, any one of those three cities would presumably do as well as any other.

The report of the pioneers' misadventures released by the State Department also led to some mellow reflections by the New York *World,* the newspaper which had been most devoted to the detailing of the project during a better and earlier time. "The 'Back to the Old Home Land' pilgrimage of the American negroes who listened to the Prophet Chief in 1914 has come to a sad ending," the *World* reported. Labelling Sam as "an intelligent black man," the newspaper added the startling bit of information that he "is said to have drifted to a West Coast native tribe and influenced them so strongly that they made him their chief." The *World* was optimistic about the fate of the destitute colonists, and predicted that "the chances are that the United States will get them back," though a large number of the migrants had left the Gold Coast and disappeared somewhere in Africa since the landing.[24]

The *World* clip elicited an angry letter from Frederick S. Simons, an attorney in New York who was now serving as counsel for the Akim Trading Company, and who felt that the harm done to his client by the British merited some consideration. If a compromise could be reached, Simons noted, then the money could be used to return the stranded pilgrims to the United States. Simons wanted to know what the procedure was for presenting his claim against the British government.

These were the "real facts" relative to the *Liberia* as Simons saw them:

The ship had been purchased free and clear by the Akim Trading Company, Ltd., of "Weleetka, Oklahoma" for $69,000. He then proceeded to the details of the sailing from New York to Portland to Galveston, and the stop-over at Barbados. Then he came to the heart of the claim, the delay of the *Liberia* at Sierra Leone:

> The vessel was subsequently released after a delay of forty-three days. By this delay, the Akim Trading Company, which paid the entire expense of the trip, was greatly damaged and was compelled to disburse more money than was contemplated or anticipated, so that when the vessel arrived at Salt Pond, the company's representative was without the required funds to meet the demands of the vessel.[25]

To correct this injustice and restore solvency to the company, Simons asked for compensation amounting to $11,000.

The State Department's response to Simons was cold and formal. Enclosed, it said, was a circular "with regard to diplomatic claims against foreign governments." If Simons felt that he had a case, he should prepare the papers in accordance with the instructions, and forward them to the State Department which would, "in due time give the matter careful consideration with a view to determining whether diplomatic intervention in support thereof would be justifiable." [26] Simons, apparently discouraged by the complicated procedure which was involved, and by the lack of interest shown by the State Department, never filed the claim.

Within the State Department, there was a flurry of renewed interest in preparing a criminal case against Sam. On June 26, the Solicitor of the Department of State prepared a memorandum to the Diplomatic Bureau suggesting the possibility of extradition and prosecution of the expedition's head.

The Gold Coast petition seemed to imply, the Solicitor wrote, that funds were probably obtained through false pretenses:

> Since it is possible that "Chief Sam" may have violated the postal or other laws of the United States or the laws of the States in which he carried on his operations, and since he may be guilty of an offense for which he could be extradited, it is suggested that it might be well to have the Ambassador's note and its enclosure copies sent to the Department of Justice, the Post Office Department, and to the Governors of Texas and Oklahoma, within which states it appears that the propaganda was principally conducted for their information and such action as they may consider proper to take in the matter.[27]

The Western European Division, wholly unimpressed with the Solicitor's eager idea, reported that it had reviewed the papers in Sam's file and had noted that both the Department of Justice and the Post Office Department had previously been unable to take any action against him.

The Solicitor, still hot on the trail, agreed that "this would seem to dispose of the Justice and Post Office" Departments, but suggested that the administrative heads of Texas and Oklahoma be contacted.[28] Letters were therefore sent to them on July 19, though no responses were ever forthcoming.

For people in the United States, Sam and his unfortunate migrants simply ceased to exist. The newspapers dropped the issue entirely, and federal authorities retired the files containing the materials that were for so many years the source of lively correspondence. Time went on, and the Negroes of the country had other battles to fight and other causes with which to identify themselves. Garvey, the flamboyant "black Moses" of the post-war period, had begun his Universal Negro Improvement Association, and was attracting an advertised million followers to his cause. Northern cities were being packed with Negro migrants from the South, embittered, disillusioned, but sufficiently practical to intend wrenching their freedom from the whites on their own geographical grounds rather than retreating off to a "fatherland."

The pioneers in Africa continued their attempts to return to the United States; and ultimately, most of them found ways and means of accomplishing their end. Many were as disgusted with themselves and their puerile involvement in the movement as they were with Sam. Time, however, according to one survivor, blunted much of the anger they felt, and mellowed their reflections on the hardships they endured in Africa. Never had anything more exciting happened to them, and never again would they have experiences to match those they had had on the Gold Coast. For the returnees, Africa took on a new color, and provided a basis on which they could differentiate themselves from their fellows who had remained in the United States and lived out their humdrum, often depressed, existence in this country.

Only a few of the pioneers remained permanently on the Gold Coast. Dr. Dorman returned and died a few months after his arrival. Will Hurt, the *Liberia*'s engineer, eventually settled down in Bristow, Oklahoma, cherishing his records of the migration and his part in it, despite his intense disillusionment with Sam. He died early in 1957, highly respected locally as an exceptional mechanic on oil field installations.

Parts of the Taylor family remained in Africa and blended, though never quite completely, into the local population. Taylor's wife died in Saltpond, but their descendants are scattered still over the Gold Coast. Best known is Willie Taylor, who maintained a fitter's shop at Agona Swedru, and did a thriving business until, according to local tradition, he had some kind of "lorry palaver" and apparently relocated in Liberia.

Vague memories of the Americans still remain on the Gold Coast, where the arrival of the migrants must have provided a more dramatic chapter in the limited context of local life than their departure had in the United States. K. B. Sam, a nephew of Chief Sam, who now lives with his adopted mother in the very house where ten of the pioneers lived while they were in Saltpond, remembers the arrival. Though he was only nine years old at the time, he "recalls seeing the boat as it lay at anchor in Saltpond." Sam's younger brother, Kofie Nyanme, still lives in the same town in the Ada district as did Alfred Sam. He, too, remembers Sam's arrival with some sixty colonists, and the difficulties they encountered with the British. Another old man, now seventy-five, "recalls the occasion of the coming of Chief Sam and the American Negroes very vividly." [29] He states emphatically that Chief Sam was well known to the Chief of Saltpond and that he was warmly received by him.

Others remember the departure of the *Liberia*. One woman, living in a large cement house in Saltpond, remembers the day very well, "for she gave birth to a son on that day." [30]

But more generally, the Sam movement and its various episodes has passed vaguely and quietly out of the memories of those persons who are even old enough to have had contact with it.

It remained for Sam to provide a typically romantic finish for a scheme which was itself so inherently romantic. Despite the wide discrepancy of their ages, Sam eventually married little Lucille Garrett, the Clearview girl who had christened the *Liberia* at Galveston. But tragedy and disorder plagued Sam even in this venture, and their three children died shortly after birth. Lucille finally left Sam and returned to the United States, while Sam moved once more, this time to Liberia, where he became a cocoa buyer. At some unknown date, he died there on the West African coast, which had once held so much promise for him and his followers.

10

"To Canaan Return"

$\mathbf{S}$ OCIAL MOVEMENTS, as general phenomena in human experience seldom, if ever, just happen. They are produced by a variety of circumstances which precede them in time, and by a complex, often inextricable, array of human interpretations of these circumstances. The events which ultimately give rise to the often cataclysmic decisions of people to rebel, to run away, to reform, to fight, take time to unfold. As a leading social psychologist has pointed out: "Collective interaction and other activities contributing to a social movement are not usually affairs that occur within a few episodes. Their scope extends far beyond the face-to-face encounters of a given number of individuals." [1]

People do not make important decisions quickly; nor are these decisions, when they run counter to prevailing mores, reinforced in a moment. It takes convincing, and convincing takes the careful rationalization of the individual's decision to lay aside his prior beliefs and commitments, a process which is at best painful and tedious. A movement which involved the number of people ultimately drawn to the African return, and which involved as well the passionate devotion to that return which most of Sam's pioneers showed, necessarily took time to develop. The diffuse uneasiness and the lingering frustration which the Negroes of Okfuskee County began to feel after statehood, took time to crystallize into action. The Sam movement represented, then, the final, fitful culmination of a long period of private talks, of intense emotional interaction, of subtle, subconscious value judgments, of uncertain decision-making among those people who sensed this frustration, and who became slowly and painfully aware that they could not relieve their tension in the more usual channels which their cultural milieu provided.

The circumstances contributing to the movement need hardly be belabored. Boley, Clearview and the other Negro communities in Oklahoma were experiments in racial self-determination.[2] If the Negroes had not believed this when they first occupied these racial islands, they soon became convinced of it, both from their own self-assurances and from the reinforcing remarks of the whites. But with the passing years, the discrepancy between the aims and aspirations of the all-Negro communities and the actualities of their life-histories illustrated vividly the lengths to which the Negro would be permitted to go—the real limits of his social tether—even if he did not come into direct and open conflict with the white group.

The Negro community was a compromise between complete integration which was then, as now, unfeasible in terms of white values, and tormenting and humiliating subordination in biracial communities. The Negro in the all-Negro community was not yet ready in 1904 to rebel against the stern racial etiquette in the United States; but he nonetheless hoped to find, in his new form of residence, a solution to a situation which showed little promise of imminent improvement. The all-Negro community was in no sense a retreat from the American standards and values which the Negroes had learned to cherish, nor was it an anachronistic revival of Africanism, but rather it constituted an attempt to develop fully and to exploit completely the American culture.

But this exploitation was refused to the Negro, not all at once to be sure, but in invidious, piecemeal fashion. Disenfranchised slowly but certainly, the Negro was obliged with each new onslaught to readjust his previous ethic. Such constant revision soon became vapid, and the Negro community relented in the face of white hostility.

Faced with bitter ambiguity, no longer certain of the direction which they should take, Oklahoma Negroes fell upon Sam as they had upon no other leader in their history. To them, Sam represented an escape which they believed was a solution; but he also represented removal to a land where they could continue their conceived roles as leaders, pioneers, and persons of prestige and importance. They were not skulking off to Africa as beaten men and women, but were instead returning proudly to their homeland, full of the ideas that residence in America had taught them, and equipped with the skills which had made the nation famous throughout the world. The Americans believed they were on their way to save the African, to "uplift" him, as the pioneers preached on their landing at Saltpond.

Sam's organization of the movement could hardly be called masterful. Though his local clubs proved an innovation, since the membership constantly reinforced its fervid belief in the wisdom of the African return, they developed almost without his urging. His appeal was enormous; and people literally flocked to purchase his stock, never questioning its value nor the validity of the claims which he was making with reference to it. The stage was perfectly set for Sam, and he came and reaped the rewards.

Whether or not Sam was a fraud is in every sense unimportant. To the Negroes preparing for the voyage, Sam was a savior. Nothing could convince them to the contrary. Though many of the middle-class Negroes of the area, those very persons who had contributed so heavily to the self-fulfillment ethic which ultimately provided the basis for the group's disillusionment, refused to accompany him, and even bitterly opposed the movement, the Negro majority, both locally and distantly, supported the scheme, at least in spirit. This was a grand experiment, a showdown experiment, in which the African, rejected in his adopted nation, was proudly packing and returning home.

Sam's claims were certainly immodest, and in some respects, altogether false. The pioneers to a man agreed that Sam had lied and cheated them. But many felt no bitterness. The trip to Africa had been worth all of the hardship they experienced.

The movement and its fantastic leader now live on only in the few disjointed recollections of a handful who survive. Its brief and hectic life attests once more to what Gunnar Myrdal has called that "basic unrest of the Negro community," a "dissatisfaction so deep that it amounts to a hopelessness of ever gaining full life in America." [3]

In these terms, the one old lady's remark becomes even more mean-

NOTES

Chapter 1

1. Spring-Rice to J. B. Moore, February 5, 1914. Correspondence of Governor Lee Cruce, Oklahoma State Capitol Library, Oklahoma City, Oklahoma. All references to the correspondence of Governor Cruce are to this collection.

2. Frederic Bancroft, *The Colonization of American Negroes: 1801-1865* (Norman, Okla.: University of Oklahoma Press, 1957), p. 155.

3. H. N. Sherwood, "Early Negro Deportation Projects," *Mississippi Valley Historical Review,* II (1916), 497-500.

4. Fyfe, Christopher, *A History of Sierra Leone.* London: Oxford University Press, 1962, pp. 13-87.

5. John Hope Franklin, *From Slavery to Freedom* (rev. ed.; New York: Alfred Knopf, 1956), p. 237.

6. Charles H. Wesley, "Lincoln's Plan for Colonizing the Emancipated Negro," *Journal of Negro History,* IV (1919), 7-21.

7. Henry Noble Sherwood, "Paul Cuffe," *Journal of Negro History,* VIII (1923), 153-232.

8. Gunnar Myrdal, *An American Dilemma* (New York: Harper Bros., 1944), p. 749.

Chapter 2

1. John Hanson Beadle, *The Undeveloped West* (Philadelphia, Chicago, etc.: National Publishing Co., 1873), pp. 378-89.

2. Sigmund Sameth, "Creek Freedmen," unpublished M. A. thesis, University of Oklahoma, 1940.

3. *Ibid.*

4. *Ibid.*

5. Interview with H. L. Chancey, Bryant, Okla., "Indian-Pioneer Papers," LXV, 80-92. Unpublished manuscript in Phillips Collection, University of Oklahoma Library, Norman, Oklahoma.

6. Indianapolis *Freeman*, July 29, 1905. Reprinted in Herbert Aptheker (ed.), *Documentary History of the Negro People in the United States* (New York: Citadel Press, 1951), p. 648-49.

7. *Christian Recorder*, June 26, 1890.

8. *The Outlook*, January 4, 1908, p. 30.

9. Boley *Progress*, March 9, 1905.

10. *Ibid.*, April 19, 1906.

11. Weleetka *American*, July 21, 1905.

12. Interview with Madison J. McLeod, Bartlesville, Okla., "Indian-Pioneer Papers," XXXV, 367-72.

13. St. Louis *Globe-Democrat*, February 22, 1912.

14. Okemah *Independent*, September 23, 1904.

15. Boley *Progress*, March 9, 1905.

16. *Ibid.*, April 19, 1906.

17. *Ibid.*, March 16, 1905.

18. *Ibid.*, March 30, 1905.

19. Interview with W. A. Stalworth, Boley, Okla., "Indian-Pioneer Papers," LIV, 80-82.

20. Boley *Progress*, April 13, 1905.

21. *Ibid.*, April 6, 1905.

22. Okemah *Independent*, March 30, 1905.

23. Boley *Progress*, May 11, 1905.

24. Okemah *Independent*, December 21, 1906.

25. As quoted in the Weleetka *American*, February 15, 1907.

26. Kingfisher *Free Press*, March 17, 1892.

27. Weleetka *American*, August 23, 1907.

28. Okemah *Ledger*, September 5, 1907.

29. Weleetka *American*, September 13, 1907.

30. Okemah *Ledger*, October 3, 1907.

31. Weleetka *American*, September 27, 1907.

Chapter 3

1. Okemah *Independent*, October 24, 1907.

2. *Ibid.*

3. *Ibid.*, December 28, 1907.

4. Boley *Beacon*, February 20, 1908.

5. Okemah *Independent*, November 14, 1907.

6. *Ibid.*, January 9, 1908.

7. Okemah *Ledger*, February 27, 1908.

8. Okemah *Independent*, January 16, 1908.

9. *Ibid.*

10. Weleetka *American*, February 28, 1908.

11. Okemah *Ledger*, March 26, 1908.

12. The *Progress* editorial is quoted from the Okemah *Independent*, April 9, 1908.

13. Quoted in the Paden *Press*, June 13, 1908.

14. Okemah *Ledger*, June 18, 1908.

15. Okemah *Independent*, July 9, 1908.

16. *Ibid.*, July 16, 1908. Excerpts from the resolution quoted in the following paragraphs are from the same issue of the *Independent*.

17. Paden *Press,* August 22, 1908.

18. *Ibid.,* August 29, 1908.

19. Okemah *Independent,* September 3, 1908.

20. *Ibid.,* February 18, 1909.

21. *Ibid.,* September 2, 1909.

22. As quoted in the Okemah *Independent,* September 2, 1909.

23. *Ibid.,* March 17, 1910.

24. *Ibid.,* March 31, 1910.

25. *Ibid.,* April 7, 1910.

26. The excerpts from the amendment, and the newspaper comments, are quoted from the *Independent,* July 21, 1910.

27. As quoted in the *Independent,* August 11, 1910.

28. *Ibid.,* September 8, 1910.

29. *Ibid.,* September 10, 1910.

30. Okemah *Ledger,* September 26, 1910. The account of Sango's experiences in Boley follows the *Ledger,* September 15, 1910.

31. Okemah *Independent,* November 3, 1910.

32. *Ibid.,* November 10, 1910.

33. *Ibid.*

34. *Federal Reporter,* Vol. 186, p. 977.

35. The account of the lynching of Laura Nelson and her son is taken from the Okemah *Independent,* May 25, 1911.

36. *Ibid.,* June 1, 1911.

37. Okemah *Ledger,* August 31, 1911.

38. *Ibid.,* August 24, 1911.

39. *Ibid.*

40. *Ibid.*

41. Okemah *Independent,* August 17, 1911.

42. *Ibid.*

43. Okemah *Ledger,* August 31, 1911.

44. *Ibid.,* November 16, 1911.

45. Okemah *Independent,* December 14, 1911.

46. Okemah *Ledger,* December 14, 1911.

47. The details of the meeting and the comments of the Boley *Progress* are quoted from the Okemah *Independent,* January 25, 1912.

48. Okemah *Ledger,* March 7, 1912.

49. Tolliver's interview with Dodson was reprinted in the *Ledger,* March 7, 1912. All quotations here are from the *Ledger.*

50. Okemah *Ledger,* March 7, 1912.

51. *Ibid.,* March 14, 1912.

52. *Ibid.,* April 18, 1912.

53. *Ibid.,* September 26, 1912.

54. *Ibid.,* October 10, 1912.

55. *Ibid.,* September 26, 1912.

56. *Ibid.,* October 31, 1912.

57. Okemah *Independent,* October 31, 1912.

58. Okemah *Independent,* November 7, 1912, and May 1, 1913.

59. *Ibid.,* May 1, 1913.

60. J. Saunders Redding, *They Came in Chains: Americans from Africa* (Philadelphia: J. P. Lippincott, 1950), p. 202.

Chapter 4

1. Okemah *Independent,* August 28, 1913.
2. Luther Fort to Lee Cruce, July 1913.
3. See note 1, above.
4. Articles of Incorporation, Akim Trading Company. Secretary of State, Albany, New York. Quotations from the company's prospectus are from this source.
5. New York *Age,* January 29, 1914.
6. *Ibid.*
7. " 'Chief' Sam and the Negro 'Exodus,' " *Literary Digest,* March 21, 1914, p. 647.
8. Articles of Incorporation, Akim Trading Company, Limited. Secretary of State, Pierre, South Dakota.
9. Alexander Johnson to Cruce, August 30, 1913.
10. Cruce to Johnson, September 2, 1913.
11. Okemah *Independent,* September 4, 1913.
12. *Ibid.*
13. Tom Hazlewood to Cruce, December 12, 1913.
14. C. G. Samuels to Cruce, September 29, 1913.
15. Tulsa *Star,* October 4, 1913.
16. James G. Fair to Cruce, October 6, 1913.
17. Cruce to Fair, n.d.
18. Richard J. Hill to Robert Owens, October 7, 1913. Correspondence of Governor Lee Cruce.
19. R. C. Lee to Secretary of the Interior, October 17, 1913. Correspondence of Governor Lee Cruce.
20. Quoted in the Okemah *Ledger,* October 30, 1913.
21. C. M. Pearson to Cruce, October 31, 1913.
22. Cruce to C. L. Hill, November 4, 1913.
23. The description of the Weleetka gathering follows the Wewoka and Lima *Courier,* October 31, 1913.
24. Pearson to Cruce, November 7, 1913.
25. The meeting at the Lima school house is described in the Wewoka and Lima *Courier,* November 11, 1913.
26. Cruce to Pearson, November 10, 1913.
27. Okemah *Independent,* November 13, 1913.
28. S. W. Butler to Cruce, November 24, 1913.
29. Cruce to Butler, November 26, 1913.
30. Okemah *Independent,* November 27, 1913.
31. The account of the Weleetka meeting is drawn from the Wewoka and Lima *Courier,* November 28, 1913.
32. *Ibid.,* December 5, 1913.
33. Cruce to Hill, December 5, 1913.
34. Hill to Cruce. December 8, 1913.
35. Hazlewood to Cruce, December 12, 1913.
36. Colville Barclay to John Bassett Moore, December 17, 1913. Correspondence of Governor Lee Cruce.
37. Okemah *Independent,* December 25, 1913.

38. Moore to Cruce, December 27, 1913.

39. Okemah *Ledger,* January 1, 1914.

40. *African Pioneer,* quoted in the Okemah *Ledger,* January 1, 1914.

41. Tulsa *Star,* January 3, 1914.

42. Oklahoma City *Daily Oklahoman,* January 16, 1914.

43. Cruce to Spring-Rice, January 17, 1914.

44. Wewoka and Lima *Courier,* January 23, 1914.

45. Spring-Rice to Moore. February 5, 1914. Correspondence of Governor Lee Cruce.

Chapter 5

1. Smith's remarks to the reporters are quoted from the New York *Times,* February 11, 1914.

2. New York *Age,* February 5, 1914.

3. New York *World,* February 10, 1914.

4. Edmund D. Cronon, *Black Moses: The Story of Marcus Garvey and the Universal Negro Improvement Association* (Madison: University of Wisconsin Press, 1955).

5. New York *World,* February 10, 1914.

6. *Ibid.*

7. Brooklyn *Eagle,* February 10, 1914.

8. Associated Press dispatch to the Guthrie *Daily Leader,* February 10, 1914.

9. Oklahoma City *Times,* February 10, 1914.

10. New York *World,* February 11, 1914.

11. Tulsa *Democrat,* February 11, 1914.

12. Quoted in the Okemah *Independent,* February 12, 1914.

13. New York *Age,* February 12, 1914.

14. *Ibid.*

15. *Ibid.*

16. New York *American,* February 12, 1914.

17. New York *Sun,* February 13, 1914.

18. *Ibid.*

19. Quoted in the New York *Sun,* February 26, 1914.

20. New York *American,* February 12, 1914.

21. New York *Age,* February 12, 1914.

22. New York *Sun,* February 14, 1914.

23. The remarks of the two Liberian officials, Dr. Ernest Lyons and J. Edmestone Barnes, are quoted from the *Sun,* February 14, 1914.

24. New York *Age,* February 19, 1914.

25. *Ibid.*

26. The account of Sam's return to the ship and of the scene on board is drawn from the New York *Sun,* February 17, 1914.

27. Brooklyn *Eagle,* February 17, 1914.

28. As quoted, *ibid.*

29. New York *Age,* February 19, 1914.

30. Letter from Courtenay W. Bennett to Cecil Arthur Spring-Rice, February 19, 1914. The account of the discussion between Bennett and Sam is drawn from this letter, which is collected in the Correspondence of Governor Lee Cruce.

31. C. W. Bennett to United States District Attorney, New York City, and New York City Attorney, February 19, 1914. Correspondence of Governor Lee Cruce.

32. New York *Times,* February 26, 1914.

33. Spring-Rice to John B. Moore, February 21, 1914. Correspondence of Governor Lee Cruce.

34. British Foreign Office to Walter Hines Page, February 21, 1914. State Department Decimal File 811.7111. National Archives, Washington, D. C. Hereafter cited as National Archives, File 811.7111.

35. Guthrie *Daily Leader,* February 21, 1914.

36. New York *Times,* February 26, 1914.

37. *Ibid.*

38. Brooklyn *Eagle,* February 26, 1914.

39. New York *Times,* February 26, 1914.

40. New York *Sun,* February 26, 1914.

41. Brooklyn *Eagle,* February 27, 1914.

42. Governor Lee Cruce to J. B. Moore, February 27, 1914.

43. Brooklyn *Eagle,* February 27, 1914.

44. New York *Sun,* February 28, 1914.

45. *Ibid.*

46. New York *World,* February 27, 1914.

47. Quoted in the Muskogee *Times Democrat,* March 6, 1914.

48. New York *Sun,* February 26, 1914.

49. See note 47, above.

50. New York *World,* March 8, 1914. The ensuing account of the *World* reporter's interview with Sam is from the same source.

51. New York *Times,* March 8, 1914.

52. *Ibid.*

53. Brooklyn *Eagle,* March 7, 1914.

54. New York *World,* March 8, 1914.

55. New York *Times,* March 8, 1914.

Chapter 6

1. Portland *Sunday Telegram,* March 8, 1914.

2. Frederick I. Anderson, "The Man Who Heard Voices," *Harper's Weekly,* February 15, 1908, pp. 10-12. The description of Sandford's career is drawn from this source.

3. *Ibid.*

4. Portland *Sunday Telegram,* March 8, 1914.

5. *Ibid.*

6. Portland *Evening Express and Daily Advertiser,* March 9, 1914. The account of the *Liberia's* arrival is drawn from the same issue.

7. C. E. Booth to the Inspector in Charge, New York Division, United States Post Office, Division of Mail Fraud, March 9, 1914. National Archives, File 711.8111.

8. *Ibid.*

9. Portland *Evening Express and Daily Advertiser,* March 10, 1914.

10. *Ibid.,* March 11, 1914.

11. *Ibid.*

12. Cecil Spring-Rice to the United States Secretary of State, March 12, 1914. National Archives, File 711.8111.

13. J. O. Sanders to the United States Secretary of State, March 12, 1914. *Ibid.*

14. Cecil Spring-Rice to the United States Secretary of State, March 17, 1914. Correspondence of Governor Lee Cruce.

15. Manila *Times,* n.d. National Archives, File 711.8111.

16. Guthrie *Daily Leader*, March 14, 1914.

17. Portland *Evening Express and Daily Advertiser*, March 28, 1914.

18. The account of the newspaper reporter's attempt to elicit information from Sam and McKenzie follows the Portland *Evening Express and Daily Advertiser*, March 28, 1914.

19. *Ibid.*, April 1, 1914.

20. As quoted, *ibid.*

21. *Ibid.*

22. Oklahoma *Guide*, April 2, 1914.

23. *Ibid.*

24. Muskogee *Times-Democrat*, April 8, 1914.

25. Portland *Evening Express and Daily Advertiser*, May 19, 1914.

26. *Ibid.*, May 21, 1914.

27. *Ibid.*

28. *Ibid.*, June 1, 1914.

29. *Ibid.*, June 2, 1914.

30. *Ibid.*, June 3, 1914.

Chapter 7

1. Oklahoma City *Times*, February 13, 1914.

2. Tulsa *Star*, February 14, 1914.

3. *Ibid.*

4. Guthrie *Daily Leader*, February 5, 1914.

5. Oklahoma *Guide*, February 19, 1914.

6. Galveston *Tribune*, February 18, 1914.

7. Oklahoma *Guide*, February 26, 1914.

8. Muskogee *Times-Democrat*, March 5, 1914.

9. Galveston *Tribune*, March 6, 1914. Burt's other comments are quoted from the same source.

10. *Ibid.*

11. *Ibid.*, March 25, 1914.

12. Tulsa *Star*, March 28, 1914.

13. The description of the camp-out in MacGuire's Park follows the Galveston *Tribune*, April 2, 1914.

14. Mayor Lewis Fisher to William Jennings Bryan, April 2, 1914. National Archives, File 711.8111.

15. Quoted in Oklahoma *Guide*, April 16, 1914.

16. "WP" to Mr. Cooke, April 6, 1914. National Archives, File 711.8111.

17. Okfuskee County *News*, April 30, 1914.

18. *Ibid.*

19. As quoted, *ibid.*

20. Clearview *Patriarch*, May 30, 1914.

21. Galveston *Daily News*, June 4, 1914.

22. Garrett's account, quoted in the following paragraphs, is taken from the Okemah *Ledger*, June 11, 1914.

23. Galveston *Daily News*, June 18, 1914.

24. Galveston *Tribune*, June 18, 1914.

25. *Ibid.*

26. *Ibid.*

27. Wichita *Daily Times* (Wichita Falls, Texas), June 19, 1914.

28. The account of the *Liberia*'s arrival at Galveston is drawn from the Galveston *Daily News,* June 19, 1914.

29. Galveston *Tribune,* June 19, 1914.

30. San Antonio *Express,* August 23, 1914.

31. *Ibid.*

32. Galveston *Daily News,* July 5, 1914.

33. Details of the delays and compromise christening follow the Galveston *Daily News,* July 10, 1914.

34. The description of the second christening follows the Galveston *Daily News,* July 12, 1914.

35. Guthrie *Daily Leader,* July 11, 1914.

36. Oklahoma City *News,* July 30, 1914.

37. *Ibid.*

38. Galveston *Daily News,* June 19, 1914.

39. Guthrie *Daily Leader,* August 3, 1914.

40. *Daily Ardmoreite,* July 30, 1914.

41. Quoted in the Seminole County *Capital,* August 20, 1914.

42. Tulsa *Star,* September 5, 1914.

43. *Ibid.*

44. Galveston *Daily News,* August 21, 1914.

45. Dallas *Morning News,* August 21, 1914.

46. Galveston *Daily News,* August 21, 1914.

47. *Ibid.*

48. San Antonio *Express,* August 22, 1914.

Chapter 8

1. W. G. Swain to Inspector in Charge, New York Division, United States Post Office Department, August 25, 1914. National Archives, File 711.8111.

2. Tulsa *Star,* September 5, 1914.

3. Certificate of Registry, *S.S. Liberia.* Ministry of Transport and Civil Aviation, General Register and Record Office of Shipping and Seamen, Cardiff, Wales.

4. Guthrie *Daily Leader,* December 21, 1914.

5. Rev. W. F. Taylor to William Jennings Bryan, January 4, 1915. National Archives, File 711.8111.

6. John E. Osborne to W. F. Taylor, January 14, 1915. *Ibid.*

7. The details of the Liberia's seizure and of the Sierra Leone investigation are from the Okfuskee County *News,* February 25, 1915.

8. Gold Coast *Leader,* January 30, 1915.

Chapter 9

1. The Gold Coast *Leader,* January 30, 1915, is the source for the account of the *Liberia*'s arrival in Saltpond, and of the formal reception, with the addresses by Chief Sam, Sorrell, Mrs. Hall, and Mrs. Lewis.

2. Hurt's letter was printed in the Tulsa *Star,* May 1, 1915.

3. W. H. Claridge, *A History of the Gold Coast and Ashanti* (2 vols.; London: John Murray, 1915), I, 596.

4. *Ibid.,* II, 551.

5. Tulsa *Star,* May 8, 1915.

6. Letter to the authors from David L. Stratmon, Cultural Affairs Officer, U.S. Information Service, Accra, Gold Coast, December 11, 1956.

7. C. W. Joshua to William Jennings Bryan, May 8, 1915. National Archives, File 711.8111.

8. Robert Lansing to C. W. Joshua, May 12, 1915. *Ibid.*

9. New York *Times,* June 12, 1915.

10. *Ibid.*

11. Tulsa *Star,* July 17, 1915.

12. Okemah *Ledger,* July 22, 1915.

13. Oklahoma City *Daily Oklahoman,* October 6, 1915.

14. Petition from L. E. Woods, *et al.,* to Alexander Ransford Slater, October 26, 1915. National Archives, File 711.8111.

15. See note 2, above.

16. Tulsa *Star,* July 17, 1915.

17. Certificate of Registry, *S.S. Liberia.*

18. New York *Times,* December 4, 1916.

19. Cecil Spring-Rice to United States Department of State, May 8, 1917. National Archives, File 711.8111.

20. Robert Lansing to Spring-Rice, May 23, 1917. *Ibid.*

21. J. P. Liddell to United States Department of State, June 1, 1917. *Ibid.*

22. J. W. Stevens to Editor, Washington *Post,* May 3. 1917. *Ibid.*

23. Alvey A. Abee to G. W. Stephens, June 9, 1917. *Ibid.*

24. New York *World,* July 16, 1917.

25. F. S. Simons to Robert Lansing, June 16, 1917. National Archives, File 711.8111.

26. "BLH," Office of the Solicitor, Department of State to Western European Division, June 26, 1917. *Ibid.*

27. *Ibid.*

28. *Ibid.*

29. Letter to authors from David Stratmon, cited above, note 6.

30. *Ibid.*

Chapter 10

1. Muzafer and Carolyn Sherif, *An Outline of Social Psychology* (rev. ed.; Harper Bros., 1956), p. 722.

2. William E. Bittle and Gilbert L. Geis, "Racial Self-Fulfillment and the Rise of an All-Negro Community in Oklahoma," *Phylon,* XVIII, No. 3 (1957), 246-60.

3. Gunnar Myrdal, *An American Dilemma* p. 749.

INDEX

The manuscript was edited by Barbara C. Woodward. The book was de-signed by Richard Kinney. The text type is Linotype Granjon based on a design by Claude Garamond and redesigned under the supervision of George W. Jones for the Linotype Corporation. The display face is Neuland designed by Rudolf Koch for Klingspor, 1923.

The book is printed on S. D. Warren's Olde Style Antique and bound in Columbia Mills' Riverside vellum. Manufactured in the United States of America.